Queer Notions
New Plays and Performances
from Ireland

Fintan Walsh is Government of Ireland Post-Doctoral Research Fellow in Drama Studies at the School of Drama, Film and Music, Trinity College Dublin. He is co-editor of *Crossroads: Performance Studies and Irish Culture* (Palgrave Macmillan, 2009) and author of *Male Trouble: Masculinity and the Performance of Crisis* (Palgrave Macmillan, 2010). He has worked as a script reader at the Abbey Theatre and is a critic with *Irish Theatre Magazine*.

Queer Notions
New Plays and Performances
from Ireland

Edited by
FINTAN WALSH

CORK UNIVERSITY PRESS

First published in 2010 by
Cork University Press
Youngline Industrial Estate
Pouladuff Road, Togher
Cork, Ireland

Performance rights should be sought directly from individual playwrights

British Library Cataloguing in Publication Data

A CIP catalogue record for this book is available from the British Library.

ISBN-13: 978-185918-469-1

Printed in the UK by J.F. Print
Typeset by Tower Books, Ballincollig, Co. Cork
www.corkuniversitypress.com

Contents

Foreword

There is strength in numbers, so they say. I've never believed it, and I'm glad that I haven't. Crowds wear uniforms, and we know where those outfits can lead us. Theatre is a perfect, subversive place for resisting the herd instinct. People gather there to watch in the darkness light emanating from the truth, or the masks of truth. These plays are a collection of masks, masks of many shades, all of them saying something I'm glad I've heard in all their defiance and despair, their sorrowful, joyous and glorious mysteries, the spite of their loving and the pleasure of their hatred, all moving like fire, warm and dangerous and inviting through the book, ending as it does with the wonderful, devastating P.S. of Panti's letter to someone remarkably like so many of us, a line which even standing on its own, as we all must stand on our own, makes *Queer Notions* essential.

Frank McGuinness
March 2010

Acknowledgements

I have wanted to publish this book for some time now. Over the past decade, I have seen almost all of the plays included here in performance, noted how they have resonated with audiences, but also feared that they would get lost and be forgotten about without being published. Ephemerality is part of the allure of the performance encounter, and queer practices tend to thrive on this dynamic, but it is also one of the obstacles to documenting cultural history. For recognizing the importance of this project, I am very grateful to Cork University Press. I am particularly thankful to the external reviewers for their comments, and to Sophie Watson and Maria O'Donovan for leading the book through to completion. A special thanks goes to Hilary Bell for her discerning copy-editing.

I would like to acknowledge the support of my colleagues at the Samuel Beckett Centre, Trinity College Dublin. Funding from the Irish Research Council for the Humanities and Social Sciences assisted final preparations of the manuscript.

All edited collections are collaborative endeavours, but perhaps this is especially true of an anthology of this kind. In preparing the book I have been mindful of the complex networks of people involved in the initial production and reception of the plays and performances before they were assembled in words and visuals here: the festivals or companies that first put the work on stage; the audiences that turned up to show their interest and encouragement; the agencies that supplied valuable funding along the way, and those who worked for free to help make things happen. I also think of the people who lived outside of the temporal and even geographic parameters of the project, who might never have imagined a book like this being possible.

Of course, I am especially indebted to the artists whose material is included here. The experience of publishing this collection has been made extra special by virtue of the fact that I know some of the contributors personally. A special thanks goes to Phillip McMahon for discussing the project at various stages of its development. Thanks also to Niall Sweeney for designing such a beautiful cover at such short notice. Also, I greatly appreciate Frank McGuinness's thoughtful Foreword. Finally, I would like to dedicate the book to those who have made, or continue to make, unsettling theatre, and theatre that refuses to settle.

Fintan Walsh
Trinity College Dublin
March 2010

Introduction:
The Flaming Archive

FINTAN WALSH

[Y]ou must never underestimate the sheer historical depth of homophobia in Ireland. And that exists in the theatre as well – perhaps it's even more pronounced in the theatre, where there is this almost heterosexual panic in case you engage too deeply with gay issues.

Frank McGuinness, Irish Times[1]

'Archival' memory exists as documents, maps, literary texts, letters, archaeological remains, bones, videos, films, CDs, all those items supposedly resistant to change . . . the repertoire, on the other hand, enacts embodied memory: performances, gestures, orality, movement, dance, singing – in short, all those acts usually thought of as ephemeral, nonreproducible knowledge.

Diana Taylor, The Archive and the Repertoire[2]

[A]n archive of sexuality, and gay and lesbian life . . . must preserve and produce not just knowledge but feeling.

Ann Cvetkovich, An Archive of Feelings[3]

A Queer Climate

It is 14 January 2010, and I am listening to RTÉ Radio 1 while preparing this manuscript. Pat Kenny introduces a panel on homosexuality and religion. In the wake of the Ryan and Murphy reports, and ongoing debates concerning same-sex partnership and marriage legislation, this kind of discussion is not unusual. Although many people have been celebrating the secularization of Irish society for some time now, it still remains commonplace for sexual matters to be measured against religious convention. Much of this pattern has recently been shaped by attempts to hold the Catholic Church accountable for the sexual violence it inflicted on its faithful, while simultaneously regulating dogmatic morality. However, the constant recourse to religious tenets also reveals the nation's continued difficulty with thinking about sexuality almost as anything other than a matter of religious reference. There is a Kafkaesque quality to this dynamic, as authority is unveiled as corrupt, and ostensibly rejected, only to be preserved through the repetition of a nuanced form of antagonism.

On this occasion, four speakers are present: Brian Finnegan, editor of *Gay Community News*; Gina Menzies, a liberal theologian; John Murray, lecturer in moral theology at Mater Dei Institute of Education in Dublin; and Ali Saleem, theologian and secretary to the imam at the Islamic Cultural Centre of Ireland. While Finnegan describes how the Church has isolated him and many of his generation, and Menzies challenges readings of the Bible used to condemn gay people, the other two speakers provide more stringent contributions. Murray underscores the natural 'complementarity of the male and female body', while Saleem appeals to his belief that God created the world 'in pairs' as evidence for the immorality of homosexuality.[4]

This debate followed a number of other high-profile instances of sexual panic that ushered in the new year. The first included the revelation that Democratic Unionist Party politician and Evangelical Pentecostalist Iris Robinson had an illicit relationship with a nineteen-year-old family friend in 2007, while also acquiring him money from two separate property developers to establish a small business. The affair took place around the time Robinson denounced homosexuality as an 'abomination' on BBC Radio Ulster, while advising that she knew a 'lovely psychiatrist' who could help those afflicted.[5] Another incident involved Pope Benedict XVI embellishing his well-known thoughts on same-sex relationships, by criticizing 'laws or proposals which, in the name of fighting discrimination, strike at the biological basis of the difference between the sexes', while stressing that 'for man, the path to be taken cannot be determined by caprice or wilfulness, but must rather correspond to the structure willed by the creator.'[6] This comment came one year after his suggestion in December 2008 that 'saving humanity from homosexual or transsexual behaviour was just as important as saving the rainforest from destruction.'[7] But perhaps the most significant event of all was the amendment of the Defamation Act that took effect on 1 January 2010, and which rendered blasphemy illegal under Irish law.

While listening to the panel discussion on the day in question, I received an e-mail from my contact at Cork University Press. The board had concerns that some of the material included here might contravene the blasphemy law, and suggested that sections should be cut. Understandably, perhaps, there were concerns surrounding section 36 of the Act, which states:

(1) A person who publishes or utters blasphemous matter shall be guilty of an offence and shall be liable upon conviction on indictment to a fine not exceeding €100,000 [amended to €25,000].

(2) For the purposes of this section, a person publishes or utters blasphemous matter if (a) he or she publishes or utters matter that is grossly abusive or insulting in relation to matters held sacred by any religion, thereby causing outrage among a substantial number of the adherents of that religion, and (b) he or she intends, by the publication or utterance of the matter concerned, to cause such outrage.[8]

While the publisher had reservations with specific references to religion within the anthology, the truth is that any text invested in the support of any form of sexual liberty might resonate as blasphemous. Although I had largely considered the new law laughable since it was first discussed in 2009, and felt partly reassured by the government's claim that it was ratified just to solve a technical hitch and not easy to enforce, the possibility that it might have an impact on the freedom of expression in more covert, insidious ways suddenly seemed very real, and unsettling. If the Vatican is allowed to issue documents that maintain that 'the particular inclination of the homosexual person . . . is a more or less strong tendency ordered toward an intrinsic moral evil',[9] then those affected by such outbursts must surely be allowed to disagree with similar conviction. Thankfully, the publisher was in agreement, encouraged by the Act's protection of 'literary, artistic, political, scientific, or academic value in the matter to which the offence relates'.[10]

Despite the concerns raised on this occasion, the reality is that in the plays and performance documents assembled in this book, religion rarely appears as the archenemy, although on occasion specific formations and expressions of religious belief come under focus. Written and performed between 2000 and 2010, the pieces both challenge exclusionary ideologies and hegemonic practices quite generally, but also strive to imagine alternative ways of being with others, and being in the world. The works are queer in so far as they explore tensions surrounding sexual difference in the broadest sense, in a manner that illuminates and interrogates issues that affect a wide range of people, including those who neither identify as Irish nor queer. Sexuality is explored in the familiar contexts of family, religion, society and nation, while alternative modes of relationality are simultaneously rehearsed.

While many of these pieces broach issues related to homosexuality, I should say that I do not think of them as 'gay plays' for a number of reasons. First, it seems reductive to try to attribute sexuality to a text or a performance. As I understand it, gay is an elected, subjective position, and not a genre. Second, and more importantly, gay and lesbian politics have changed to the extent that while there may still be some consensus surrounding certain shared goals, there are also many differences. For example, while it seems that same-sex partnership legislation is increasingly important to many, for others only marriage is an acceptable form of legal recognition. But at all levels of society there are many people who have no interest in legally binding unions whatsoever. Within certain strands of queer studies too, for instance, there is a growing recognition of the necessity for minorities to engage in political networks that target the production of violence and inequality on systemic rather than just subjective domains. For the purposes of this collection, the word 'queer' seems to be the most useful term for holding in place the varied and shifting concerns of lesbian, gay, bisexual, trans, and queer-identifying individuals (LGBTQ), while extending an invitation of engagement to those who are curious, questioning, or just straight with a twist. Understood in this way, the title *Queer Notions* denotes an array of thematic, aesthetic and political positions that work in different ways to critique heteronormativity, with an eye to the future, and the possibilities it engenders.

The primary aim of this collection is to document some of the ideas and embodied interventions that have shaped Irish LGBTQ culture(s) in recent times, principally in the years following the decriminalization of male homosexuality in 1993 and up to the present, which has been politically dominated by calls for civil partnership and/or marriage provision. Decriminalization and discussions surrounding partnership legislation are important benchmarks in the development of sexual politics in Ireland, and theatre and performance have been among the most important fora through which these issues have been negotiated. In various ways, the plays and performances represented here have reflected, sustained and influenced queer lives, enriched Irish theatre and performance practice, and vigorously contested the homogenizing project of nation-building on which the Irish Literary Theatre was established. The anthology strives to provide a home to a representative selection of as yet unsettled material that is always at risk of being lost in the fissures of dominant historiographical practice, and to make possible the formation of a repertoire of this work for future generations to reflect upon. On 16 June 2008, the Irish Queer Archives were officially handed over to the National Library of Ireland for collection. This marked an important turning point in the country's recognition of the enormous contribution of queer lives to Irish culture, and served as a reminder of the necessity to register ongoing activity. While it is now commonplace to record live theatre digitally, in the past a lot of performance has gone undocumented even in literary and visual form. This is especially true of work that emerges within the context of community arts practice.

In addition to vitalizing Irish LGBTQ studies, this book also makes a significant contribution to Irish theatre and performance studies. Many of the people involved in the writing, production and performance of the events documented here move between the fringe and the mainstream, rendering these distinctions less stable in the process. These artists have been integral to the enrichment of Irish theatre and performance, not only in the exploration of alternative themes, but in developing a range of dramaturgical strategies, theatrical languages and aesthetic devices that have shifted the focus of Irish theatre from being both logo- and author-centric, to being a more collaborative, participatory, performance-focused form. In short, this book, and the performances on which it is based, seeks to articulate important developments within Irish LGBTQ studies and Irish theatre and performance studies, offering itself as an archive of knowledge and feeling,[11] that goes some way to reveal the passion and creativity that invigorate and agitate the margins of culture.

Queering the Canon, Redressing the Archive

It has been well documented that the leading mode of theatrical practice in Ireland throughout the twentieth century was primarily literary, often naturalist, and frequently concerned with questions of nationhood. Established at the turn of the twentieth century, the Irish Literary Theatre was primarily a postcolonial exercise and its work often bore the features common to the produce of cultural nationalism, not least of all in its frequent idealization of national subjects as part of a strategic fortifying response to colonial dominance. As has been frequently observed, not only have female characters been typically confined to the imaginary realm in Irish drama, as a currency or site of contestation over which male characters might battle, but female authorship and theatre participation has gone largely ignored until quite recently.[12] Similarly, gay and lesbian characters, themes, authors and practitioners have frequently been rendered invisible, even as they literally and symbolically disturbed the terms by which Irish culture and citizenship were defined.

Within the context of Irish literary studies, a good deal of attention has been paid to the development of gay and lesbian writing in the twentieth century. In this respect, Éibhear Walshe's *Sex, Nation and Dissent in Irish Writing* (1997) is a seminal collection in the analysis of gender and sexuality.[13] So too are Walshe's essays on Oscar Wilde, Kate O'Brien, Emma Donoghue and Colm Tóibín, for example. But within the context of Irish theatre and performance studies, arguably less attention has been paid to divergent sexualities. While the growth of the independent theatre sector in the 1980s created a platform for the articulation of new voices via new forms, many groups remained silent and/or unspoken of. In the introduction to a special edition of *Modern Drama* (2004) devoted to Irish theatre criticism, editors Brian Singleton and Karen Fricker draw attention to their contributors' claims that the voices of the urban working class, certain women and homosexuals have continued to remain relatively mute in Irish culture.[14]

On the issue of homosexuality, this critical silence is somewhat surprising, given that the subject has often featured in work by leading playwrights including Thomas Kilroy and Brian Friel. Indeed, both Kilroy's *The Death and Resurrection of Mr Roche* (1968) and Friel's *The Gentle Island* (1971) were met with hostility when they premiered at the Dublin Theatre Festival. More recently, however, Kilroy's *Christ Deliver Us!* (after Frank Wedekin's *Spring Awakening*) featured a giddy dance and lingering kiss between two teenage boys in a diocesan secondary school in 1950s Ireland. When it opened on 16 February 2010, beautifully directed by Wayne Jordan, the scene took place downstage centre, and worked powerfully to critique other instances of sexual oppression in the play world, as well as in Irish culture more generally. This was *Dancing at Lughnasa* for a post-*Billy Elliot* generation. Still remaining within the canonical tradition, virtually all of Frank McGuinness's dramatic writing pivots on a queer dramaturgy. In these examples (which are not exhaustive) homosexuality and queerness typically function to destabilize history, widely accepted truths and grand narratives. This is especially true of McGuinness's *oeuvre*, which has consistently explored the relationship between homosexuality and the production of knowledge in an Irish context. Until very recently, however, this dimension to McGuinness's work has largely gone unnoticed. For instance, David Cregan exposes how, for a long time, critics typically deferred engagement with issues of homosexuality in the playwright's work, preferring to 'subvert or skirt these contentious themes'.[15] Further, he suggests that this myopia has been shaped by the strong Catholic, nationalist traditions in Ireland. Drawing attention to this oversight, Cregan emphasizes the importance of giving due attention to how figurations of queer sexuality work to unsettle the theatrical canon and the heterogeneous nationalism with which it is associated: 'Representations of homosexuality and gay characters are often the sexual dynamite McGuinness ignites to blow up the organization of history that dominates and dictates solidified or essentialized Irish identities.'[16]

While Cregan's call is a timely intervention in analysing representations of non-normative sexualities in Irish drama and theatre, it also prompts us to think about how LGBTQ people make meaning beyond the national stage. Indeed, Cregan's edited collection *Deviant Acts* (2009) goes some way to analysing a wider spectrum of practices and representations.[17] Although one of the earliest controversies involving homosexuality in Irish theatre included the UK-based Gay Sweatshop's production of *Mister X* and *Any Woman Can* in 1976, it was not until the late 1980s, and tentatively throughout the 1990s, that Irish theatre began exploring issues surrounding homosexuality with any consistency. The correlative of this, of course, is that the same might be said of any expression of sexuality. To this I would say that while the combined efforts of those working in women's and gay rights were crucial to Irish culture's reckoning with these matters around this time, the illegality of male homosexuality created an atmosphere where issues concerning non-normative sexualities were more contentious.

One of the earliest theatre groups to exclusively explore gay and lesbian experience was Muted Cupid (1991), a Dublin-based company that staged plays often with a more optimistic nuance, in contrast to less favourable media coverage and public perception. As member Frank Thackaberry puts it, the focus was 'nearer to the issues of day-to-day

living than issues of life and death'.[18] Prior to its establishment, directed
by Des Braiden for Acorn Productions at the Hawk's Well Theatre, Sligo,
Aodhán Madden's *Sea Urchins* (1988) explored the murder of a young
gay man on Dún Laoghaire pier. The production resonated with the
murder of Declan Flynn in Fairview Park, Dublin, in 1982 by a gang
who were eventually given suspended sentences of manslaughter. Later,
another important production included Wet Paint Art's *Tangles* (1990),
directed and developed with the company by David Grant, which
explored tensions surrounding being a gay teenager in working-class
Dublin. The production went on national tour, prompting one reviewer
who saw the show at the Old Museum Arts Centre in Belfast to pick up
on the play's broader critique of discrimination by stressing that the
main character Kevin (played by Anthony Brophy) could have been
'Black, Protestant, or whatever'.[19] In the same year, Geraldine Aron's *The
Stanley Parkers* (1990), produced by Druid Lane Theatre and directed
by Garry Hynes, explored the life of a gay couple dealing with AIDS.
When Stanley (played by Des Keogh) becomes ill, he and his partner
Dimitri (played by Michael Roberts) reflect upon their lives together.

In the middle of the 1990s, Patrick Mason directed Tony Kushner's
Angels in America: The Millennium Approaches at the Abbey Theatre
(1995). This was one of the most commercially and critically successful
plays of the decade which dealt explicitly with the AIDS crisis under
Ronald Reagan's administration. However, its Irish premiere was a relative failure. While there has never been a clear consensus as to why this
was the case, Mason suggests that Irish audiences thought it was 'about
queers', and consequently felt that it was not 'about us'. Perhaps this was
the case, or maybe, as Patrick Lonergan suggests, people stayed away
because they considered it an American play, and not about Ireland.[20]
Either way, the event underscores the importance of context to the res-
onance of queer theatre and performance.

Despite the apparent failure of *Angels*, Gerry Stembridge's *The Gay
Detective* garnered considerable success when it was produced at the
Project Arts Centre in Dublin one year later in 1996, after which it trans-
ferred to the Tricycle in London. Set in 1993, the year of
decriminalization, the play is both a thriller and a love story that includes
gay-bashing, romantic entanglements, and a maze of moral quandaries.
The reference to a gay politician also resonated with the real-life incident
in 1994 that involved Junior Minister Emmet Stagg being arrested in the
Phoenix Park on suspicion of soliciting sex with men.

In addition to these theatrical endeavours, a discrete and increasingly commercialized gay and lesbian culture was experimenting with different performance idioms that did not necessarily rely upon well-crafted scripts. The activist initiatives of groups such as the National Gay and Lesbian Federation (1979) and the Gay and Lesbian Equality Network (1988), as well as events such as Pride (which began as a one-day event in Dublin in 1983), often drew on performative approaches to politics, as do similar groups today, such as MarriagEquality (2008). We might also think of aLAF (a Lesbian Arts Festival, 1999) in this regard. Also, it is important to note how significant pub, club and popular culture were in the development of queer performance in Ireland, especially during the 1980s and 1990s. The careers of per-formers such as Shirley Temple Bar and Panti, as well as the lesbian performance troupe the Shamcocks, developed in bars and clubs before they crossed over to the mainstream. First established in Sides nightclub in 1987, the subversive beauty pageant the Alternative Miss Ireland (AMI) has continued to be a central force in the queer per-formance calendar, harnessing boundless creativity to raise awareness and finance for HIV and AIDS organizations. Indeed, many of the contributors to this book have also been involved with this event.[21] This is especially true of Panti, founding organizer and emcee, who has had three plays staged since 2007, and Neil Watkins, whose cross-dressed alter ego Heidi Konnt won the competition in 2005.

In addition to AMI, the establishment of the International Dublin Gay Theatre Festival in 2004 marked another significant turn in the life of queer theatre and performance in Ireland. The fortnight-long fes-tival was initially started to coincide with the 150th anniversary of the birth of Oscar Wilde, and reputed to be the first of its kind in Europe. While the festival initially sought, somewhat problematically, to 'cele-brate gay men's contribution to the arts',[22] it soon broadened its scope, identifying criteria for admission to include 'works by gay writers, works that have a gay relevance or theme, or works that include either performance or another artistic contribution by gay people'.[23] Both Verity-Alicia Mavenawitz's *The Drowning Room* and Neil Watkins's *A Cure for Homosexuality* first appeared as part of this festival. However, a split in the core organizing committee has meant that two separate festivals will take place for the first time in 2010: the International Dublin Gay Theatre Festival and the Absolut Gay Theatre Festival Dublin. Whatever the precise reason behind this development, the division, or rather multiplication, of the festival reminds us that there is no such thing as a unified gay agenda.

More recently still, another interesting development has been the addition of the Queer Notions programme to the Dublin Pride Festival in June 2009, curated by THISISPOPBABY in association with Calipo Theatre Company. Led by Jenny Jennings and Phillip McMahon, whose play *Danny and Chantelle (Still Here)* appears in this book, THISISPOP-BABY is dedicated to exploring the intersection of popular and queer culture across a wide range of activity, from new writing to music to experimental performance. Although Queer Notions has only taken place one year so far, it has already registered as a potentially important arena for nurturing and showcasing the best of local talent, while also providing a platform for encountering the work of international artists.[24] For example, Úna McKevitt's devised piece *Victor and Gord, Ali and Michael*, which was initially developed as part of Project Brand New early in 2009, was given its first full staging in Queer Notions, as was a version of Panti's *A Woman in Progress*.

Plays and Performance Documents

While this volume aims to include work that is representative and varied, as is the nature of edited collections, it is not the complete picture of queer performance in Ireland. Despite my efforts to uncover recently produced work worth publishing in more regional centres, including Northern Ireland (although there is no neat parallel in the development of LGBTQ culture to be observed), the Republic's capital still appears to be one the most active centres of both theatre and queer culture. Suffice to say, there is room for more research into this field.

The plays are organized chronologically, according to their premiere dates. Loughlin Deegan's *The Queen & Peacock* (2000) opens the collection, and it explores the phenomenon of the Irish in London. However, Deegan's play takes place as Ireland's economy is improving, and many of those who once emigrated are returning home. Despite this trend, in an old gay bar in London, Donegal man Paul still cannot bring himself to tell his family that he is gay. His inability to come out is not just explained by variations in the cultural mores of Ireland and England. When he meets Willie, an openly gay teenager from Dublin who does not understand his reservations, a ten-year age gap seems to render them worlds apart, and a difference in rural and urban attitudes is thrown into relief.

Deirdre Kinahan's *Passage* (2001) similarly explores the issue of emigration. Following her mother's death in London, Kate sorts through her few belongings with her partner Sara, trying to piece together a picture of a highly private life. Following a rift, Kate did not see her mother for years and had never met her relatives in Ireland. Her relationship to her family and nation is deeply divided, and her mother's death exposes deep wounds. Hidden truths gradually emerge and precipitate a process of healing.

In *A Cure for Homosexuality* (2005) Neil Watkins explores the darker side of male sexuality. The play examines religious and political violence against gays, while also considering issues surrounding the erotic attachment to subjection in the character Paddy Doyle. The narrative crosses time and place, passing references to Ireland, Germany and the USA. First performed in a gay bar in Dublin as part of the International Dublin Gay Theatre Festival, Watkins abandoned the fourth wall to deliver his performance up close and personal to those present. Featuring an unsettling mix of humour, carnality and brute realism, Watkins's play is foremost a hard-hitting exploration of the psychology that propels people to denounce gays and stigmatize those with HIV and AIDS, while claiming that homosexuality can be cured through recourse to psychiatry or religion.

Also first produced at the International Dublin Gay Theatre Festival, Verity-Alicia Mavenawitz's *The Drowning Room* (2006) is a more restrained reflection on what drives people to commit hate crimes, with a focus on a homophobic attack that leads to one man's death. More importantly, however, the play is a study of how the family and friends of both victim and perpetrator cope with their respective losses. Over the course of one evening, a group meet to scatter the ashes of their recently deceased friend and relative, Seán. The play is both a work of mourning and an affirmation of life, which calls for society to learn from its violence.

Currently Writer in Association at the Abbey Theatre, Phillip McMahon's two-hander *Danny and Chantelle (Still Here)* (2006) is also a mixture of loss and celebration. Two twenty-something, working-class Dubliners take a bus to the inner city, plotting the night ahead as they hurtle towards their destination. Reaching a nightclub, they bump into man-about-town Swiss-Tony, who introduces queer desire into the mix. The excitement of clubbing and sexual awakening is counterpointed by the demolition of the Ballymun tower blocks, which forms the play's dramatic backdrop, and frames the piece as a melancholic poem about a range of people and places in a time of radical transition.

An interesting feature of queer performance practice is that often it resists its own documentation. This is especially true of devised work, solo performance or experimental theatre that does not anticipate repeated runs. Quite often too, this approach actually thrives on ephemerality: quickly created to speak to and resonate within the moment, and never recorded. Nonetheless, while these works may be difficult to incorporate into a repertoire, they are valuable additions to the archive. Here, we might also blur the boundary between the terms 'archive' and 'repertoire': after all, isn't it true that new performance often manages somewhat mysteriously to absorb the trace of its formally undocumented antecedent? Often too, this transmission is actually recognizable to audiences, especially in localized or community contexts. Nonetheless, the book also includes examples of visual and literary documentation of performances that, while perhaps difficult to restage, are of central significance.

The contribution of a photo-essay by graphic artist Niall Sweeney is a wonderful example of how visual and performance cultures interact. For nearly two decades Sweeney's own work has been extremely important in the visual imagining and documentation of queer culture in Ireland, and his images take us back to 1987. A founding member of AMI, Sweeney has continued to design for the annual event. Further, he was behind the organization and design of important queer club nights throughout the 1990s, such as Elevator, Powderbubble, HAM and GAG, which extended the boundaries of performance and visual culture. These events were also where theatre companies such as Corn Exchange and visual artists such as Anne Seagrave made fledgling career appearances. On 11 October 2007, Sweeney's five-hour performance *The Story of 'O'* played at the Sugar Club, Dublin. Combining visual and performance media, it explored queer culture in Ireland, and included participation by a range of other artists, including Panti, Watkins and McMahon. Produced by THISISPOPBABY, Sweeney performed his show *Revolver* as part of the Darklight Film Festival at the Lighthouse Cinema, Dublin, on 3 October 2009. This live production combined lecture, storytelling and performance, juxtaposed against mediated visuals of Sweeney's graphic design from the 1980s right up to the present.

Devised by Úna McKevitt, *Victor and Gord, Ali and Michael* (2009) is a performance piece that marks a shift in theatrical form within the collection. The script and performance emerged through workshops led by McKevitt with the cast, and it is based on very personal exposition. While the production was first developed early in 2009, the piece included here was staged as part of the Queer Notion's programme in June of the same year. It was later restaged with some new cast members for the Dublin Fringe Festival in October 2009, and again in February 2010 – the script altered to reflect the stories of the new performers. The work is of interest to a collection like this, not only because the performers include gay people who discuss sexuality on stage, but that the process of theatre-making, and the reality style of performance, explore a form of intimacy between the people on stage and in the audience quite unique to Irish theatre.

The inclusion of Panti's *A Woman in Progress* (2009) is important for many reasons. While Panti has been performing in Ireland in pubs and clubs for nearly two decades, and recently made acclaimed forays into more conventional theatre spaces, this is the first script that the performer has published. Again, this is something of a performance document rather than a play to be restaged. Given that the material is so specific to Panti's persona, it is unlikely to be produced by anyone else, although I am sure somebody would have lots of fun trying. The play is additionally significant for premiering at the Ulster Bank Dublin Theatre Festival in 2009, which marked a significant moment in the centralizing of queer performance within the mainstream. Beginning with Pope John Paul II's visit to Ireland in 1979, Panti explores changes in Irish culture, and the fashioning of her persona in the intervening years. While certain conservative attitudes and institutions are challenged, Panti reserves her strongest criticism for the gay community, which she sees as being commercially obsessed and politically indifferent.

Performing the Future

The performance artist Guillermo Gómez-Peña describes the fetishizing of transgression as culture's growing obsession with the 'mainstream bizarre'.[25] When it comes to queer theatre and performance, this tendency is especially pertinent. Typically, queer artists and audiences are mobilized to challenge normativity, to the extent that a certain transgressive erotics underpin this kind of arts practice. The great irony, of course, is that if and when what appear as central battles for LGBTQ people are won – such as same-sex partnership legislation, for instance – queer culture will have to continue to rethink its relationship to the status quo if it is to remain of any critical value. This will certainly necessitate thinking beyond issues deemed to affect LGBTQ people alone, in order to address connections with other marginalized groups. On this note, Brokentalkers' production of Seán Millar's *Silver Stars* (2008), a song-cycle based on interviews with older gay Irishmen, and largely performed by non-actors, might be seen to reflect a new shift in queer culture's youth-bias.[26] Evolving the meaning of 'queer' will also involve exploring how violence and inequality are produced on systemic levels, not least of all by the global capitalism and neoliberal processes that actually rendered LGBTQ people visible, as was the case in Ireland during the Celtic Tiger era. For those working in theatre and perform-ance, this will surely involve developing new theses, dramaturgical strategies and performance aesthetics, inside and outside of conven-tional spaces, in order to stage what Jacques Rancière had referred to as scenes of dissensus that continually destabilize the co-ordinates of agreement in a range of unforeseen and productive ways.[27]

In Jacques Derrida's *Archive Fever* (1998), a title which perversely inflects the title of this introductory essay, the philosopher claims that the archive is about a responsibility to the future: 'It is a question of the future, the question of the future itself, the question of a response, of a promise and of a responsibility for tomorrow.'[28] Following on, while *Queer Notions* offers itself as a record of what *was*, its most important contribution is to what *might be*. As Derrida continues: 'The archive: if we want to know what that will have meant, we will only know in times to come.'[29] Meanwhile, from the present-past, this book suggests that the queerest notion of all might be to do something with the notions that flit across its pages: to embody the ideas, to run with them, to act up and act out; in short, to perform.

Notes and References

1 Frank McGuinness quoted in interview with Sara Keating, 'Observe a Son of Ulster', *Irish Times*, 14 September 2009. Read online at http://www.irishtimes.com/newspaper/features/2009/0914/1224254469314.html
2 Diana Taylor, *The Archive and the Repertoire: Performing Cultural Memory in the Americas* (Durham, NC: Duke University Press, 2003), pp. 19–20.
3 Ann Cvetkovich, *An Archive of Feelings: Trauma, Sexuality, and Lesbian Public Cultures* (Durham, NC: Duke University Press, 2003), p. 241.
4 *Today with Pat Kenny*, RTÉ Radio 1, 14 January 2010.
5 *Stephen Nolan Show*, BBC Radio Ulster, 6 June 2008.
6 See Philip Pullella, 'Same-sex Marriage is Threat to Creation, Says Pope', *Irish*

Independent, 12 January 2010. Read online at http://www.independent.ie/world-news/samesex-marriage-is-threat-to-creation-says-pope-2009445.html

7 Phillipe Naughton, 'Pope Accused of Stoking Homophobia after He Equates Homosexuality to Climate Change, *The Times*, 23 December 2008. Read online at http://www.timesonline.co.uk/tol/comment/faith/article5387858.ece

8 Defamation Act 2009. Read online at http://www.oireachtas.ie/documents/bills28/acts/2009/a3109.pdf

9 Joseph Cardinal Ratzinger, 'Letter to the Bishops of the Catholic Church on the Pastoral Care of Homosexual Persons'. Given at Rome, 1 October 1986. Read online at http://www.vatican.va/roman_curia/congregations/cfaith/documents/rc_con_cfaith_doc_19861001_homosexual-persons_en.html

10 Defamation Act 2009.

11 In *An Archive of Feelings*, Cvetkovich emphasizes that archives must tend to knowledge and feeling.

12 See, for example, Catherine Lynette Innes, *Woman and Nation in Irish Literature and Society, 1880–1935* (London: Harvester Wheatsheaf, 1993), and Melissa Sihra (ed.), *Women in Irish Drama: A Century of Authorship and Representation* (Basingstoke and New York: Palgrave Macmillan, 2007).

13 Éibhear Walshe (ed.), *Sex, Nation and Dissent in Irish Writing* (Cork: Cork University Press, 1997).

14 Brian Singleton and Karen Fricker (eds), 'Irish Theatre: Conditions of Criticism', *Modern Drama*, vol. 47, no. 4 (2004), pp. 561–72.

15 David Cregan, 'Irish Theatrical Celebrity and the Critical Subjugation of Difference in the Work of Frank McGuinness', *Modern Drama*, vol. 47, no. 4 (2004), pp. 671–85, at p. 671.

16 Ibid., p. 672.

17 David Cregan (ed.), *Deviant Acts: Essays on Queer Performance* (Dublin: Carysfort Press, 2009).

18 Frank Thackaberry, *Theatre Ireland*, no. 27 (1991), pp. 12–13.

19 Mark Carruthers, '(Gay) Pride and Prejudice', *Fortnight*, no. 38 (July–August 1992), p. 34.

20 In *Theatre and Globalization: Irish Drama in the Celtic Tiger Era* (Basingstoke and New York: Palgrave Macmillan, 2009), Patrick Lonergan discusses this occasion, suggesting that audiences might also have felt alienated by the fact that the play was American. For an extensive discussion, see pp. 128–62.

21 For a study of the Alternative Miss Ireland, see Fintan Walsh, 'Homelysexuality and the "Beauty" Pageant', in Sara Brady and Fintan Walsh (eds.), *Crossroads: Performance Studies and Irish Culture* (Basingstoke and New York: Palgrave Macmillan, 2009), pp. 196–210.

22 See 2004 overview posted on the organization's website. Read online at http://www.gaytheatre.ie/archive/html/2004_overview.html

23 See 2005 overview posted on the organization's website. Read online at http://www.gaytheatre.ie/archive/html/2005_overview.html

24 For example, Queer Notions hosted celebrated UK performer David Hoyle and cabaret duo Bourgeois & Maurice.

25 Guillermo Gómez-Peña, 'Culturas in Extremis: Performing against the Cultural

Backdrop of the Mainstream Bizzare', in Henry Bial (ed.), *The Performance Studies Reader*, 2nd edn (London and New York: Routledge, 2004), pp. 345–56, at p. 346.

26 The show was first performed at the Bealtaine Festival in 2008, and it went on to play at the Ulster Bank Dublin Theatre Festival in 2009, before being programmed in New York's Under the Radar Festival in January 2010. So far, the production has also been booked to play in Paris and a selection of other international venues in 2010.

27 See Jacques Rancière, *Dissensus: On Politics and Aesthetics*, trans. Steven Corcoran (London and New York: Continuum, 2010).

28 Jacques Derrida, *Archive Fever: A Freudian Impression*, trans. Eric Prenowitz (Chicago: University of Chicago Press, 1998), p. 36.

29 Ibid.

The Queen & Peacock

LOUGHLIN DEEGAN

Dedicated to the memory of Jim Daly
and John Hewitt

The Queen & Peacock was first presented at the Garter Lange Arts Centre, Waterford, on 31 August 2000 by Red Kettle Theatre Company.

CAST

Mark	Tony Flynn
Bob	John Hewitt
Willie	Alan Leech
Paul	Charlie Bonner

PRODUCTION TEAM

Director	Jim Nolan
Designer	Moggie Douglas
Lighting designer	Jim Daly
Costume designer	Mona Manahan

CHARACTERS

Mark, *thirty-two*
Bob, *late forties*
Willie, *nineteen*
Paul, *late twenties*

Act One

It is early evening in the Queen & Peacock bar in Brixton, London – a beautiful old establishment that has seen better days. In view is a long, wooden counter, backed by mirrors and glass shelves, which are stacked with bottles of spirits, glasses, bar memorabilia and various oddities. A 'fruit machine' stands against the stage-right wall. There is a number of stools along the counter and around the bar are a few tables surrounded by lower stools. Stage left is the door to the street, complete with brass fittings and stained-glass panels (a few of which have been replaced by ordinary smoked glass). Stage right is a blind corridor, which leads to the toilets. There is also a door behind the counter, which leads to a storeroom offstage. As the lights come up WILLIE *is playing the fruit machine.* BOB, *the barman, is busy polishing glasses.* MARK, *dressed in loud street drag, is dancing provocatively to Suede's album* Coming Up, *which is playing loudly from the CD player behind the bar. He prances, panther-like, conscious of every inch of his ornamented body, covering the entire stage area. He is empathizing animatedly with the words of 'Trash' until the music stops suddenly.*

MARK: (*To* BOB) Hey, leave that on. I'm warming up here.

BOB: Enough.

MARK: Bob!

BOB: I said, enough. It's giving me a headache.

MARK: Oh typical, darling. Ruin the fun then, why don't you? What a pity I don't have a rattle for you to steal as well, that would make your day altogether.

BOB: Would it now?

MARK: It would, darling, I'm sure it would. (*He moves over to* WILLIE.) I'm terribly sorry, Mavis, he's not always this cross.

WILLIE: (*Looking around, uninterested*) What?

BOB: Just sit down, Mark.

MARK: You have a problem with my dancing?

BOB: No.

MARK: With the music, is it?

BOB: Not with the music, no.

MARK: Well what, then? This is a public house, is it not? A place where people come to enjoy themselves, to let their hair down a little; it's like a bloody morgue in here this evening.

BOB: I wonder how that could be, then?

          (*Pause*)

MARK: I have no idea. (*Changing the subject quickly, he wanders over to* WILLIE.) So what do you think of him then, Bob? My latest find.

WILLIE: Me! Me bollix, I am.

MARK: Charming, isn't he?

BOB: Indeed.

WILLIE: Fuck off.

MARK: Irish, he is. From Dublin.

BOB: I see.

MARK: Cute, eh?

WILLIE: Ah Jaysus.

BOB: Whatever you say, Mark.

MARK: Another one to add to my collection. The latest in a long line.

WILLIE: What bleedin' line?

MARK: The latest in the longest line, looking for love.

WILLIE: He's a fucking lunatic, he is.

BOB: You could say that.

MARK: Oh but I've found him now. This is the one, don't you think? My search is over.

WILLIE: Ah Jaysus!

BOB: If *you* say so.

MARK: No, no. I want to know what *you* think.

BOB: (*Slight pause*) I can't imagine why.

MARK: Because Gertie seeks Bobbie's approval on all matters of the heart. (*Beat*) You know this.

BOB: Does she really?

MARK: Yes, she does. So go on, admit it, he's adorable, isn't he?

BOB: (*Pause*) I wouldn't know, Mark.

MARK: What? Whatever can you mean? Surely even you can recognize unspoilt beauty when you see it.

WILLIE: Hey. (*Slightly coy*) Shag off, would ya?

MARK: Well, Bobbie?

BOB: (*Sternly*) I said, I wouldn't know. OK, Mark?

MARK: Oh! Touchy, touchy.

BOB: Do you need me to write it down for you?

MARK: Somebody got out of bed the wrong side this morning, then, didn't they?

BOB: (*Beat*) So, been in London long, then, Willie?

MARK: He only arrived yesterday – if you're so interested.

WILLIE: I can speak for meself, I can.

MARK: Came over on the boat.

WILLIE: Flew over actually. Can't stand boats, me.

MARK: His first night in London and who do you think he bumps into?

WILLIE: (*To* BOB) They make me sick, they do.

MARK: Just his luck, eh?

WILLIE: We took the boat to France on our school tour last year and I puked me bleedin' ring up for a solid twenty hours, no joking.

MARK: Standing at the bar, he was, looking all lost and lonely.

WILLIE: I was in me hole.

MARK: Just my type, eh Bob?

WILLIE: I wasn't a bit lost. I was having a great fucking time.

MARK: Poor little Paddy, all on his own in the big city.

WILLIE: Bollix. I was grand, I was. Giving it socks, Bob, in this club, you know? Hadn't a clue where I was going to kip, but I couldn't give a shite. You should have seen this place. Jaysus!

MARK: Heaven!

WILLIE: Heaven is right. Thank you, God, I said, I'll never ask for another thing again. I promise.

MARK: You're so sweet, Mavis.

WILLIE: When I walked in there, first I says, fuck this, like, this is me, Bob, you know? This is the place for me. The size of it, like. Don't get me wrong now, we have clubs an' all in Dublin, loads of them, but nothing like this place.

MARK: Why doesn't that surprise me?

WILLIE: There must have been a couple of thousand men in this joint, no joking.

MARK: Slight exaggeration, darling.

WILLIE: Muscle Marys most of them.

MARK: Fake tans and a bucket of steroids! Not a real man amongst them.

WILLIE: Your eyes would be out on stilts.

MARK: Running around sticking their tits into each other's faces.

WILLIE: I was tripping over me tongue, Bob. (*He sticks out his tongue, pointing at it.*)

MARK: Oh please, Mavis.

WILLIE: Footprints, you know, like?

MARK: He couldn't take his eyes off me as soon as I walked in the door.

WILLIE: What? Fuck off. One guy even asked me if I did rubber. I hadn't a bleedin' clue what he was on about. I thought he meant condoms, safe sex, like, so I said I did. He wanted me to head home with him, and get all dressed up! He had the gear too, head to toe. Fucked if I know what he'd have done to me. Remoulded me probably, into the bleedin' Michelin Man.

MARK: No chance, Mavis. Those queens never live up to their butch promises. Wrapping last night's quiche in cling film would be more like it.

WILLIE: And you'd know, would you?

MARK: Indeed I would. Gertie's been there before, remember. (*Beat*) Many, many times.

WILLIE: From home, he was. A big redneck of a culchie from Mayo, packed into tight black rubber.

MARK: No surprise there.

WILLIE: We ended up talking about the Ga after.

MARK: See? Told you.

BOB: The Ga? What's that, then?

WILLIE: You know, the GAA, like. The hurling and the football.

BOB: Oh right.

MARK: Scintillating conversation, I'm sure. It's no wonder you're such a big hit with the boys.

WILLIE: (*Getting annoyed with* MARK) Oh yeah? Well maybe I should have gone back to his gaff then.

MARK: (*Embracing* WILLIE *now*) Yes, but then you would never have met Gertrude here, would you my sweet?

WILLIE: (*Shrugging him off*) Exactly.

MARK: And what's that supposed to mean? I didn't hear you complain last night when you needed somewhere to sleep, did I?

WILLIE: Yeah well. (*To* BOB) I was supposed to be kipping with a friend of me neighbour's cousin, I was, but when I rang the bleedin' number, they'd never even heard of the fucker.

BOB: People move on, I suppose.

MARK: Exactly, Mavis. And Bobbie here doesn't need to know the intimate details of your sleeping arrangements, do you, darling? What possible interest could he have in where *you* spent the night? (*He kisses* WILLIE *on the head.*)

WILLIE: Hey, leave it, will ya? I don't like people touching me hair.

MARK: Mousse abuse, Mavis, that's what that is, mousse abuse.

WILLIE: Piss off, would ya? You said it was fine earlier. And stop calling me Mavis. My name is Willie, OK?

MARK: We all have our crosses to bear.

WILLIE: (*Checking his hair*) It looks OK, does it, Bob? It doesn't look stupid or anything?

BOB: It looks fine to me, Willie.

MARK: I thought you said you couldn't tell how he looked? Changed your mind all of a sudden, have you?

BOB: He looks fine to me.

WILLIE: We're off out again tonight; where is it again you said?

MARK: I can't remember.

WILLIE: No, that place you said earlier. The Meat Hook or something?

MARK: The Hoist, darling, the Hoist.

WILLIE: Sounds bleedin' deadly.

MARK: Separates the men from the boys, I assure you.

WILLIE: I can't fucking wait.

MARK: I'm just not sure that you're up to it yet, Mavis. In a few more years maybe.

WILLIE: Fuck off, would ya? I'm nineteen, I am. I've seen much worse than that place, I have.

MARK: I wouldn't bet on it.

WILLIE: Have you ever been, Bob?

MARK: Him! Ha!

WILLIE: What?

BOB: No. Not my scene, I'm afraid, Willie.

WILLIE: Oh sorry. I thought . . .

MARK: What? That . . . that Bob was a fairy? Oh perish the thought, darling. Who'd have him, for pity's sake, an old man like him? Bob doesn't get involved in any of that *messy* stuff, do you, Bob? Mr. Private is what he is, Mavis. Mr. Hands off. (*Pause*) Why, Bobbie here defined the term 'asexual', didn't you, darling?

(BOB *doesn't respond.*)

WILLIE: What? The silent but deadly type, is it? Eh Bob?

MARK: Take my advice, Mavis, the quiet silent types are the ones you have to watch. They tend to creep up on you when you least expect it. (*Pause*) My long-suffering mother always warned me about the quiet ones, but do you think I listened?

BOB: Your mother, you say?

WILLIE: Warned you about what?

BOB: I wasn't aware that you actually had a mother, Mark.

MARK: Everybody has a mother, don't they?

WILLIE: Unless they were grown in a test tube or something, like a bleedin' fungus.

BOB: So where is she, then, this mother of yours?

MARK: She lives in Kent.

BOB: Kent?!

MARK: Yes, Kent, what's wrong with that? You have heard of Kent, haven't you? It's . . . in a small town, a village. You wouldn't know it.

BOB: Really?

MARK: Yes, really.

BOB: And you go to Kent a lot, do you?

MARK: No, but . . . I speak to her almost every day.

BOB: Do you now?

MARK: All the time, yes. We talk for hours on the telephone, every single day.

BOB: I've just never heard you mentioning her before, that's all.

MARK: I always mention my mother, always.

WILLIE: My ma is bleedin' great, she is.

MARK: Never stop talking about her actually.

WILLIE: Raised five of us, on her own an' all.

MARK: You mustn't have been around at the time, Bobbie dear. Funny that; you don't know every small detail about us, now do you? Despite all your eavesdropping.

WILLIE: Gave me no grief about coming here nor nothing.

BOB: (*To* MARK) Is that so?

MARK: It is.

WILLIE: It is, yeah.

BOB: Where did you say you were off to again, Willie?

WILLIE: Yeah, yeah. The Pulley, no, no –

MARK: (*Very cross now*) The Hoist!

WILLIE: The Hoist, that's it. Can't wait to get all tied up, me. (*To* BOB) Hung, drawn and quartered, more like. Shouldn't we be heading, then?

BOB: Wouldn't want to miss any of the excitement, eh Mark?

WILLIE: Exactly. (*To* BOB) No offence, like, but it's as quiet as a nun's orgasm in here, it is.

BOB: (*To* MARK) Then there's nothing to wait around for, is there?

WILLIE: Unless the woodworm come out later and start lap-dancing or something?

BOB: Nothing Willie would be interested in at least.

WILLIE: So what are we waiting for?

MARK: One for the road, then. If you insist, Bob.

WILLIE: (*Looks at his watch*) Ah Jaysus, but it's nearly –

MARK: Is that a problem?

WILLIE: Well no, it's just that –

MARK: What, darling?

WILLIE: I thought we were going after this one. (*Trying not to let* BOB *hear*)

You said we might go to that bar in Soho first. The one where –

MARK: Well Gertie's just changed her mind, hasn't she?

WILLIE: Ah fuck.

MARK: A woman's prerogative, sweetie. And besides, what Bob's not telling you, Mavis, is that it's a special occasion in the Queen's tonight. Maybe we should stick around after all.

WILLIE: What occasion? (*Pause*) A geriatric's tea party, is it?

MARK: Not a party, no.

WILLIE: What then?

MARK: Mine's a vodka and tonic. No ice. No slice.

WILLIE: Fuck off, it's your fuckin' round.

MARK: I'm going for a waz.

(MARK *exits*)

WILLIE: Jaysus! Did you hear that?

BOB: (*Cold*) The same again then, is it, Willie?

WILLIE: (*Checks his pockets for money*) It's not as if I have a choice, like, is it?

BOB: Not really, no.

WILLIE: Just a quick one, that bollix said. Just the one in some boozer halfway across the bleedin' city. I didn't know where we were going and now that we're here, he's acting like a right bleedin' wanker.

BOB: (*Placing the drink on the counter*) One bottle of Bud.

WILLIE: He'd want to cop-on pretty soon, or I'll be out of here on me own, I will. And he could start buying a round or two any minute now as well. Spend money for England that fucker would – my money! – and win bleedin' medals at it too.

BOB: (*Placing* MARK's *drink on the counter*) And one vodka and tonic.

WILLIE: I'd better be sorting meself out with a job pretty sharpish, like, or it'll be me eating dead cats out of dustbins, with no bleedin' curry sauce on 'em neither. (*Giving* BOB *a fiver*) Cheers, Bob. (WILLIE *takes his Bud and moves to one of the lower tables.*) May the bollix choke on it.

(*The door from the street opens and* PAUL *enters.*)

PAUL: Bob. (*To* WILLIE) How's it going?

BOB: Pint of ale?

PAUL: Aye.

(MARK *returns from the toilet.*)

MARK: Oh! The Laughing Cavalier has landed, then, I see.

PAUL: And the Mona Lisa is on her perch as usual.

MARK: Not my style, darling. Too dowdy by far. 'The Rape of Venus', now that's a painting.

PAUL: I wouldn't know it.

MARK: (*Takes his drink from the counter*) No, you wouldn't, I suppose. Ooh! Look at you. We *are* all dressed up this evening, aren't we? (*He sniffs.*) Tell me, that's never cheap aftershave I smell. Going out, are we?

         (PAUL *doesn't answer.*)

MARK: A little freakish, isn't it, Paul? Under the circumstances?

PAUL: And what circumstances would they be?

MARK: Florence Nightingale is never gallivanting with other men whilst her poor boyfriend is lying sick in his hospital bed, is she?

PAUL: Fuck you, Mark, OK?

MARK: Ouch! Touchy subject, is it, dear?

PAUL: It's not a subject at all actually, as well you know.

MARK: Oh really? Just good friends, was it, all that time?

PAUL: Something like that, yeah.

MARK: Speaking of which – have you met Willie, Paul?

PAUL: I don't believe I have.

MARK: My new toy boy.

PAUL: Oh great.

WILLIE: Oh no, don't mind me at all, lads. You fuckers just fight away amongst yourselves. I'm having a brilliant time here on me own, I am; can't wait to tell 'em back home about all the great times I'm having over here in London, oh no.

MARK: Just put a sock in it, Mavis, will you?

WILLIE: As opposed to a pair of fishnets, is it?

MARK: Oh touché, Fifi, touché!

PAUL: (*Brightening now*) Dublin I take it?

WILLIE: Yeah. Ballyfermot. So?

PAUL: Paul, Paul Brennan, from Dungloe.

MARK: Mary to his friends, of course.

WILLIE: What? Never heard of it.

PAUL: In Donegal, like.

WILLIE: Oh yeah. Mountains and stuff. We did it in school. (*Beat*) Fluky bastards.

PAUL: What?

WILLIE: The All-Ireland, like. 'Ninety-two. Yous were steeped.

PAUL: Fuck off, would ya? Yous were well beaten.

WILLIE: Me bollix we were. If Charlie Redmond hadn't missed that penalty, dozy fucker.

PAUL: Do you hear this lad? The same crowd wouldn't beat carpets. And when's the last time you fuckers won anything anyway?

WILLIE: Only . . . 'Ninety-five, sure.

PAUL: An awful bad year for the football, that.

WILLIE: Well, it took yous long enough, didn't it?

PAUL: It was worth waiting for, I'll tell you. (*To* BOB) The biggest deal it was at home, Bob. The whole county was covered in flags and banners and . . . they even had the roads painted green and gold, for fuck's sake.

MARK: Oh my God, Bob. The emigrants are bonding. Pass me a tissue quick. They'll start singing soon.

PAUL: (*To* WILLIE) You follow the Ga, then, Willie, I take it?

WILLIE: I do, yeah. Born with a hurley up me arse, I was.

MARK: That would explain a lot.

WILLIE: And we'd a mad bastard of a Brother in school who played football for Kerry, or so he said anyways.

PAUL: Jaysus, but I miss talking about the football. Nobody in here has a fucking clue what I'd be on about, not since . . . anyway.

MARK: Oh no, here we go again.

PAUL: If himself was here now, eh Bob?

WILLIE: Who's this?

PAUL: A friend of ours, Willie.

WILLIE: From home?

PAUL: From Wicklow, he is.

WILLIE: Ah Jaysus.

PAUL: I know. Never won a thing in their lives, but do you think he'd admit that?

WILLIE: They still play with bleedin' pigs' bladders down there. Think the Sam Maguire is a fucking *céilí* dance or something.

PAUL: (*Enjoying this so much*) He's quick enough to say he's from Wexford all right, when it suits him.

WILLIE: A bleedin' turncoat, eh?

PAUL: From the border, he claims. Two hundred yards or something. (*Pause*) Anyway. (*He pauses again.*) Cheers, Willie.

WILLIE: Yeah, cheers.

(*They drink.* PAUL *places a letter on the counter for* BOB.)

PAUL: That's for you.

MARK: Oh, Postman Paddy is still working, then, is he?

PAUL: My last port of call, as always.

MARK: How cosy.

BOB: (*Taking the letter*) Thank you, Paul.

PAUL: Don't mention it.

(BOB *places the letter on the shelf behind him without opening it.*)

MARK: Another bill, I presume?

BOB: I'm sure it is.

MARK: You're getting a few of those.

BOB: Really? Who's counting? (*To* PAUL) You were up at the hospital, then, were you?

PAUL: I was, yeah. And it's a hospice actually, not a hospital, which you would know of course if either of yous bothered your arses to call up and visit the poor fucker.

MARK: Oh Bob's a very busy man, aren't you, Bob?

PAUL: And what's your excuse?

WILLIE: Who's this? Who's in hospital?

MARK: The Wild Colonial Boy, Mavis. Who else?

WILLIE: Yer man from Wicklow?

MARK: The very same.

WILLIE: And what's wrong with him? Is it serious?

MARK: Very good question. Paul?

PAUL: Ah you know yourself, Willie. He's not at all well. (*Pause*) Not for a while now.

MARK: You haven't found the Queen & Peacock at its best, I'm afraid, my dear. In the absence of its number one customer. Isn't that right, Bob?

BOB: Whatever you say, Mark.

MARK: Kept this place open, he did, with the amount he put away.

WILLIE: Really?

MARK: See that stool there? That's out of bounds, that is.

WILLIE: Yer man's stool?

MARK: Do you know the Turin Shroud, Mavis?

WILLIE: Yeah.

MARK: Well that humble barstool there is almost as precious and venerated as any shroud. Except that it's only some Paddy's bony ass you see imprinted there, not the face of the saviour of mankind at all.

BOB: Leave it out, Mark.

MARK: Oh what? Sensitive all of a sudden, are we? (*Pause*) So what is the news from the bedside, then? Do tell.

PAUL: I didn't think you cared.

MARK: I don't. I just thought it would be polite to ask. (*He finishes his drink.*) Barman, another when you're ready.

WILLIE: But I thought we were –

MARK: And make this one a double. Lover-boy is paying.

WILLIE: Me again! Fuck off with your lover-boy. I'm bleedin' skint, me.

MARK: Jesus, Mavis! What are you wittering on about now?

WILLIE: But I bought the last two, so I did. I'm only saying, like.

MARK: Well don't say, OK? We get the picture, dear. I can't bloody stand it the way you keep wittering on like that.

WILLIE: I'm not the bleedin' Bank of Ireland, I'm not.

MARK: (*Shouting at him, he is suddenly very angry*) Just shut up for two fucking seconds and pay for the fucking drinks, would you?

(WILLIE *is speechless for a moment.*)

WILLIE: Jaysus! (*He looks at* BOB, *then roots in his pockets once more for change. He is now very low on cash.*) You'd better give the fucker a drink, so, if he wants the bleedin' thing that bad. Fucking hell!

(*There is an awkward silence.*)

PAUL: I wouldn't be paying too much attention to us this evening, Willie, if I was you.

WILLIE: Bloody right, I wouldn't.

PAUL: It's nothing personal, like.

MARK: And why is that, Paul? Oh yes, of course, I forgot. We're supposed to be in mourning, aren't we? And I neglected to wear my little black number as well, how remiss of me.

WILLIE: In mourning! But the poor fucker isn't dead, is he?

MARK: Almost, darling. Very, very nearly.

WILLIE: Oh really. Jaysus! Sorry to hear it.

MARK: Yes, well. Maybe that's worth hanging around for, eh Mavis? Maybe we should stick around for that famous Irish wake we hear so much about. The opportunity of seeing a bunch of Irish queens mourning one of their own is not a sight I'd want to miss.

WILLIE: Ah fuck off.

PAUL: You don't have a wake until after the person is dead.

WILLIE: Exactly.

MARK: But Paulie, dear, yesterday you said it was only a matter of hours. He could be dead right now for all we know. Who's to say he's not lying on some cold slab in there now, limp and wasted and no more.

WILLIE: Ah steady on, Mark.

MARK: Well, he could be.

PAUL: He's not. I just came from there.

MARK: The true little Irish saint.

PAUL: A lot you'd know about it.

MARK: Maybe more than you think, darling.

WILLIE: One of them plastic Paddys, is it?

MARK: Good God no. I've just seen quite a few Paddys pass through here, Mavis, that's all. There has been a steady trail of your kind to London for as long as anyone cares to remember. The gay Irish. Hibernoqueer! A particular breed of immigrant. Unique in many ways and not to be mistaken with the common or garden Paddy who's natural habitat is down Kilburn way, and who hangs out on building sites all day, eats greasy fry-ups every evening, the remains of which he vomits onto somebody's doorstep after 'a good feed of pints' later that night. Oh no, Hibernoqueer is a different class of asylum seeker altogether.

WILLIE: What the fuck's he talking about now?

PAUL: He's spouting shite again.

MARK: They're in hiding, Mavis, aren't they? From their families and their friends and from the prying eye of our good friend, Holy Catholic Ireland.

WILLIE: Holy Catholic Ireland! Jaysus! I haven't heard that one in a while.

MARK: And our absent friend there is a prime example of the species. Best specimen you'd find under any rock in London. Except maybe Paulie here of course.

BOB: Not now, Mark.

MARK: Why, it's the truth, isn't it? Our friend before and now you, there's a bit of a pattern developing, wouldn't you say? (*He sings.*) 'Just a little bit of history repeating'.

PAUL: Not from where I'm standing, it's not.

MARK: Oh I wouldn't be so sure, there are quite a few similarities when you think about it.

PAUL: I'm not a bit like him, and well you know.

MARK: Oh what? Re-established contact with the outside world, then, have you?

BOB: Shut it, Mark.

PAUL: Bastard!

WILLIE: What are you on about now?

PAUL: He thinks he's being smart, Willie, that's all, thinks he knows everything about everyone. Well he's not nearly as smart as he thinks.

MARK: You've been in contact with your family, then, have you?

PAUL: So what if I have?

MARK: Well that's a first.

PAUL: What's it to you?

MARK: (*Clapping*) Clap, clap, clap. How long have you been in London now, twelve months is it?

PAUL: Fuck you, Mark, OK?

MARK: And?

PAUL: What? And what?

MARK: Did you tell them, then?

PAUL: That's none of your fucking business.

MARK: I'll take that as a no, then. Oh well, maybe next time, yeah? Maybe next time.

(MARK *exits to the toilets.*)

BOB: Just ignore him.

PAUL: That's easier said. (*Pause*) I know I shouldn't let him get to me. It's just . . . They wrote to me, Bob. The day before yesterday. They're selling the place.

BOB: What, the bar?

PAUL: And the house. Unless I go back, it's going in the paper next week.

WILLIE: (*Looking from one to the other*) What bar?

PAUL: Home, Willie.

WILLIE: What about it?

PAUL: I'm the only son. I've worked there all me life, but . . .

WILLIE: But what?

PAUL: Since I wasn't in touch and all, the ole lad says he's going to sell it. There's no point in him wearing his fingers to the bone, he says, if I don't want it. (*Pause*) It's up to me.

WILLIE: So what's stopping you? I'll bleedin' take it if you don't want it. What did you say?

PAUL: Nothing yet. They want me to ring them to let them know once and for all.

WILLIE: Free beer all night every night! So what are you waiting for? Ring them now for fuck's sake. Go on, will ya?

(*A mobile phone rings somewhere.*)

WILLIE: (*Joking*) Maybe that's them, Paul.

PAUL: Fuck off.

WILLIE: I'm telling ya. Answer the bloody thing.

(MARK *enters from the toilet.*)

MARK: My phone! (*Delighted*) At last!

PAUL: Oh bloody typical, here we go again.

WILLIE: What?

PAUL: Tonight of all nights.

(MARK *runs to his large shoulder bag, digging desperately for the phone.*)

MARK: (*In an exaggerated female voice*) Hello, Gertrude speaking. How may I help you? (*Pause*) Of course, darling, of course. Any time, any place.

WILLIE: Who's he talking to?

PAUL: You don't want to know, trust me.

(MARK *turns to* WILLIE, *covering the phone with his hand.*)

MARK: A pen, Mavis, quick. In the bag, a pen. (*Into phone again*) Just bear with me for two ticks, duckie.

(WILLIE *moves to the bag and starts searching.*)

WILLIE: What's he need a pen for now?

(WILLIE *hands the pen to* MARK *and stands listening as* MARK *calls out an address and writes it on his hand.*)

MARK: Seventeen, yes, Josephine Avenue, ah Brixton, what luck, I'm just around the corner. I'll only be two minutes. Looking forward to meeting you too. Bye-bye.

WILLIE: Who was that?

MARK: (*Beginning to gather up his belongings*) Nobody, darling, nobody. I've a little job to do.

WILLIE: Where are you going?

MARK: Nowhere, you just wait here, sweetheart. I'll be back for you, I promise.

WILLIE: Wait here? What for? What's going on, Mark?

MARK: Do you want to have a good time tonight, darling, or don't you?

WILLIE: Yeah, I do but –

MARK: But what?

WILLIE: That call, what was that about?

MARK: Money, darling.

WILLIE: What?

MARK: We need money for the gear, don't we? The happy powder, remember? Gertie said she'd look after it, didn't she?

WILLIE: Yeah but –

MARK: Well then. Stop moaning. I haven't all day. Leave everything to Gertie. OK?

BOB: I warned you about this, Mark. I told you.

MARK: I hear you loud and clear, captain.

BOB: Don't go bringing that stuff back here neither.

MARK: Of course not, darling. No need to get your knickers in a twist. I'm well aware of the house rules. More aware than anyone, really. Ten minutes, Mavis, I promise.

(MARK *blows him a kiss and leaves with his belongings. There is silence in the bar.* WILLIE *eventually speaks.*)

WILLIE: Is that fucker coming back, or what? (BOB *turns away from him without speaking.*) Oh that's bleedin' great, that is. So much for the Irish looking out for each other, then. (*Pause*) What the fuck am I doing in this fucking hole anyways? Fuck this. (*He finishes his drink in a hurry.*) I'm going . . . (*He can't decide.*) I'm going for a piss.

(WILLIE *exits to the toilets.* PAUL *and* BOB *are silent for a few moments.*)

BOB: He seems like a nice lad. How long will he last, do you think?

(PAUL *doesn't respond.*)

BOB: As long as his money does, I suppose.

(*Again, no response*)

BOB: Oh well, he'll learn, I'm sure, like they all do.

(BOB *takes the envelope from the counter and rips it opens. He starts to read.*)

PAUL: Listen, Bob, I couldn't give two fucks what he learns, OK? If you play with fire, you're going to get burnt, that's how it works nowadays; it's a big bad world out there and the sooner he realizes it the better.

BOB: The voice of experience now, is it?

PAUL: Something like that, yeah.

BOB: Fine. Fine. It has nothing to do with me in any case. (*Pause*) Can I get you another drink? (*Pause*) Suit yourself. (*Pause*) I'll just be inside, then. I've a few things to look after.

PAUL: How long was he coming in here, eh?

BOB: Who's this, then?

PAUL: You know bloody well who I'm talking about. Fifteen years it is.

BOB: Is that so?

PAUL: Only you'd swear to God he'd never put his foot over the door there, the way you're carrying on now. This bar is the only place he felt at home over here, do you know that? He told me that, one night when we were totally pissed, the only other person in this whole city that he regarded as a friend.

BOB: Well good for him, then.

PAUL: And now that he's drawing his last in there you don't even have the decency to drop in for two minutes and say goodbye to the poor fucker.

BOB: What you do is your business; what I do is mine.

PAUL: Oh really, and that's the end of it, is it? No discussion. That's the way it is because Bob says so.

BOB: Something like that, yes.

    (*Pause*)

PAUL: I don't understand you, do you know that?

BOB: And nobody is asking you to, are they?

    (*Pause*)

BOB: (*Ripping up the letter as he goes*) Now I have some business to attend to.

PAUL: That's from the brewery, isn't it?

BOB: What is?

PAUL: That fucking letter.

BOB: It's addressed to me, I think.

PAUL: Oh fine, fuck off, so, why don't you? Don't know why I give a shite anyways.

(PAUL *finishes his drink.* BOB *opens a bottle of Budweiser and places it on the counter.*)

BOB: That's for the young lad when he comes out. He might need it. You can look after yourself.

PAUL: I wouldn't want to be relying on you anyway, would I?

(BOB *exits without answering him. Pause.*)

PAUL: Stubborn old bollocks.

PAUL *finishes his pint, moves behind the bar and begins pulling a new pint for himself.* WILLIE *enters. He is sheepish now. A little embarrassed.*)

PAUL: There's another drink there for you.

WILLIE: Jaysus, thanks. I can't buy you one back though.

PAUL: It's not me you need to be thanking at all, it's Bob who left it for you.

WILLIE: Oh right, well cheers anyway.

PAUL: Yeah, cheers.

WILLIE: Listen, Paul . . .

PAUL: Don't mention it, Willie.

WILLIE: What I said there earlier, like.

PAUL: It's grand, Willie. Grand.

WILLIE: Right.

(PAUL *leaves money by the till and comes back out in front of the bar with his new pint. They are silent briefly.*)

PAUL: I don't mean to be telling you your business nor nothing, Willie, but I'd be careful, you know? You never know who you're going to get mixed up with over here.

WILLIE: What? In the big city, is it? You're as bad as he is.

PAUL: I'm just saying, that's all.

WILLIE: Well don't bother, I'm nearly twenty, I am, and I think it's deadly over here, bleedin' deadly.

PAUL: Good for you, then.

WILLIE: For fuck's sake, like. Do you not?

PAUL: Ah, you know. (*Pause*) I'm a bit of a home bird, me. Ireland makes sense to me, you know how it is. I understand things over there.

WILLIE: So what are you doing over here, so?

PAUL: I'd go home in the morning if I could, to be honest with you. I'd be on that bloody plane first thing tomorrow morning if I could at all, nothing in the whole world would stop me.

WILLIE: Why don't you then?

PAUL: Things are never that simple. It's a small town so it is.

WILLIE: Bally-whatyamacallit?

PAUL: *Dungloe*, we call it.

WILLIE: Right, yeah!

PAUL: A great place it is too, you should pop up there sometime. Some sessions, I'll tell ya.

WILLIE: Ah, I'm OK here, thanks, for the time being anyway.

PAUL: Jack the lad, I was, at home. With the pub, the lads, the training, the few pints, you know how it is. But then this happened and sure you know the rest.

WILLIE: What? What happened?

PAUL: Ah you know, like. Mark was right earlier when he said about . . . nobody at home knows anything about . . . you know.

WILLIE: What? Being a big homo, like?

PAUL: (*Smiling*) Aye. They'd fucking die if they did, the auld lad would have a heart attack on the spot; no joking, it'd kill him and me ma as well. They're set in their ways, so they are.

WILLIE: My ma knew I was a bleedin' Nellie years before I did. I was sent home from school for kissing me best mate in front of the whole of junior infants. I think that convinced her.

PAUL: You're having me on.

WILLIE: No, no, he was fucking gorgeous, he was.

PAUL: Jaysus! That's a good one. You were an early starter, so.

WILLIE: First out of the traps, yeah. And now look at me.

PAUL: Fair play to you, Willie. Fair play to you.

(*Pause*)

WILLIE: Do you never go into the city at all then?

PAUL: Ah you know, I used to when I came over first. I couldn't get enough of it at first, thought it was the business altogether.

WILLIE: The clubs like?

PAUL: Well yeah, yeah, and you know . . . all the men, like.

WILLIE: (*Relishing the thought*) I know. Tell me about it!

PAUL: Just getting on with it, not caring about anything. They couldn't give a shite about anything over here, and you think that's the fucking business when you come over first.

WILLIE: I know!

PAUL: But you get tired of it all soon enough, let me tell you.

WILLIE: No way!

PAUL: All they ever think about, all they ever talk about, is themselves – their hair, their clothes, their drugs and their fucking bastardin' pecs. Jesus Christ, but if I have to listen to one more conversation in a bar about good fucking pecs, I'll fucking kill someone.

WILLIE: I thought pecs were trainers, I did, when I heard of them first. 'Nike pecs', like – sounded like they cost a fortune.

PAUL: They do! Three years in a some gym at least. And like, why is it, Willie, that there's not one fecking homo over here who follows the soccer?

WILLIE: I fucking do!

PAUL: They all think that they're so bloody cool and gorgeous. And different – different, my hole. They're all the same, Willie, all of them. You should see them in these clubs. It's like an identical twins convention or one of those, except that they're all from the same fecking family or something. I'm surprised some of them can find themselves to go home at all, that they don't mistake themselves for somebody else on the way out. That would be great, eh? Half three some morning in Heaven and total chaos breaks out because nobody knows who's who, and they all lose it – freak out – because they suddenly see that they are all the same – that nobody is anybody any more.

WILLIE: It'd be like something out of the *Twilight Zone* or one of those.

PAUL: They'd all have to go home together, to the same flat, because nobody would remember where home was!

WILLIE: But to whose flat?

PAUL: Jaysus, yeah! Two thousand faggots crammed into a single bed in a grotty dive in Neasden or somewhere – two thousand pairs of perfect pecs lying there wondering who was going to get up and turn the light off. (*They laugh heartily.*)

PAUL: Of course they'd probably love that – being in the one bed – the perverts.

WILLIE: You're only jealous, you are.

PAUL: Fuck off. I am not. Why be jealous of them eejits. Out of their heads on E most of them.

WILLIE: And what's wrong with that?

PAUL: When I came over to London first, Willie, I was the only one drinking pints. Everyone else was drinking water from plastic bottles.

WILLIE: You're joking.

PAUL: Honest to God. Yer man here was the only person I could have a few decent pints with. (*He indicates towards the stool.*)

WILLIE: Your mate.

PAUL: This was one of the first places I wandered into when I came over. There used to be a real gay bar down the street there and I couldn't bring meself to go in, so I popped in here for a quick pint instead.

WILLIE: A pint of courage, like?

PAUL: Yeah, and I've hardly left the place since.

WILLIE: (*Looking around the bar*) I know the feeling.

PAUL: This place was busier back then, and yer man would be sitting up on his stool there, taking everything in. The quiet silent type, you know the ones.

WILLIE: Oh fuck yeah, they're the dangerous bastards, according to Mark.

PAUL: I sat up beside him here that first time and we got chatting and sure every evening I came in after that it was the same thing. Great craic we used to have, you know? (*Pause*) He was a strange fish, Willie. He'd never talk about . . . you know? . . . being *gay* an' all.

WILLIE: Bit of a closet case, was he?

PAUL: Never be seen dead in a gay bar. Well . . . until he was bollocked altogether. He . . . well you know the drink, like. He could be pretty messy on the drink.

WILLIE: Right.

PAUL: Irish bars mostly, and in here of course; he didn't seem to mind in here.

WILLIE: He wasn't very fussy, then, was he?

PAUL: No, no, not just in here. Went on mad sprees, the two of us did, all over the city. Every Friday night we'd meet in here and head off all over, talking and laughing.

WILLIE: Having the craic, like.

PAUL: But the talking and laughing would always stop, so it would, when he'd had enough to drink, like. You could set your watch by him. Sitting in the back of a taxi, then, without a word between us. (*Pause*) Like a lamb, I used to be, Willie, following him wherever he wanted to go – the Market Tavern or Sub-Station or wherever. The same story every time, it was. Standing guard against a wall in the dark somewhere, a corridor or a corner maybe. Young lads dancing and shite, and us as pissed as two farts. And then some other guy would wander past, you know? Some young lad half his age with big open eyes and no T-shirt on him, and he'd look and yer man would look and that'd be it, he'd be gone, just like that, without even saying goodbye, without even glancing in my direction. (*Pause*) And I wouldn't have wanted him to go, Willie. Even though we wouldn't be saying a word, I wanted him to stay there, in the dark, you know . . . *with me.*

(*Pause.* BOB *re-enters from the storeroom.*)

PAUL: But, do you know, the surest thing was that he'd be in here the next day? No matter where he'd been or who he was with, he'd be sitting on that stool there when I came in the next morning. And it'd be me he'd want to talk to then. Just me and him, talking about the football and the racing and . . . and home, you know?

(*Pause*)

PAUL: (*Looking at* BOB) Yeah well, there's no point going on about it now, Willie, eh? The poor fucker is dying now and nobody here wants to listen to me harping on about it for the next fifteen years or so, do they?

BOB: I don't suppose they do.

(*Pause.* PAUL *exits to the toilet as* MARK *re-enters from the street. His mood has visibly changed.*)

MARK: You're still here, I see.

WILLIE: (*He's not impressed.*) Oh! You're back.

MARK: (*Walking into the pub*) Of course I'm back, why wouldn't I be? This is *my* local, is it not?

WILLIE: Well, yeah.

MARK: I thought you might have gone by now.

WILLIE: No, no, I was waiting. For you!

MARK: Whatever for, darling? (*Taking money out of his jacket*) The lady can pay for her own drinks now.

WILLIE: What?

MARK: A vodka and tonic, barman, please. I don't need your money any more, Mavis, and I don't need to listen to you complaining about paying for things either.

WILLIE: What do you mean? I was only saying, like.

MARK: Well don't, darling, don't say. You're beginning to bore me, as it happens. I think I might be going off you now that I think about it; maybe it's time for a replacement already.

WILLIE: But you can't, you said –

MARK: Oh don't go getting all upset about it. These things happen.

WILLIE: But Mark?

MARK: Maybe you should just fuck off. (BOB *places his drink on the counter.*)

MARK: Cheers, Bob. You're a dear.

WILLIE: What did I do?

MARK: Nothing, darling, nothing. It doesn't matter what you've done.

WILLIE: For fuck's sake.

MARK: Don't go on, you know how I hate it when you go on. Just take the fucking hint, Mavis, OK? Get out of here, go on, go.

BOB: Stay where you are, Willie.

WILLIE: I don't fucking believe this!

(PAUL *returns from the toilet.*)

PAUL: Oh the prodigal son has returned, has he, or should I say, daughter, Mark? That was a quick one.

MARK: Speed is of the essence, dear. In my line of work at least.

PAUL: I wouldn't know.

MARK: I don't believe that for a second.

WILLIE: What line of work?

MARK: (*Turning back to him quickly*) Oh you're still here, are you? I thought I told you to leave?

PAUL: Don't you listen to that fucker.

MARK: Oh what, the emigrants have fully bonded, have they? Why am I not surprised? (*He moves to the lower table with his drink.*) And the waiting continues, then, I take it?

PAUL: Does it? I thought you and Willie were going out for the night.

MARK: Oh we're all waiting. All of us. Bob and I just as much as anybody else.

(*Pause*)

PAUL: (*To* WILLIE, *changing the subject*) Has he been giving you grief?

MARK: Why of course not, what are you suggesting? Gertrude couldn't possibly be capable of such acts. But thank you for your concern, darling, it's so nice to see you're all so fond of my latest toy boy all of a sudden. Made an impression, have you, Mavis?

Maybe I shouldn't be so quick to dispose of you after all.

PAUL: (*Aside to* WILLIE) Ignore him. He often gets like this after *a job*.

(MARK *takes a small envelope from his pocket and turns to* WILLIE.)

MARK: Here it is anyway. As requested. Your Colombian Marching Powder!

BOB: Hey, put that away.

MARK: He's never tried it, you see, always wanted to, didn't you, darling? Well now's your chance.

BOB: I told you before.

WILLIE: What? In here, like?

(MARK *goes through the motions of cutting up the cocaine*.)

MARK: Don't worry about him darling, he'll be fine, won't you, Bob?

BOB: Put it away, I said!

MARK: That's exactly what I intend to do. Any minute now.

BOB: I warned you about this.

MARK: You've warned me about so many things, which one could you possibly be referring to now?

BOB: Just take that shit and get out of here.

MARK: I'm just going to powder my nose, sweetheart. That's allowed, isn't it, Bobbie dear, in your little book of rules? But then, we don't want to go down that road, now do we?

(*Pause*. BOB *backs off*.)

MARK: Mavis, dear? After you.

(WILLIE *walks towards* MARK.)

PAUL: Willie!

(WILLIE *hesitates*.)

MARK: Oh for God's sake. Have it your way, then. (*He snorts the first line of coke, rubs his nose and holds the note out to* WILLIE *again*.) You'll never know what you're missing. (*Pause*) Fine, then, Mavis. All the more for Gertrude. It was she who paid for it after all. (*He snorts the second line of coke*.)

PAUL: With her hard-earned cash.

MARK: No harder than delivering letters, Paul. It's just another service.

PAUL: Oh really? I would have thought it was a damn sight harder, the service you provide.

WILLIE: What service?

MARK: You're just jealous, darling, because you couldn't get anyone to do it with you, even if you did pay them.

WILLIE: Pay them! But . . .

MARK: You couldn't even get it off with that drunken Irish friend of yours, for God's sake, and everybody knows that he's slept with half the faggots in London.

PAUL: Cunt.

MARK: Not that he'd remember, state he was in.

WILLIE: You mean you're a –

MARK: Oh for God's sake, Mavis, use your imagination, will you?

WILLIE: Ah fuck!

MARK: You have a problem with that, do you?

WILLIE: I've been kipping with a bleedin' prostitute!

MARK: Oh please. Such a vulgar word. There are so many more elegant descriptions.

WILLIE: Like what?

MARK: Escort, darling. I'm a professional escort.

WILLIE: You escort them to the bleedin' scratcher, is it?

PAUL: Up against the beer kegs round the back of a pub would be more like it.

MARK: (*Suddenly harsher*) Fuck you, *Paddy*, OK?

BOB: One more word and I promise you, you're out of here.

MARK: Oh! What's this? What has Bobbie so cross all of a sudden, then?

BOB: You heard me.

MARK: Not sensitive, I hope?

BOB: Just don't push it, OK?

MARK: You're never barring me, are you? Again!

BOB: If I have to, yes.

MARK: Oh this really is *so* tedious. Mavis, what time is it?

WILLIE: (*Rubbing at his nose*) What?

MARK: I said, what time is it? Are you stupid or something?

WILLIE: Fuck off. It's half past nine.

MARK: Half past nine!

WILLIE: Yeah. And I'm not bleedin' –

MARK: (*Interrupting him*) Look around you, Mavis, and tell me what you see.

WILLIE: What I see?

MARK: Yes, what you see. How many people, Mavis. How many people do you see?

WILLIE: Well four, like.

MARK: Exactly. Four! Only four. One of whom is the barman, correct?

WILLIE: Yeah. What the fuck is –

MARK: It's half past nine on a Saturday night, the place is practically deserted, except for a sad, lonely, old barman and his *three* customers, and he thinks I believe him when he says that he's about to bar one of them.

BOB: I'd survive.

MARK: Oh would you really? Without your favourite customer and all?

        (*Pause*)

WILLIE: So what are we waiting for, then? You said so yourself, this place is –

MARK: Just sit down and shut up, Mavis.

WILLIE: For fuck's sake.

MARK: For the last time, I said we were going nowhere, OK?

PAUL: And why not?

MARK: Excuse me?

PAUL: If this is such a sad place, as you keep saying, why don't you go out with the lad. If you have such an aversion to us Paddys, what are you doing hanging out in an Irish bar for the last ten years anyway?

MARK: An Irish bar! This is not an Irish bar, this is the Queen's, darling! Do you really think that Gertrude would be seen dead in an Irish bar? I don't think so, Paul.

PAUL: Well maybe it's time you left, then.

BOB: Paul! Don't you start.

MARK: No, no, he's right, Bob, standards are slipping. You'd let any kind of a tart in here these days. Maybe it is time I left. Maybe it's time Gertrude dragged herself out of this hole and left these crass, vulgar people behind her.

PAUL: You said it.

BOB: Mark!

PAUL: The door's over there.

BOB: Take it outside.

MARK: There's something rancid going on here. Something foul. He called this place an Irish bar, for fuck's sake.

BOB: I couldn't care less what he called it.

MARK: You've got to stop it, you know. It's no wonder the place is deserted, if that's the case. It's beginning to smell of them.

PAUL: Be very careful now.

MARK: Crawling out from the taps, they are, and up from the sewers.

PAUL: It'd shut it now, if I were you.

MARK: (*He moves over to the stool again.*) Sickly. Like this one. Coughing and spluttering and spreading disease. Drowning his sorrows and waiting. For what, though?

PAUL: Shut the fuck up.

MARK: To get drunk enough, that's what. To get pissed off his fucking face, so he'd have the courage to crawl out of that pathetic closet of his and go hunting down some young, unsuspecting innocent. No need for talking, just wham, bam and thank you ma'am.

PAUL: I'm warning you, Mark.

MARK: Well, sir actually. When you think about it. Thank you, sir. Probably infected half of London with his carry on, dirty bastard.

PAUL: One more word and I'll –

MARK: You'll what? Give me one, is it?

PAUL: Maybe.

MARK: Another big Irishman, is it? Another big Paddy!

BOB: I said outside.

MARK: Can't you put up one of those signs, Bob, you know – no blacks, dogs or Irish. That might keep them out.

PAUL: OK. That's it! (*He grabs* MARK.)

BOB: Paul!

PAUL: You're nothing but a bollocks, Mark, do you know that? A fucking bollocks is what you are.

MARK: Why thank you, Paul, you're too kind.

PAUL: A bloody freak show with your make-up and your dresses and your high-fucking-heels. You don't even know what it is to be normal, so you don't, to be decent and to give a shit about somebody other than yourself. You're not half the person he is, not even now when he's faded away to nothing in there. He has a bigger heart in him than you'll ever have, even now. (*He pushes* MARK *away.*)

MARK: I'm glad you think so.

BOB: Leave it, Paul. Now.

PAUL: I will, yeah. I'll leave it.' Cause I don't even want to touch the fucker. I don't want to have a single thing to do with him.

(PAUL *moves back to his seat and sits down with his back to the others.*)

WILLIE: Does this mean that yer man who's sick –

MARK: Yer man who's sick could have been a little bit more selective about where he stuck his cock, Mavis, *comprende*?

WILLIE: (*Slowly*) Oh right.

(MARK *takes his glass and throws back the vodka.*)

MARK: Another drink, barman. I think I need another drink.
(BOB *doesn't respond.*)

MARK: I said a vodka and tonic, Bob, are you fucking deaf? What does a girl have to do to get a drink around here?

(BOB *still doesn't move.*)

MARK: You might as well give it to me, because then I'll fall down and you can throw me out.

(*Pause.* BOB *turns to prepare the drinks.*)

MARK: And for God's sake turn on a bit of music or something, will you? This is fucking morbid, this is, standing around waiting for the fucker to die. Come on. Music, Bob, quick, liven the place up a bit. That's what you need, you see, get some bands in or a drag act maybe, bring in some real punters.

BOB: (*Placing the drink on the counter*) Why would I need to, I have you, don't I?

MARK: Or a bit of flesh. What do you say? A small PA system, a big prick, and we're in business. (*He sings 'I Will Survive'.*) 'First I was afraid, I was petrified. Thinking I could never live without you by my side.' (*He takes a long drink from his new glass.*)

BOB: OK, OK, very funny, Mark.

MARK: (MARK *continues with the song.*) 'I spent oh so many nights just feeling sorry for myself, I used to cry . . .'

BOB: That's enough now.

MARK: '. . . But now I hold my head up high . . .' (*He jumps up onto one of the lower stools.*)

BOB: Come on, get down from there.

MARK: '. . . And you'll see me. Somebody new.' (*He points towards* WILLIE.) 'Not that fucked up little Paddy who's so in love with me . . .'

BOB: Mark! (*He comes out in front of the bar.*) I said, get down from there.

MARK: '. . . And so you felt like dropping in and just expect me to be true . . .'

BOB: I'm not going to tell you again.

MARK: '. . . But I'm saving all my loving . . .'

(*The public phone on the wall starts to ring.*)

MARK: '. . . For someone who's . . . (*Long pause as they listen to the phone ringing*) loving me.'

(MARK *stops singing as they all stare at the phone.* BOB *eventually answers it.*)

BOB: Hello? The Queen & Peacock.

(*Pause.* MARK *stumbles down from the stool and sits.*)

BOB: Yes, speaking. (*Pause*) That's right. (*Pause*) Yes. (*Pause*) Yes I see. (*Pause*) OK. (*Pause*) Yes, yes. (*Pause*) Yes OK, yes thank you. (*Pause*) Thank you. Goodbye.

(BOB *replaces the receiver. They remain silent for a number of moments.*)

PAUL: The hospice?

BOB: Yes. (*Pause*) They want somebody to go over.

(*Pause*)

PAUL: This is your last chance, Bob.

BOB: (*After some hesitation*) I can't leave the bar.

PAUL: You could shut it. (*Pause*) Fine. Have it your own way, then. (*He moves towards the door.*)

WILLIE: Can I come with you, Paul. Please? I'm not staying here with this fucker.

PAUL: (*Pause*) You're dead fucking right, Willie. Come on, then.

(WILLIE *takes his jacket and they exit. Long pause.* BOB *stands staring at* MARK, *who sits with his head bowed. Slowly* MARK *begins to sob.* BOB *doesn't respond. After a few moments, he fills a whiskey for himself. He then walks out in front of the bar and sits on a high stool, looking at* MARK.)

BOB: Mark. Mark!

(MARK *doesn't respond.* BOB *checks his watch and thinks for a moment.*)

BOB: OK then. (*He moves to the street door, which he bolts, first at the top and then at the bottom. At the sound of the second bolt* MARK *sits upright suddenly.*)

MARK: What are you doing?

(BOB *doesn't answer.*)

MARK: It's not closing time yet.

BOB: I know.

MARK: But you've locked the door.

BOB: So? They're not breaking it down. You said so yourself.

MARK: No . . . But it's . . .

BOB: And they're not likely to now, are they?

(MARK *stands slowly, unsteady on his feet.* BOB *returns behind the bar.*)

MARK: I want to go home.

BOB: Nobody is stopping you.

(*They stand silent for a few moments.* BOB *moves to the storeroom door.*)

MARK: Where are you going?

BOB: Upstairs.

MARK: But . . .

BOB: What?

(MARK *doesn't answer.*)

BOB: Go home. (*Pause*) If that's what you want.

MARK: What do you mean . . .?

BOB: You know what I mean.

MARK: Again? (*Pause*) Now?

BOB: Why not?

MARK: But . . . Willie. I . . . I don't want to.

(*From behind the counter,* BOB *turns off the main light, leaving the bar lit from the street, the toilets, the storeroom and the fruit machine only. He stands silently by the door now, with his hand on the switch.*)

BOB: Go home, then. It's up to you.

MARK *hesitates for some time but then reluctantly moves slowly towards the storeroom. As he does so,* BOB *switches off the light from the toilets and exits. When* MARK *exits behind the bar, the light in the storeroom goes off, leaving the stage lit by the street and the fruit machine only. The light from the street begins to fade slowly and the music rises – 'Saturday Night' by Suede.*

Act Two

It is later the same evening and the Queen & Peacock remains in relative darkness. A face appears at the door from the street, followed by a knocking.

WILLIE: (*Offstage*) Hello! Hello! Are you in there, Bob? Bob! Bob!
(*The knocking continues, more persistent now.*)

WILLIE: (*Offstage*) Where the fuck are ya? Open the bleedin' door, will ya?

(*Eventually a light is turned on in the storeroom and* BOB *appears. He is hassled, but not panicked. He readjusts his clothes as he makes his way to the door.*)

BOB: OK. OK. I'm coming.

(*When he eventually manages to open it,* WILLIE *enters, looking confused.*)

WILLIE: What are you closed for?

BOB: I was . . . I had something to look after.

WILLIE: But it's not even closing yet.

BOB: I was upstairs.

WILLIE: Upstairs! What were you doing up there?

BOB: Well . . .

WILLIE: (*Moving into the bar*) Skiving off, were you? Oh yeah.

BOB: I, 'em, yeah, I wasn't expecting you back. I thought you'd be there all night.

WILLIE: You'd never see that in Dublin, you wouldn't. A pub shut before closing. No way.

BOB: Well you're not in Dublin now, are you?

WILLIE: Dead right, I'm not. Dead bleedin' right.

BOB: What can I do for you, Willie?

WILLIE: What? But I'm . . . Paul asked me to come back, like. He's still filling out forms and that.

BOB: Oh yes.

WILLIE: He asked me to . . . you know? . . . let yous know, like. (*Pause*) About your mate. (*Pause*) Ciarán. (*Pause*) He's dead, so he is. (*Pause*) Shocked, are you?

BOB: (*Beat*) I expected as much.

WILLIE: Before we got there and all. Paul is really cut up about it, you know, about him dying on his own and all. But as I says to him, people die on their own all the time. It can't be that bad, can it? It's not as if anyone can do anything for you at that stage, like.

BOB: I wouldn't know, Willie.

WILLIE: A good mate of yours, was he?

(BOB *just shrugs his shoulders.*)

WILLIE: Yous will miss him, though, eh?

BOB: *Paul* will miss him, yes.

WILLIE: Are you upset, like?

BOB: Well . . . you know.

(*They are silent for a moment.*)

WILLIE: So are you going to give me a drink or what? I need a bleedin' drink, I do, all I've been through. You are open now, aren't you? I wouldn't like to disturb you if you've other things to be doing, like.

BOB: One, then, Willie. A quick one.

(BOB *moves back behind the counter, turning the main lights on again.*)

WILLIE: Oh I've seen it all now, I'm telling you.

BOB: Have you really?

WILLIE: I bleedin' well have.

BOB: Good for you, Willie.

WILLIE: Not meaning to upset you or anything like, but it scared the shite out of me, it did. I'd never seen a dead body before and . . . The state of the poor fucker. He wasn't the size of a dipstick inside in the bed. All *collapsed*, kind of. His eyes were still open and he was staring at the door, he was. They were looking at you no matter where you stood, like one of those paintings you know, and there was no life left in them . . . his eyes . . . all grey, they were.

BOB: Yes. (*Pause*) Thank you, Willie, I . . .

WILLIE: You'd think they'd close the poor bastard's eyes at least, wouldn't ya?

BOB: (*Pause*) I'm sure they will.

WILLIE: Grey, like. Jaysus! (*He stops and takes another drink from the bottle and calms down a little.*) Where's Mark got to then? Head home, did he, or what?

BOB: Mark? Oh he . . .

WILLIE: I'm not surprised, fucking state he was in. Back to the gaff, like?

BOB: Just after you left, Willie. (*He glances into the storeroom briefly.*)

WILLIE: First time he got to bed before midnight in a long time, so. Since his testicles dropped, I'd say. (*He drinks again.*) I was thinking coming over, in the taxi, you know? One of those black jobbies. There're real London them, aren't they?

BOB: So I believe.

WILLIE: Fit a whole Bosnian republic in the back of one of those machines, you would. And I was sitting there, Bob, thinking, you know? About tonight and that, and all the antics in here, like.

(*Pause.* BOB *doesn't respond.*)

WILLIE: That's all a show, that is.

BOB: A show?

WILLIE: There's a lot more between yous crowd than you're letting on. You're not fooling me at all. I know what you're up to all right.

BOB: (*Pause*) What *are* you talking about?

WILLIE: I think you have a bit of a soft spot for our Mark, that's what.

BOB: You what?

WILLIE: For them all, I'd say. You know what I mean.

BOB: Do I now?

WILLIE: The two of yous are great friends behind it all, yourself and Markie Mark. I'll bet ya anything.

(*Pause*)

BOB: I'm a barman, Willie. I open up, I serve drinks, I close. That's it, end of story. I don't get involved.

WILLIE: Ah that's bollix, and you know it. It's all 'cause of yer man, it is. Ciarán!

BOB: What is all because of Ciarán?

WILLIE: Yous are all upset about it, and why wouldn't yous be? But nobody wants to just come out and say it. Real hard chaws, yous think you are.

BOB: You think so?

WILLIE: I do. Mark as well. He's different, he is, when he's not in here. All that Gertie stuff is just an act for when he's in here.

BOB: I'm glad to hear there's some excuse, then.

WILLIE: I was thinking, you see, sitting in the back of Bosnia-Herzegovina there, thinking about why he was so different tonight to last night. He was really sound last night. Came on heavy enough at the club all right, but when we got back to his gaff, he was all quiet, you know? Shy and that. I don't mean to be telling tales from school nor nothing, but he wasn't really into ... you know, like? I wasn't really pushed meself, to be honest with you.

BOB: Oh no?

WILLIE: Well, you know, he's not exactly today's bread today, is he? And the outfit and that. But he just sat there in this long pyjama thingy and we talked, so we did. He was all questions, you know, asking me about Dublin and home and then when I was really pissed, he was all on about minding me, you know? Looking after me and not letting anything happen to me. And then we fell asleep, so we did, the two of us on the bed, without taking our clothes off nor nothing.

BOB: (*Getting flustered*) I'm not sure I need to know all of this, Willie.

WILLIE: What? No! We didn't ... you know, like? ... at all. He just wanted to ... hug me and kiss me neck and that, Jaysus, like. I don't think he's interested much in sex to be honest with you, Bob.

BOB: Is he not?

WILLIE: 'Cause of all that Ford Escort business, I suppose.

BOB: What?

WILLIE: All those auld fuckers slobbering all over him.

BOB: Willie ...

WILLIE: I wouldn't be interested in sex after that neither. Dirty bastards.

BOB: Willie!

WILLIE: What? What?

BOB: (*He hesitates*) Maybe you should go home, Willie.

WILLIE: Home? I don't have a bleedin' home.

BOB: Maybe you should just finish up your drink and go.

WILLIE: Why? What have I done now?

BOB: The bar is closed. I shouldn't have opened. I ... (*He stops.*) Just go, Willie.

(*The street door opens suddenly and* PAUL *enters. Pause.*)

PAUL: (*To* BOB) He told you, I presume.

BOB: Yes. Yes, he did.

WILLIE: I came straight back, like you said.

PAUL: Good. Good man.

WILLIE: Did you get all that stuff sorted, then?

PAUL: The stuff? No I ... (*He turns to* BOB, *changing the subject.*) You weren't rushed off your feet in here, I take it?

BOB: No. (*Pause*) All was quiet.

PAUL: Would've been too late anyway. He was gone before we got there.

    (*Pause.* PAUL *sits*)

WILLIE: So is he down in the freezers now, is he?

PAUL: In the morgue, yeah.

WILLIE: That's what one of the porters says to me, Bob – 'We'll take him down to the freezers now, young lad.' Gas bastards, they were, eh Paul? Innocent as you like, they were, wheeling in this metal jobbie. Dum di dum di dum. Made up like a bed, it was, but when they whipped off the sheet, what was it only a fucking coffin? No joking, like, a metal one, wasn't it, Paul?

PAUL: (*Reluctant*) It was.

WILLIE: So as not to upset the other patients, yer man told me. I didn't think people died of that any more. Are there not drugs, like?

PAUL: Well, there are sometimes, but . . .

WILLIE: So why? Why didn't he just take those?

PAUL: (*Exasperated*) It was too late for any drugs by the time he'd . . . by the time they'd found out.

WILLIE: Oh typical Irishman, eh Paul? Don't go to the hospital unless your two bleedin' legs are hanging off.

    (*Pause. Nobody speaks.* BOB *gives* PAUL *a glass of whiskey without speaking or looking at him.*)

WILLIE: So what do we do now, then, eh? Get all drunk and maudlin, is it, Paul? Start singing and shite? That'll get the punters in all right, Bob.

PAUL: Not sure that I'm up to that just now.

WILLIE: And why not? You're just feeling guilty, you are.

PAUL: Guilty?

WILLIE: Yeah guilty. You just think –

PAUL: In all fairness, Willie, it's a lot you'd know about it.

WILLIE: No, no, I was just saying that –

PAUL: What the fuck's it got to do with you anyway? You never even met Ciarán, so fuck off for a minute with your telling me how I should be feeling, OK?

WILLIE: OK.

PAUL: Feeling guilty, he says. What the fuck do I have to be feeling guilty about? I was the only visitor he got in that place since he went in. It was me who sat with him all day every day, bringing him cigarettes and bottles of Guinness that he couldn't even drink because he was in a coma for fuck's sake. Is that it? Is that what I should be feeling guilty about?

WILLIE: I said, OK!

PAUL: Since when did it become a crime to visit someone in hospital? It's the only fucking decent thing to do, isn't it? Where I come from it is anyway.

WILLIE: Paul, nobody's saying –

PAUL: And what, I should be feeling guilty because I put on a new shirt and got dressed up a bit? Jesus Christ, like. I was planning on going out afterwards, if you must know.

WILLIE: Sure there's nothing wrong with –

PAUL: Planning on copping myself on. Getting a bit of a life, like.

WILLIE: So why the hell didn't you, then?

PAUL: 'Cause I had to do the decent fucking thing, didn't I? Had to call into the hospice after work, like I did every day; like the good fucking friend that I am.

WILLIE: Ah Jaysus.

PAUL: And I sat there talking shite as usual of course. Talking shite to a fucking corpse practically. Until the nurse came over, that is. Told me I looked nice, she did, that I smelt nice as well. The cheap aftershave didn't seem to bother her at all. She took my hand, as if I was his . . . you know. Took my hand and told me not to be upset . . . that he was on his way out. (*Pause. His anger abates a little.*) 'His vital signs are very weak' was how she put it. She gave me a cup of tea and left me there, the chief mourner, you know? I didn't know what to do. I should have said something, but . . . I just sat there, drinking me tea and talking to him, telling him all this crap about work and me supposed to be living the high fucking life in the big city, sitting there holding back the tears and trying to pretend that everything was normal, that this was normal, that I . . . that I was just his friend and . . . and I did feel guilty, oh yeah. But not for leaving him, not for heading back here for a few pints and leaving the poor fucker to die on his own; I felt guilty for sitting there, Willie, and for pretending to be his boyfriend, for fuck's sake. 'Cause that's what I was doing, you see, day after day, sitting there, in me good shirt, yeah, and pretending to meself, taking all their sympathy and . . . And then this evening there, when I was all business, all talk about arrangements and making plans and getting his body home ... this matron type comes in and takes the nurse aside and whispers to her, and looks over at me and whispers some more, and comes over to me then and says in this sorry kind of a voice, as if I'm a child or simple or something, 'Mr. Brennan,' she says, 'I'm afraid we can't let you sign these forms, Mr. Brennan; I know you were very fond of your friend, Mr. Brennan, but it's not up to you, you see, it's the next of kin who must sign these forms.' Not me at all.

WILLIE: Sure who, then, if not you?

(*Pause.* PAUL *looks at* BOB.)

PAUL: Him there, Willie. (*Pause*) His best friend, it would appear.

WILLIE: Did you know about this, Bob?

(*Pause*)

PAUL: Oh he knew all right, didn't you? (*Pause*) That's why they rang here earlier, he had given them this number.

WILLIE: Is that true? (*Pause*) Jaysus!

PAUL: So what are you going to do about it, then?

BOB: About what, Paul?

PAUL: Ah for fuck's sake. The funeral. Getting him home. His family. Who's going to do that, then?

BOB: Nobody.

PAUL: What do you mean 'nobody'? Their son is dead, Bob.

WILLIE: Exactly.

BOB: He doesn't have a family, you know that.

PAUL: That's a load of bollocks, that is.

BOB: He hasn't seen them, or spoken to them, for fifteen years.

PAUL: But that's just families. Irish families. Tell him, Willie.

BOB: They'll arrange it at the hospice. A cremation.

PAUL: A cremation!

WILLIE: Ah Jaysus.

PAUL: Hold on a minute now. He's going back to Ireland. He'll be buried there.

BOB: No. He won't.

PAUL: You can't do that. You can't bury him on his own in a strange fucking city.

BOB: He's been here for fifteen years. That's not strange.

PAUL: It's still not home, though.

WILLIE: It's never home unless there's a family.

BOB: Is that so?

(*A mobile phone rings.* WILLIE *sees* MARK's *bag over by the fruit machine. He walks towards it.*)

PAUL: Fuck you, Bob.

WILLIE: It's Mark's.

PAUL: Fuck you.

WILLIE: What's his bag doing here?

BOB: He must have . . . when he left.

(WILLIE *answers the phone.*)

WILLIE: Hello? (*Pause*) No this is not Gertrude. (*Pause*) No she's . . . *he's* not here. What? What do you mean? (*Pause*) Fuck off! I'll do no such thing, ya bleedin' perv ya. (*Pause*) It doesn't matter who I am. I said . . . No, I won't tell him actually. No, fuck you, ya bollix. OK? Fine, fine. Do so. Fuck off so. And don't ever ring this bleedin' number a– (*The call ends.*) The bollix hung up on me. Do you know what he wanted me to . . . (*He stops, thinking.*). But what's Mark's phone doing –

BOB: He left it behind him, Willie.

WILLIE: (*Taking a step towards the storeroom door*) And earlier, when you were –

BOB: He went home, I told you.

WILLIE: (*Suddenly pointing to the storeroom*) There's somebody in there.

PAUL: What?

BOB: There's nobody there, Willie.

WILLIE: Yous two are never –

BOB: I said there was nobody there.

(MARK *suddenly appears through the storeroom door.*)

MARK: Looking for me, are you, darlings?

(MARK *is no longer in drag. He is barefoot and wearing a pair of black trousers and white shirt that belong to* BOB. *The clothes are obviously too big for* MARK, *but he has arranged them, nevertheless, with a certain 'feminine' grace.*)

PAUL: Jesus Christ!

WILLIE: I knew it. I fucking knew it.

MARK: Did you, sweetie? Well wasn't that smart of you? Somebody give him a gold star, why don't they?

PAUL: Bob?

(MARK *saunters over to* BOB *and kisses him on the cheek.*)

MARK: Thank you, my dear, that was wonderful.

BOB: (*Grabbing* MARK's *arm*) Don't!

MARK: (*Yanking his arm away*) Oh not so rough, darling. Not so rough. (*He rubs at his arm.*) You've changed your tune, haven't you? So gentle before. (*He saunters over to* WILLIE *and takes his phone.*) Mine, I believe.

(WILLIE *relinquishes the phone without speaking.*)

PAUL: What's going on?

MARK: What does it look like, sweetie?

PAUL: I don't believe this.

WILLIE: You don't? I'm fucking speechless.

MARK: (*Approaching* WILLIE) Oh Mavis, dear. Don't be like that.

WILLIE: (*Stepping back*) Stay away from me, you. I've had just about enough of you, I have.

MARK: Oh don't be getting your knickers in a twist, lovie.

WILLIE: Fuck you and your fucking knickers, OK?

BOB: I want you all to leave.

WILLIE: What? Again, is it? Oh I know why you wanted me to go earlier now, so I do, why the fucking door was locked and all.

BOB: I said, I want you all to leave.

WILLIE: Me telling him everything down here.

MARK: Oh but darling, you can't possibly ask us to leave now.

WILLIE: And behind me back . . .

MARK: Things are only beginning to get interesting.

WILLIE: He was rogering fucking Scary Spice upstairs there.

BOB: I'm warning you, Mark. Just leave. (*Loudly*) Now!

MARK: (*Defiant*) Force me, then. Go on. Physically eject me from the building. You'd enjoy that, wouldn't you? A bit of rough and tumble. (*He stares at* BOB *for a few seconds.*) I'm not going anywhere, Bobbie dear. I'm going to have a drink, I am.

(BOB *tries to block his way.*)

BOB: I wouldn't if –

MARK: Don't you even think of touching me, or I swear to Christ I will scream so fucking loud that this whole building will come falling down around your ears and there will be more people in that door within the next ten seconds than there has been in the last three fucking years.

(BOB *hesitates, then stands back.* MARK *takes a bottle of vodka from behind the counter.*)

MARK: Drinks, anyone? They're on the house. (*Pause*) Oh go on, you will. Force yourselves. Bob doesn't mind, do you Bob? (*Pause*) OK then. Abstain if you must. I'll just have to help myself, won't I? (*He moves back in front of the counter, taking the bottle of vodka with him.*) We're all very quiet all of a sudden. Officially in mourning now, is it? We can have that wake at last, can we, now that he's clinically dead and everything?

PAUL: Oh lovely, Mark. Fucking lovely.

MARK: What? What? You have to 'give him a good send off', don't you? It's traditional. (*Rubbing* WILLIE's *head*) What do you think, Mavis?

WILLIE: (*Shrugging him off*) Fuck off and leave me out of this.

MARK: (*Pretending to be shocked*) What, you mean you don't fancy me any more!

WILLIE: Piss off.

MARK: You've gone off me, haven't you? Admit it. I know you have.

WILLIE: So what if I have, what's it to you anyway?

MARK: It'll be the outfit, darling, that's all. I wasn't sure myself. Is it me, do you think?

BOB: Take off those clothes.

MARK: What! Here? No, surely not! You want me to strip here?

BOB: What are you doing wearing my clothes?

MARK: I'm wearing your clothes, darling, because Gertrude wasn't feeling so well all of a sudden, if you must know. She's not feeling nearly as fabulous as she was, Bobbie dear. I wonder why?

BOB: Take them off.

MARK: In my own good time.

PAUL: Will you for fuck's sake just do what he's telling you?

MARK: Oh no, Paul. No no no. (*He takes a swig out of the vodka bottle.*) I'm not going to do what he tells me to do any more, not any more, I'm not. Sick and tired of doing what *he* tells me, I am.

PAUL: Just go home, Mark.

MARK: You see, everybody thinks they can order me around. Everybody in here thinks they can do what they like with me. Even your boyfriend was at it (*He indicates Ciarán's stool.*) before he went and . . . (*He takes another swig.*) Used to tell me

I was a slut, he did. A tart! And, well, he'd know. Isn't that right, Bob?

(BOB *doesn't respond.*)

MARK: You see, Bob knows all about sluts as well, Paul. He likes them like that, he does. Sad miserable sluts. The sadder the better, as it happens.

BOB: Just shut it, Mark.

MARK: (*Approaching* BOB) He likes them desperate, he does. Picks them off when they're weak, when they're down. When they're too pissed to put up any resistance.

BOB: I said, shut your filthy mouth.

MARK: (*Into his face*) Afraid I might reveal something, are we? Afraid I might give away some of your secrets, some of those secrets that you keep locked up in that private room of yours, with your private games and your private, greasy hands.

(BOB *attempts to grab* MARK, *but he shrugs him off easily.*)

MARK: You make me feel ill, you do – bile, darling, vomit – every time. It was never me up there with you. I was miles away, I was. I'm good at that, learned it years ago and it sure comes in handy now and again.

PAUL: This is fucking ridiculous.

MARK: Oh really, and why's that, then?

PAUL: Just not tonight, Mark, please. This is between you and Bob, for another time.

MARK: Oh but tonight is exactly the night, Paulie. What other time could possibly be more appropriate?

BOB: I'm warning you!

MARK: Don't you get it, Paul?

PAUL: (*Angry*) No Mark, I don't get it. I don't fucking get it, and do you know something –

MARK: Ask your boyfriend, Paul, if you don't believe me. (*He turns back to* BOB.) Isn't that right, Bob? Ask Ciarán, if he doesn't believe me.

PAUL: No.

MARK: Oops sorry, I forgot. You can't ask him, can you? He's dead, isn't he?

PAUL: This has absolutely nothing to do with Ciarán.

MARK: Oh Paul, for Christ's sake. How simple do I have to make it for you? He uses people. Like slabs of meat, he does. Your precious Ciarán long before me. (*Pause*)

PAUL: No. That's not true.

MARK: Of course it's true. For the past ten fucking years or something. What? You mean you really didn't know? And there was me thinking you were the best of mates.

PAUL: Bob? (*Pause*) Talk to me. Is this . . . It's not true, is it?

MARK: Oh it's true all right. And do you want to know why? Because your lover-boy was weak, dearie – lonely, sad, weak and drunk, always drunk. Lying on his stomach up there with his hands tied behind his back. Pissed out of his brains, being fucked up the arse by that fat slob there.

WILLIE: Jaysus!

MARK: Better off dead, darling, that's what he is.

PAUL: No.

MARK: Better off dead.

PAUL: No.

MARK: And me? The replacement is all I am. I've only recently been blessed with all this attention, since your good buddy fucked off into that hospice, as it happens. The replacement is all. (*Pause*) A balm for a broken heart maybe. Eh Bobbie?

BOB: (*Turning quickly*) I told you to get out of my bar. All of you. Take your things, and your drinks and (*very loud*) get the fuck out of here.

(*There is silence.*)

PAUL: That's fine by me. (*He takes his jacket from the stool, preparing to leave.*)

WILLIE: Hold on a minute, will you? Where are *you* going?

PAUL: I'm out of my depth here.

WILLIE: What, and I'm Michelle bleedin' Smith, am I?

PAUL: I'm going home.

WILLIE: And what about me, where am I supposed to kip? (*Quickly to* BOB) And don't even think of suggesting that fucking room up there.

PAUL: You can stay with me, till you get yourself sorted out.

WILLIE: Deadly.

MARK: Oh go on then, Paul. Run, why don't you? Away from this mess. Since you're next.

(PAUL *continues towards the door.*)

MARK: Because you're desperate as well, darling. Don't you see that?

PAUL: Not that desperate. Not by a long shot.

MARK: Off with you, then. Go on.

PAUL: I'm not running, Mark. Not from you, not from here, not from anything.

BOB: Unlike himself. (*Pause*)

MARK: What did you say?

BOB: I said, unlike himself.

(*They all look at* BOB, *waiting for him to speak, but he doesn't.*)

MARK: (*Trying to be jovial*) What do you mean? Run, is it? I don't think so, Bobbie. Gertie doesn't do exercise, you should know that by now, you've seen those heels.

BOB: I know what I know.

MARK: What are you saying exactly?

BOB: A barman knows everything, about everyone, you know that. He stands here quietly, sober, watching you all. He sees things, things you don't think he sees, and he hears things, things you wouldn't want him to hear.

MARK: (*Anxious now, nervous*) Oh you're so full of shit, do you know that? Nostradamus now, is it? The oracle in the alehouse!

BOB: Kent, you said, Mark, wasn't it? Your mother.

(MARK *suddenly looks at* BOB, *horrified. He begins to laugh now, desperately seeking a way out.*)

MARK: Kent . . . My mother, yes. So what? An old dear, she is. I've told you this.

BOB: Yes. You have.

MARK: A small village and . . . Blue rinses, you know the type.

BOB: Blue rinses?

MARK: Bridge and bowling. She . . . she's old now, on her own. She says –

BOB: Yes, what is it she says again?

MARK: She says, Gertrude darling . . .

BOB: Yes. Gertrude darling!

MARK: . . . you will be good to me now, won't you, Gertrude?

BOB: Does she now?

MARK: Yes, yes, she does. I'll need somebody, she says, somebody graceful and sweet to take the bare look off her at parties, that's what she always says, to take the bare look off her at parties.

BOB: Fourteen years of age, he was.

MARK: (*Quickly*) What?

BOB: In a park at night, it was.

MARK: What? What's this?

BOB: Men, older than his father, paid him, they did.

MARK: No.

BOB: But he was caught one night, by the police, and he was arrested, wasn't he, Mark?

MARK: Stop it.

BOB: Which caused quite the row at home, I believe, seeing as how there was a report in the papers and everything.

MARK: Don't listen to him, Mavis, he's –

BOB: And how his father wasn't one little bit happy about the family name being dragged through the dirt like that.

MARK: (*Shouts*) Shut up!

BOB: Hit him, I believe, and not for the first time neither.

MARK: Shut up. Shut up.

BOB: So he runs, doesn't he?

MARK: No.

BOB: Over to London, he runs.

WILLIE: London?

MARK: (*Shouting now, with his hands over his ears*) No, I won't listen to this.

BOB: (*Over* MARK's *protests*) Homeless.

MARK: I won't listen to this.

BOB: On the job.

MARK: I won't listen to this.

BOB: Irish!

(MARK *suddenly grabs a flick knife from his bag and jabs it to* BOB's *throat.*)

WILLIE: Irish!

MARK: I said, stop it or I swear to God I'll fucking kill you!

(WILLIE *approaches* MARK *slowly.*)

WILLIE: Mark, listen to me. Easy now. Take it easy, will ya?

MARK: I won't listen to this crap. I won't listen to him making up stories.

WILLIE: Please, just put the knife down.

MARK: Fucking Irish. (*Screaming, he pulls the knife back as if to slash* BOB *with it.*) Jesus Christ, I'll fucking kill you.

(*Pause.* MARK *considers striking* BOB. *They stare at each other for a few moments, until, gradually,* MARK *releases his grip on* BOB. *He appears to almost crumple as his arm lowers and the knife drops from his hand. He slowly moves across the bar, away from the others. Long pause.*)

PAUL: A fucking Paddy all this time? (*Pause*) All the shite we've had to listen to from this bollocks. Going on and on in here as if us Irish were the scum of the earth.

WILLIE: Leave it, Paul, will ya?

PAUL: And if it wasn't in here he was, bad mouthing us, it was out there, looking for any young Irish lad he could find to feed his fucking fetish on.

MARK: Stop it.

WILLIE: Fetish! What fetish?!

PAUL: Fresh off the boat if possible, isn't that right, Mark?

MARK: Shut up.

PAUL: Innocent and scared and needing to be looked after.

MARK: Shut up.

BOB: The longest line, is what he called it.

MARK: No.

BOB: But where do you think that line started, Paul?

MARK: Leave her alone.

BOB: Developed quite the obsession for one of her young tricks, Paul, didn't she?

MARK: Leave Gertie alone.

BOB: One of her Irish customers.

          (MARK *backs further away into a corner.*)

MARK: No.

BOB: Dragged her in on his shoe, he did.

MARK: Not that.

BOB: Fifteen years ago, wasn't it? And she's been fouling up this place ever since.

PAUL: What's going on?

MARK: Stop it, please.

BOB: Followed him around like a bitch in heat. No matter how many times he slapped her down.

MARK: (*To* PAUL *now*) Make him stop. Please, Paul.

BOB: He wouldn't even look at you. Wouldn't even piss in your direction.

MARK: Gertie hated him, she hated him. Gertie hated him, she did.

PAUL: What's going on, Bob? Who's he talking about?

BOB: Who do you think, Paul? You don't think it was me he was coming in to see all those years, do you?

(MARK *slumps onto the table and begins to sob quietly.*)

MARK: No!

BOB: (*To* MARK) Love of your sorry little life, wasn't he, Mark? Broke your tiny little heart, and now you have to keep it hidden like everything else behind that pathetic disguise of yours. (*Pause*) Oh your beloved told me all the sordid details of your life, he did. Told me exactly what he thought of *you*. (*Pause*) I think that makes us quits now, don't you?

PAUL: Oh my God.

(*Pause. They are silent as* MARK *continues to sob.* WILLIE *goes to him. He places a hand on his shoulder affectionately. He leans down and embraces him. Pause.*)

WILLIE: (*Looking up again*) It'll be OK, Mark.

BOB: But I told you before. It's not Mark at all.

WILLIE: Just leave it, Bob.

BOB: It's not Gertrude. He's nobody. Nothing.

MARK: No!

BOB: Behind all the make-up and the clothes there's nothing left any more.

MARK: No!

BOB: Just a shell. There's nothing in there but air, stale, foul-smelling, filthy air.

(MARK *suddenly overturns the table.*)

MARK: Nothing! Not nobody. Gertie's not nobody. She's somebody, she's . . . (*Pause. He is completely defeated.*) She's your slave, that's what she is – no – your peacock! Your fancy peacock with all these gaudy feathers shoved up her arse, strutting about this place, cooing and making you feel majestic. That's it, yes. Majestic Bob – King of all he surveys! (*Pause*) Well, who does that make the Queen then? (*He looks around at the others, as if waiting for an answer. He turns and knocks Ciarán's stool to the floor.*) The Queen is dead, darlings. Our Queen is dead.

(MARK *stands silently for a few moments, then stumbles slightly, straightens himself, looks around the room and sees his bag, the contents of which have been scattered somewhat during the foray. He begins picking up the contents as the others stand watching him silently; maybe* WILLIE *hands him a lipstick or some such. When he has everything gathered up, he begins to move towards the exit. He stops momentarily, realizing he is barefoot. He crosses to the store-room door, but he can't go back up there. He turns and enters the toilets. The others stand silently.)*

PAUL: (*Trying to remain calm*) So it looks like I was the gooseberry in the pile all along, then. (*Pause*) Him too.

WILLIE: Just leave it, Paul.

PAUL: They were all having a right fucking orgy behind Paul's back, so they were.

WILLIE: It was a long time ago.

PAUL: It didn't quite add up, so it didn't. Bad-mouthing Ciarán, *and me*, at every turn, while he practically lived in this place. Well now we know why, don't we? Another fully signed-up member of the Ciarán fucking fan club. (*Pause*) And what about this dark horse here? A right cosy little set-up he had made for himself, eh Willie?

BOB: I thought you were just leaving.

PAUL: And there was me thinking he was on our side all along.

BOB: Just doing my job. (*He begins to clean up the mess, ignoring* PAUL *as he does so.*)

PAUL: And was that part of your job description as well, eh? To go sneaking about behind people's backs, preying on their friends, taking fucking advantage?

BOB: Taking advantage of whom?

PAUL: Who the fuck do you think?

BOB: Oh we're all big boys here. Nobody was forced to do anything they didn't want to.

PAUL: Oh really?

BOB: I didn't hear any complaints.

PAUL: And they were completely sober all this time as well, I suppose.

BOB: Not always, no. But what's that got to do with me? At the end of the day we all make our own decisions.

(*Pause*)

PAUL: Didn't you care for him at all, then?

BOB: Care for him?

PAUL: So it was just sex, then, all that time?

BOB: (*Pause*) We all get . . . *urges* Paul. You know that, you're a man. Not everybody insists on complicating things with emotions.

PAUL: But you're fucking gay, so you are.

BOB: What! Gay! Oh no. Who said anything about being gay? Sex is just sex. Whenever the opportunity presents itself, we take it. Man, woman . . . (*He shrugs.*) I didn't have much of a choice in here, did I? (*Pause*) It's all about *release*, Paul.

PAUL: Release?

BOB: Yes. Release.

PAUL: That's bollocks, that is.

BOB: Oh yeah?

PAUL: There's more to it than that.

BOB: Like what?

PAUL: Love!

BOB: (*Laughing*) Love!

PAUL: Yes, love! There's love, so there is. There's caring for somebody and just wanting to be with them.

BOB: Like today you mean? Like you sitting by his bed, cooing into his ear, telling him you *loved* him? A lot of good love did him today . . . or you for that matter. He didn't even know you were there.

PAUL: You're some bastard, you are. Do you know that?

BOB: Oh I think I know what your real problem is, Paul. You're jealous.

PAUL: Jealous!

BOB: You're jealous, because you wanted him and you couldn't have him . . . drunk *or* sober.

PAUL: (*Desperately trying to control his temper*) I see. (*Pause*) Well maybe I am. And more fool me. (*He moves to the door.*) Come on, Willie.

WILLIE: But what about Mark?

PAUL: What about him? You and me are going to get as far away from this place as we possibly can.

WILLIE: (*Beat*) To a club, you mean?

PAUL: Why not?

WILLIE: Deadly.

PAUL: We'll get so bloody rat-arsed we won't give two shites where we are or what fucking city we're in. (*Beat*) Just like old times in a way.

WILLIE: Come on, so. (*He runs to the door.*)

BOB: But haven't you forgotten one tiny detail?

WILLIE: Oh Jaysus. What now?

BOB: Just the small matter of a decomposing corpse that has yet to be disposed of. In their rush to get off the sinking ship, the rats have forgotten about the body, then, have they?

PAUL: Oh that's fucking lovely, that is.

WILLIE: Well . . . his family, Paul.

PAUL: What about them? (*Pause*) They kicked him out fifteen years ago, they didn't care very much about him then, why should I go bothering them now?

WILLIE: The funeral then. The cremation.

(*Pause*)

PAUL: He named him next of kin. Let him sort it out.

WILLIE: But he's still your mate, you still have to go to the funeral.

(*Pause*)

PAUL: One less isn't going to make any difference.

WILLIE: What? But that just leaves Bob, then.

PAUL: If he's planning on going, that is.

(*Pause*)

WILLIE: Bob?

(*Pause.* BOB *doesn't answer.*)

WILLIE: Ah Jaysus, lads, that's not good enough, not good enough at all now. He was your mate, Paul, and he's Irish, and he's over here on his own and he can't be buried, or burnt or whatever, without someone there to say a few bleedin' prayers over him. (*Pause*) What are you saying, like? Just because he was shagging a few people that you didn't know about or . . .

PAUL: It's not that simple.

WILLIE: . . . or just because you went all soft on him. You're his mate. You're his only mate. You still have to go to the poor bastard's funeral.

(*Pause.* PAUL *doesn't respond.*)

WILLIE: Oh fuck this. You're as bad as the rest of them, you are. Just as fucking bad. In fact yous are the saddest of bastards that I've ever met in me whole life.

PAUL: Wait a minute, will ya?

WILLIE: (*To* BOB) The Hoist, wasn't it, that club?

BOB: That's right.

PAUL: You can't go there on your own. That's a bloody S & M bar, that is.

WILLIE: Oh don't you worry about me, Paul.

PAUL: They'll never let you in. You've no money.

WILLIE: See you, Bob. You can tell that other bollix I said goodbye as well. You're welcome to him.

PAUL: You need leathers and shite. Military stuff.

WILLIE: (*With the door open, he hesitates.*) That's it. (*Pause*) I've been trying to think of it all evening and now I have it.

PAUL: What?

WILLIE: What yous guys all remind me of. I have it now.

PAUL: Listen, Willie, wait a minute, will you?

WILLIE: The Jap soldier.

PAUL: (*Beat*) We remind you of a Japanese soldier?

WILLIE: Yeah, yeah. The one after the war.

PAUL: (*To* BOB) What the fuck is he –

WILLIE: The one who was still guarding that tiny island 'cause nobody had bothered to tell him that the war had ended forty years ago or something. His bleedin' radio had gone on the blink and the poor fucker was still fighting with his fucking tommy guns when some gammy tourists stumbled on him a few years back.

PAUL: What?

WILLIE: Seventy-nine he was, or something. Living in a tiny shack made from leaves and shite, with only the bleedin' parrots for company. The whole world had changed since he'd left but he still wouldn't accept that it was over, that they'd lost it all years ago, that it was time to give it up. (*Pause*) That's what yous are like.

PAUL: Oh really?

WILLIE: Only worse. 'Cause that poor bastard didn't know any better. He'd ran out of Duracell for fuck's sake, how could he? Yous, though, yous are a totally different story. You guys have nobody to blame but yourselves. Not your mas nor your das, not nobody.

PAUL: Is that so?

WILLIE: It is, yeah. People are having a great fucking time at home, Paul. Just getting on with it, you know? having the craic, getting the odd shag – it's no big deal. (*Beat*) Haven't you heard of Temple fucking Bar, for fuck's sake?

(PAUL *laughs nervously.*)

WILLIE: The war is over, Paul. And the sooner yous in here realize it the better.

PAUL: You're a gas man, Willie, do you know that?

WILLIE: Oh I do, yeah, I'm a fucking riot, I am. Now, see yous. I'm off to get me hole.

(WILLIE *exits.* PAUL *stands watching the door for a few moments. They are silent.*)

PAUL: (*Eventually*) He's gone. (*Pause*) Cheeky little fucker. Did you hear what he . . . (*He stops, knowing that* BOB *won't respond.*) That's fucking great, that is. (*Pause*) Where is he going to stay, like? He'll freeze to death out there if he's not careful. (*Pause*) Fucking Japanese soldiers. What kind of shite was that he was talking?

BOB: There's an old Chinese saying, Paul.

PAUL: Oh Chinese now, fucking great.

BOB: It says: 'When six people tell you you're dead, lie down and die.' (*Pause*)

PAUL: And what the fuck is that supposed to mean when it's at home?

BOB: Listen to the bloke, will you? He might be young, but you'd still do well to listen to him.

PAUL: Oh and I'm supposed to take your advice now, am I, supposed to listen to *you*?

BOB: Fine, then. Don't. I was just going to suggest that you put us all out of our misery.

PAUL: And how do you suggest I do that then?

BOB: (*Beat*) Ring them, Paul.

PAUL: Ring them? Ring them! Oh that's a great fucking idea that is. (*Pause*) He's a seventy-two-year-old man, Bob. I'm his only son. He's never been out of the town in his whole fucking life. What do you suggest I tell him, then?

BOB: Tell him you're a faggot, Paul. Tell him you're a big fairy who likes men's dicks up your arse. That's what it boils down to, isn't it? Not that big a deal when you think about it. I'm a shirt-lifter, Father, a good old-fashioned arse bandit who's hiding out in London because I ain't got the courage to be doing it back in small town wherever. What is it Mark calls it again? Queen Paddy and his Catholic Cock. Tell him that, why don't you?

(*Pause.* PAUL *doesn't respond.*)

BOB: And then we'd both have lost a licensed premises this evening. Make us quits too, in a way.

PAUL: What are you talking about?

BOB: It's gone. Finished.

PAUL: The brewery. All those letters.

BOB: They've decided to do the place up. Lunches and long-neck bottles.

PAUL: All those letters you just ripped up.

BOB: Lambeth needs it, they say. They're coming to *evict* me in the morning.

PAUL: But . . . They can't.

BOB: Oh yes they can. They most certainly can.

PAUL: (*Pause*) What will you do? You've been here forever.

BOB: I'll be just dandy. I always am.

PAUL: And Mark?

BOB: What about him?

PAUL: Where will he go?

BOB: We're on our own now. All of us. (*Pause*) So that's it, then. (*Pause*) It's past closing. Time to go home, Paul.

(BOB *turns away from him and returns behind the bar. He exits into the storeroom. Long pause.* PAUL *fishes for change in his pocket and moves towards the payphone. He inserts money into the phone and dials. There is silence.*)

PAUL: (*Into the phone*) Hello, Ma, is that you? Yeah, yeah, it's me. It's Paul, Ma. (*Pause*) I'm OK, I'm OK. How are you, and Daddy and . . .? (*Pause*) I know, I should have . . . I meant to ring, but . . . I got your letters, Ma. (*Pause*) I know, I know it's late, I'm sorry, I forgot, I thought it was past closing, it's just . . .

(PAUL *stops as* MARK *enters from the toilet. He is exhausted, deflated, energy-less.* MARK *crosses the bar and sits.*)

PAUL: No, no I'm fine, I'm OK, but wait, Ma. I've something to tell you, I . . . Listen to me, Ma, listen to me, will you? I've decided, I . . . sell the pub, Ma. I don't want it, I can't, I . . . Don't be upset now but the reason I . . . A friend of mine died, Ma. He was . . . I loved him, Ma. I loved him, so I did, and the reason I can't . . . Ma, I'm gay. I'm gay, so I am. (*Pause*) No, ah no don't cry, Ma, don't cry. I think I might come home, Ma. Not to the pub but

. . . I know it's busy, but Ma. (*Beat*) Aye, I'm all right, so I am. Don't be worrying about me 'cause I'm all right. (*Pause*) Yeah, yeah, you go. OK, yeah, yeah, I know, I know, I'll call tomorrow, so. (*Beat*) Bye-bye. (*He hangs up. Pause.*)

MARK: (*Softly*) You're going home?

PAUL: Well . . . (*He shrugs.*) Dublin maybe. According to Willie, it's a great fucking place these days.

MARK: And Mavis? (*He corrects himself.*) Willie. Is he gone too?

PAUL: Yes. He's gone, Mark.

(*Pause*)

MARK: That's . . . That's good.

(*Pause.* BOB *re-enters from the storeroom. He is carrying a dustpan and brush.*)

MARK: I used to know a boy who lived in Ireland once.

PAUL: Did you now?

MARK   His name was . . . His name was *Fergal*.

PAUL: Well, well. (*He smiles*) Fergal, is it?

MARK: Stupid name, don't you think? Never suited him. Gertrude never liked it, she . . . (*He pauses.*) A little sissy boy, he was, Fergal. Glasses and a cow's lick and . . . (*Pause*) A pull-through for a rifle, his father called him. (*He continues in a deeper, sterner voice.*) 'With those thin little hips on ya, a pull-through for a rifle is all you'll be good for.'

PAUL: (*Beat*) Hasn't Fergal done well, then?

MARK: Always got attention from the men, he did, too much attention, too much. So he came to London, didn't he? He was too young, Paul, too young to be on his own like that, but where else could he go? Ended up on those bloody streets out there, didn't he, making money anyway he could? (*Pause*) And then he met this other boy, this other boy from . . . *home*. (*Pause*) And he was a strong boy who wasn't a sissy and who knew how to look after himself and . . . And he held on to Fergal, he did, in his big arms, he did, and he told Fergal that everything would be all right and that he would mind him and not let anything happen to him and . . . and . . . He's dead now, isn't he? That boy is dead now.

(*Pause*)

PAUL: Yes. He is. Ciarán is dead.

(*Pause*)

MARK: Gertie misses him, Paul, Gertie misses him, she does.

PAUL: I know, Mark. We all miss him.

MARK: (*Wiping his eyes, he begins to compose himself a little.*) But she doesn't know that little sissy Fergal any more, she lost him somewhere, dead maybe as well, and good riddance to him.

PAUL: You think so?

MARK: They killed him, they killed him, Paul, but I don't care because they can't touch Gertie. Everybody just adores Gertie. He's gone for good now and Gertie's never going back there, never.

PAUL: Good for you, Mark.

MARK: She's on her own now. It's too late for . . . Much too late. This is her home now.

(*Pause.* PAUL *moves towards* MARK.)

PAUL: You take good care of Gertie now, do you hear me? And fuck the rest of them. (*He turns and moves towards the door. He stops and looks at* BOB *again.*) Goodbye, Bob.

BOB: Bye, Paul.

(PAUL *looks to* MARK *one last time and exits. Pause.*)

MARK: This is her home now. (*Pause as he looks around the bar*) Gertie will stay here now. Here's all she has left. (*He looks towards* BOB.) She'll be OK here, won't she? In the Queen & Peacock? (*Pause*) Gertie will be OK, won't she, Bob?

BOB *turns the main light off and the remaining lights fade to blackout.*

Passage

DEIRDRE KINAHAN

Passage was first presented at the Civic Theatre, Tallaght, Dublin, on 25 April 2001 by Tall Tales Theatre Company.

CAST

Kate	Phoebe Flint
Sara	Victoria Monkhouse
Nora	Julianne Mullen
Brian	Robert Shaw
Margaret	Billie Traynor

PRODUCTION TEAM

Director	Maureen Collender
Designer	Robert Lane
Producers	Rita Gray and Deirdre Kinahan
Lighting designer	Maeve Wright
Music composition	Fergal Andrews

CHARACTERS

Kate, *young London woman, twenty-eight, tight-lipped*
Sara, *young London woman, twenty-eight, arty and stylish, Kate's partner*
Nora, *young Irishwoman, early twenties, speaking from the past, Kate's mother*
Brian, *Dublin man, thirty, jocular, Kate's cousin*
Margaret, *Dublin woman, fifty-eight, homely, Kate's aunt*

In the Shadows

In the cold morning light
her fingers invaded the neat piles;
a rent book, bills, certificates, pills
all the documents of life.

The cupboard beneath the stairs
held no memoirs, secrets, keepsakes.
No lock of hair
no letters wrapped in ribbon
no childhood scribble or teenage flight.
The cupboard beneath the stairs
kept desire hidden still from sight.

Kate beheld her mother's life there
ransacked and empty.
Like a shadow she has passed over London's streets,
swathed in green
she could never be seen
behind the ballad and the reel
she thought she would cease to feel
the bitter loneliness.
Life, for Kate's mother was a journey home
To forgotten dreams and childhood schemes
To an illusory land of outstretched hand,
No need for keepsakes.

Act One

Scene One

KATE, *an attractive woman. Wears expensive and fashionable clothes. Sifts through shoeboxes of letters and neat, bull-clipped piles of documents when the play opens. The set is not realistic, but suggests the front room of a small council house in London. The year is 2001.*

SARA *enters. She is trendy, with cropped hair, and expensive clothes. She puts a mug of coffee down beside* KATE *and sits. Pause.*

SARA: Are you all right, Kate?

KATE: Yes, thanks Sara, I'm fine.

SARA: She didn't have much, did she? (*Looking around*) Everything is so bare, it's eerie. It's as if she packed up before she went.

KATE: That'd be Mum all right. Everything in order. No chance of those that follow finding a hint of her personal life.

SARA: It's freezing.

KATE: Plug in the fire.

SARA: Are you joking, Kate? It's from the Dark Ages and there's three inches of dust on the bars. It'd combust, kill the pair of us. God, is that all she had for heat?

KATE: It was always cold. I remember that. (SARA *wanders off to a window and looks out; she settles back to her tea, looking uncomfortable.* KATE *is lost in the boxes.*) This is unbelievable.

SARA: Something of interest?

KATE: None of it. Imagine – she's got bills here going back forty years. Rent books, church notices, bin collection leaflets, but nothing, absolutely nothing, to do with life. Real life.

SARA: Maybe the sentimental stuff is stashed upstairs.

KATE: There's not even a photograph. Can you believe that, Sara? Not one, no notes or cards. Not a letter. God, it's as though no one existed in her life.

SARA: Did they?

KATE: What?

SARA: Exist in her life? Anyone?

KATE: Of course, there was me! And her family in Dublin, a few women from the club and Connolly.

SARA: Was he the old boy at the funeral?

KATE: Yes. Lifelong neighbour. I can't believe she'd have nothing here.

SARA: You've been through them three times, Kate!

KATE: I just think there has to be something. She was a cold old bitch but she must have kept something somewhere – a little note, a photo, first day at school, Christmas cards – God, just a little shadow of life.

SARA: Weird all right. (*She goes over and puts a hand on* KATE's *shoulder.*) Why don't you just leave it . . . maybe she'd nothing to say, nothing to remember. She was sick for a long time; she probably just cleaned it all out.

KATE: I know how long she was sick, Sara. I've taken that smack already, thanks, I don't need it again from you.

SARA: I wasn't . . . (*Sighs. Pause*) Let's just get out of here, Kate, bring the stuff home – you might find something.

KATE   Do you know she'd enjoy this . . . wouldn't you, Mum? You'd enjoy my feeling shit. (*In imitation of her mother's Irish voice*) 'That's Katie for ya, BUSY BEE KAT-IE, getting on with her big career. No time for her poor mother. Well, when you turn your back on God, turn your back on decent living, you'd hardly spare a thought for your own.'

(SARA *looks at her amused.*)

SARA: Fuck . . .

KATE: I know. She was a sanctimonious old cow. A specialist in making you feel bad. I'm sure she gloried in the cancer, you know. Misery was the only thing that could make her happy.

SARA: Let's go, Kate, you'll get upset; I know you rarely saw her but –

KATE: Rarely! I never saw her, well not in the last few years; I escaped.

SARA   I can't even picture you here; it's so drab, it's bloody miserable.

KATE: I lived here all right, danced that jig. I wonder did she send her stuff to Margaret – she did name her as her next of kin.

SARA: That's it. She must have sent it home when she'd not seen you for years.

KATE: Nor Margaret.

SARA: What, her own sister, didn't she visit her?

KATE: In Dublin? No, not Mum; she'd sing about it, pray for it, sob over pictures of it but she'd never go there.

SARA: Really?

KATE: Her one outing was to the church. That, the Irish centre, the shops and the launderette were the extent of her world in London.

SARA: She sounds a thriller, your mum.

KATE: Just a martyr. She loved the role, enforced exile and all that.

SARA: But she could get to Dublin in an hour.

KATE: That wasn't the point; she died alone on a foreign shore. I can just see her preparing for the final journey – doused in holy water. No doubt she offered up all the pain for my sins. It's no wonder she hadn't a friend in the world; they even avoided her down in the club, or she avoided them, I could never tell. She went there every weekend but kept a distance, all those years and she never seemed close to anyone. I can't remember anyone ever visiting, except Connolly of course – another oddball. They would listen to old ballads on the record player; she'd never let me play it, it was devoted to blasting Irish rebellion all over the estate.

SARA: Bet that went down well.

KATE: (*Laughs*) Oh great, it was like declaring war on the whole community. You should hear the words of those songs – they are like death threats couched in lullabies.

SARA: And is he still at it?

KATE: Who?

SARA: The old boy next door . . . is he still singing?

KATE: No. Well I don't know, really. I should call in and talk to him, I suppose. He was with her at the end. Poor Mr. Connolly, he was caretaker in the local school or something but I think it's gone now, torn down. He's nice, you know, always very kind to me, kind to Mum.

SARA: Was he a sweetheart?

KATE: Of Mum's. God, no, are you mad? Just two lonely old souls grumbling together. He was as bad as her in a way, never settled, never really left whatever godforsaken village he came from.

SARA: In Ireland?

KATE: Yes. Just like Mum, he lived here, earned a living here but never called it home. Do you know, I had to get two tubes across London to school because of her mania? The comprehensive was taboo; I had to go to the nuns. I'd walk down that street in my green blazer, the conspicuous Paddy not allowed to mix with the other kids.

SARA: There must have been hundreds like you.

KATE: Oh there were, but I couldn't mix with them either; no one was good enough.

SARA: No one English.

KATE: No one at all. God, look around you . . . not a penny and there never was . . . a small council house in the East End, ridiculous.

SARA: (SARA *studies her.*) Kate, I can't believe you've never talked about her, told me about her.

KATE: What was there to tell?

SARA: I could have met her . . .

KATE: Mum! . . . Never. She'd never have entertained it . . . *us*! Anyway, she'd no interest in me . . .

SARA: Her own daughter? She must have, Kate.

KATE: I'm telling you. I was too much of a disappointment. I could never do anything right.

SARA: Connolly didn't seem to think so. He knew all about your work; he said she was very proud.

KATE: Well he got that wrong. Mum would never be proud of me. How could she be, she didn't even know me? . . . We were like two strangers living in this house. I always hated it; can't think why I came back.

SARA: She died, Kate, you had to, after all she was your mum, your connection . . .

KATE: Connection to what, Sara? That's the question. I thought I didn't care . . . she no longer had any part in my life but now she's gone I feel . . . I feel anchorless.

SARA: Of course you do.

KATE: When I left, I was determined to live, you know? Really live – in the now, the here and now. Mum always looked back, looked overseas, and she'd have dragged me back, back to her Ireland, her priests and her club. I just had to get out, I couldn't stand it.

SARA: You were right.

KATE: So why am I here now and why do I feel so lost?

SARA: It's perfectly natural, Kate . . .

KATE: Natural? There was nothing natural about me and Mum. I know nothing about her. That's all I was thinking right through the service. I know practically nothing about her. Why was she so alone? That's what I keep thinking, sweating her days away in a grimy launderette. Where were the big family in Dublin? Her sisters. She never saw them. She talked incessantly about them, Sara, but she never went home.

SARA: Strange.

KATE: There wasn't a single visit that I remember. I never met Margaret or Joan, Mary or Jen. Yet they were so much a part of my life, our life. I'd hear constantly about them, about their children. I thought we were a part of that big gang, big community. How? I never knew them, never even knew Mum. God, how I wish I'd talked to her. And now, now it's too late. I can't believe it . . .

SARA: (*Comforting her*) I know, it's awful . . . it will be all right, Kate.

KATE: I didn't think she'd go, you know? Didn't think we'd never meet again. You just never think, do you? I can't even remember the last time. I go through it over and over but I can't remember when we last spoke. So she was right, you see, I was too busy getting on with the big career . . .

SARA: Shhh, Kate, leave it, you weren't to know, she froze *you* out . . .

KATE: Oh God.

SARA: It's not your fault, Kate.

KATE: I know but . . . Oh I love you, Sara, you've been fantastic, you're always fantastic. I don't know what I'd do without you.

SARA: Don't worry, you'll never have to find out. What about your dad, Kate?

KATE: Dad? Daddy's dead. He was killed in an accident on a site near Hammersmith, I think.

SARA: Yeah, but what about his family?

KATE: I don't know. I never knew him. Never knew anything really; if I asked Mum, she'd get upset. So I didn't ask. You know, when I look back, my whole childhood seems a fog, a fantasy, imagining Dad, imagining Dublin. I feel like I've been pieced together by someone's scraps, someone else's memories.

SARA: It's OK, Kate. It's OK to be upset.

KATE: I'm not upset. Just confused.

SARA: Why don't we go home, Kate, before we die of cold or confusion?

KATE: OK, I'm drained. I feel suitably shit. Mum must be delighted.

SARA: Come on, Kate. I'm sure she's more on her mind . . .

KATE: Like getting through the Pearly Gates; no, locking them behind her.

SARA: Kate.

KATE: I know. I don't know what's got into me. Let's go home. *Get out of here!*

SARA   Take the boxes with you and we can come back for the bags later.

KATE: Right, thanks, Sara. I'll go through the rest at home.

They leave. Lights fade to black.

Scene Two

A mirrorball, like those you would see in a 1950s ballroom, is lowered. It spins slowly, casting its sparkle around the stage and out into the audience. A slow song from the period is being played and the voice of a young woman reading a letter fills the theatre. She appears in silhouette, dancing a waltz alone.

Dear Brendan

It's such a pity you are not in Dublin this week; the Cadets are playing at the Met, I know how much you love them. I've had a good week, Celia and me got in free to the Adelaide on Tuesday 'cause one of the committee fancies C. She doesn't fancy him but keeps him sweet on account of getting in, she's gas! I was out at the weekend with her and Liam, her latest, we cycled out to the Strawberry Beds and I THOUGHT OF YOU! Liam plays football for Laois, Celia is having a ball going to all the matches and the meals after, she thinks she's a real celeb!

The old bitch Weaver in the shop is watching me like a hawk since that Saturday I was late after meeting you. Her eyes will get stuck one of these days watching that clock. Still, make sure to send your letter to the shop 'cause Ma will read anything that comes into the house.

Have you much work now? Will Reilly give you work back down here soon, do you think? I'm just dying to see you. I was thinking we could go cycling ourselves at the weekend, out to the sea, like that beach you tell me about in Donegal. We could go to the pictures – oh Brendan, will you write to me soon, tell me what you're doing and when you'll be coming down? I miss you so much, can't wait to see you.

Love, hugs and kisses,

Nora

Scene Three

Front room of a London flat. SARA *is putting on earrings.* KATE *arrives in from work.*

KATE: Hiya, I'm bushed. That bloody new IT manager is an absolute twat.

SARA: Really? Yesterday he was 'charming'!

KATE: Well yesterday was the honeymoon period. He's an ass.

SARA: I see.

KATE: Where are you off to?

SARA: Julie's.

KATE: What, are they back?

SARA: This morning, and they have split up.

KATE: No! When?

SARA: On the skiing holiday. Julie said it was a disaster; Karen just got pissed and holed up in the hotel.

KATE: I knew it; I knew it would never be her scene – why take fresh air when you can have vodka?

SARA: Exactly. Well Julie has had enough; she kicked her out when they came home.

KATE: That was a bit drastic.

SARA: Maybe, I said I'd go over, give a bit of support.

KATE: Well, I won't come, Sara. I need to wind down from Howard.

SARA: Is that his name?

KATE: Yep.

SARA: OK, see you later.

KATE: Do you have to go? Now? I was looking forward to a nice night with you, some wine . . .

SARA: Sorry, I said I would; you said you might work late.

KATE: I know. I just couldn't be bothered.

SARA: You! Not bothered about work? That Howard has a lot to answer for.

KATE: It's not him. I don't . . . I just can't get motivated. There's no buzz in the new projects. Our new budget was announced yesterday, a huge increase and I don't care.

SARA: You've lost your mum . . . you're out of sorts. You should take some time off.

KATE: Off work, why? What would I do? No, I'm sure I'll get back on track, something will inspire me. Ah stay, Sara, we'll open that nice bottle you got from Surrinda.

SARA: No. I'm going. Julie's in a state. (*Gives her a kiss as she leaves*) Anyway sounds like you'll have company. Some man Brian called earlier, said he might drop by.

KATE: Brian? Brian who? I don't know any Brian.

SARA: I don't know, a cousin or something. Listen I'm going, I want to catch a film with Julie; it's on the machine, play it again.
       (SARA *exits.* KATE *goes over to the answering machine and hits play – a smooth Dublin voice plays.*)

BRIAN: Well hello, cuz, this is Brian Mullen here, Margaret's son from Dublin. Just phoning to catch up. I'm in London this evening, so thought I'd drop by. See how you are coping after your mam and that. If it's not convenient, you'll get me on 00353-87-4828869, but I hope to see you later. Bye.

       (KATE *stands there stunned, then replays message; as it reaches the end, the buzzer goes. She goes to the intercom.*)

KATE: Hello?

BRIAN: Hi, this is Brian Mullen here, calling for Katie Dunne.

KATE: Brian. Hi. I was just listening to your message.

BRIAN: What a coincidence. (*Silence*) Eh, is this a good time?

KATE: Of course, it's fine. You're my cousin?

BRIAN: Yep, that's right.

KATE: So who? I mean, you're my first cousin?

BRIAN: That's right, Margaret's son.

KATE: Margaret?

BRIAN: That's right.

KATE: Margaret Mullen.

BRIAN: That's right.

KATE: And you're her son.

BRIAN: That's right.

KATE: From Dublin.

BRIAN: Yep! I have a passport here if you need to take a look at it.

KATE: (*Laughs*) I'm sorry, I mean . . . Yes. Come on up.

> (KATE *presses buzzer, looks stunned – goes to mirror, goes to get a bottle of wine, starts fixing flat.* BRIAN *arrives, a bit dapper, holding out an enormous box of chocolates.*)

BRIAN: (*Proffering the chocolates*) A twenty-year supply! Thought I'd make up for lost time.

KATE: (*Totally lost*) Lovely. (*He remains at the door.*) Well come in, Brian – imagine, Brian Mullen! What a surprise, I'm delighted, a cousin. It's good of you to call.

BRIAN: Nonsense, I've been coming to Highbury for years, always meant to call, just never got around to it, too much boozing to do, you know yourself.

KATE: I do, I do of course. So are you often in London, on business, is it?

BRIAN: No, much more important than that.

KATE: Really?

BRIAN: Football.

KATE: Oh right. Would you like a drink? Sit down.

BRIAN: Thanks, a beer would be great.

> (KATE *exits to kitchen.*)

KATE: (*Offstage, from the kitchen*) So you're a fan?

BRIAN: Fanatic! Big time – been obsessed since I was about six.

KATE: As long as that.

BRIAN: Yep, since me da went missing at the match in 'Seventy-one. Arsenal won the double that year.

KATE: (*Returning with beer*) Really.

BRIAN: Yep, from then on I had to pray for Charlie George . . .

KATE: (*Bemused*) Who was he?

BRIAN: Scored the goal.

KATE: And you'd to pray for him?

BRIAN: Of course. I had a hit list. You know, to pray to the guardian angel for cousins, aunties, the whole squad – you were included: 'Aunty Nora and Kate'. (*Smiles*) Hope you'd more luck than Charlie George.

KATE: Why's that?

BRIAN: He lost his fingers in a lawnmower.

KATE: He did?

BRIAN: Yep.

KATE: I'm sorry.

BRIAN: Don't be. He'd retired.

KATE: Right. (KATE *is really quite lost, doesn't get the joke.*) So is there a match tomorrow?

BRIAN: You bet. Spurs in the League.

KATE: Is that important?

BRIAN: Critical.

KATE: I see.

BRIAN: I take it you don't follow the football?

KATE: Clueless.

BRIAN: Not to worry. So how have you been? Since Aunty Nora died?

KATE: Good, fine. You know.

BRIAN: Yeah, good . . .

KATE: And how is your mother?

BRIAN: She's great; she'll be chuffed I caught you. She's been hounding me for years to call.

KATE: Right.

BRIAN: Not that I didn't want to, like, I meant to, countless times but sure I'd only be around for a day or two, see the match and head off.

KATE: Absolutely.

BRIAN: Have you been to Dublin much yourself?

KATE: Never. Can you believe it? I was due to go on business last year but it never happened. I had actually contacted your mother. I would have loved to visit but . . .

BRIAN: That's a shame, she'd have loved to see ya!

KATE: True. I'd love to too. I'd like to see Dublin, I hear it's great.

BRIAN: It's not a bad old town. Changing though. Getting rich.

KATE: Yes.

(*Pause*)

BRIAN: Isn't it gas we've never met?

KATE: I suppose it is.

BRIAN: And you only a stone's throw from Highbury.

KATE: You could have saved a fortune on accommodation!

BRIAN: And snogged all your mates!

KATE: (*Laughs*) Is that a fact?

BRIAN: Nice place. Are you working nearby?

KATE: Liverpool Street, just a few tube stops.

BRIAN: Great. What do you do?

KATE: IT, and you?

BRIAN: SC . . .

KATE: SC?

BRIAN: Sell chocolate.

KATE: Right. Well, you'll never be out of work so long as I'm around; will you have one of these? (*She wrestles the box open.*)

BRIAN: I certainly will. There is nothing like beer and chocolate! (*Sits back*) This really is a nice place.

KATE: Thanks, we bought it a few years ago.

BRIAN: We?

KATE: Yes, myself and a friend.

BRIAN: I see. Well it's great. What is it – half a house?

KATE: Yes. We've both got access to the garden, though, which I love.

BRIAN: Do you do a lot of gardening?

KATE: Yes, I pretty much look after it.

BRIAN: There you go, green fingers, that's the *Oirish* in you!

KATE: (*Small laugh*) How about you? Are you living in Dublin?

BRIAN: I am.

KATE: With a friend?

BRIAN: Nope, all on me lonesome, but sure I'm not far from the ma.

KATE: Do you see her a lot?

BRIAN: Christ. All the time. She's great; they're all great. You should come over some time. Everyone'd love to meet you.

KATE: Really? God, I can't see why.

BRIAN: You're part of the folklore. I told you – 'Aunty Nora and Kate in London'.

KATE: Right . . . and would they all know about me?

BRIAN: For God's sake, woman, the lot, there's been an information highway operating in Cabra long before fibre optics. There are five sisters, remember. News travels in nanoseconds.

KATE: I suppose. And Mum remained part of that?

BRIAN: Well I'm sure she did. She wrote and I know she was often on the phone.

KATE: She would have been, yes, of course.

BRIAN: It's gas. I feel like I've known ya, ya know? you and your ma, but you were never actually over.

KATE: I know, I wonder now why we never visited. I never thought about it till she died. I suppose it never really came up . . . she loved to talk about Dublin, about her sisters and their life . . .

BRIAN: I know they were always asking her over, Granda especially. Apparently she was his pet.

KATE: Really?

BRIAN: Yeah, Ma says he was heartbroke when she left.

KATE: That was a long time ago.

BRIAN: It was.

KATE: I suppose it was the money, really; there certainly wasn't a lot when I was younger and, well I don't know, perhaps she lost interest later on when such an amount of time had passed. Maybe that's why she never went back. She was an odd sort of woman, really, quite dark . . .

BRIAN: Sure it was tough on her losing your da so early on.

KATE: Yes.

BRIAN: Me ma felt dreadful not coming over to her funeral, but the word came quite late . . .

KATE: I know, I'm sorry. It was all a bit of a shock. I wasn't too sure what to do. Who to contact and that.

BRIAN: For God's sake, sure it's an awful time, you just get on with it, don't you?

KATE: It was like walking in a vacuum. I didn't know, you see, that she was so sick, sick at all, really.

BRIAN: Didn't you?

KATE: No. Dreadful, isn't it? We weren't in contact, you see . . . there was a bit of a rift.

BRIAN: Oh right. I'm sorry . . . I didn't know. So much for the information highway. (*Small laugh, no response*) God, I'm sorry, that must have been tough on you.

KATE: (*Getting upset*) It was. It was awful. I got a call at work. I mean, you never imagine it could happen, Brian, I never dreamt that she would die – die, just like that. (BRIAN *sits stunned during this outburst.*) She was sick for months and I never knew, I never knew a thing about it; we hadn't spoken for years. She was such an old bitch, you know, casting comment, always raving on about my clothes, my voice, my life. She was just, just – suffocating with her codes and her bloody paranoia. I could never bring a friend to the house, you know! They'd be picked apart, no one was ever good enough, there was no one you could trust. I never knew who I could be pals with, who would possibly please. I had spent every waking hour trying to make her happy – got good marks at school, regularly went to church. I even persevered at that ridiculous dancing when I was useless and now I'm sure that that was part of the plot; I'd let her down – 'Made a show of me', as she'd say. Fail. I'd just always fail, fail, fail, fail. (*Choking back the tears*)

BRIAN: (*Stunned*) Jaysus, sorry about that. I'd no idea. I'd never have started. Look, would you like a drink?

KATE: Yes please, there's a bottle in the cabinet.

BRIAN: (*Gets a bottle of vodka and pours two large glasses*) Eh, is there a mixer?

KATE: No.

BRIAN: Fair enough. (*Comes over with the two glasses and gives one to* KATE)

KATE: (*Struggling to recover*) I'm terribly sorry. God, you must think I'm nuts. I'm a bit stressed, you see – pressure at work and what with mum, well it's all still a bit raw, you see.

BRIAN: Of course, of course it is. Don't try to talk, just get that down you and we'll, em, we'll have another chat.

KATE: Thanks.

BRIAN: Sure maybe we'll have a meal, go out on the town to cheer you up.

KATE: Oh, are you staying?

BRIAN: Here?

KATE: Here? In London?

BRIAN: I am, yeah I'm here for a few days. So do you fancy that, then, we'll go out?

KATE: Yes. Yes, I'd love to, Brian . . . just let me put on my face, I must look a state.

BRIAN: You look great.

KATE: Thanks, Brian . . . I don't know what came over me . . . I don't normally . . . I mean . . .

BRIAN: Look, relax, put on that face. I only hope it's as nice as the one I've just met.

KATE: Thanks. I won't be a minute.

KATE *smiles and the lights fade out.*

Scene Four

Another letter is read. The young woman stands in silhouette, impatiently looking at her watch as the music plays.

Dear Brendan,

Mick Connolly came into the shop with your note today. You should have seen Weaver's face at the cut of him, he must have come straight from the site. He walks straight up to me, gives Weaver a saucy wink and slips the note into me hand. He's a character. She gave me a hard time for the rest of the day but it was worth it. I was thrilled to get your note. I know it's daft but I was beginning to think you'd forgotten me! Left me for one of those Donegal girls!

So you'll be in Dublin on Friday, I can scarcely believe it, it seems so long since I saw you last – two months and two days! I wish there was a bit of work for you here but even the weekend seems like a gift. A WHOLE WEEKEND. I'm so excited, I'll be waiting at Clery's, like you said. C says we might make a foursome on Saturday but Friday I want you all to myself! I'll see what dances are on Saturday – there'll be a band in the Crystal and the Four P's.

Oh Bren, I can't wait to see you. I pretend I kiss you every night before I go to sleep. I picture every inch of you, pretend we are lying close. I miss you so much when you're away. Last Sunday I was out in Howth and threw kisses into the sea, imagining that they would find their way all around Ireland to Ballintra. Maybe we could take the tram out there this Sunday before you catch the bus – you can give me back those kisses! Anyway I'll see you on Friday – JUST THREE DAYS!

Love and kisses always,

Nora

Scene Five

The flat. SARA *is dressed up, having a cigarette before she goes out. The intercom buzzes.*

SARA: Hello?

BRIAN: Hi, is that Sara?

SARA: Yes.

BRIAN: This is Brian.

SARA: Oh right.

BRIAN: Is Kate about?

SARA: Em . . . She's not back from work . . .

BRIAN: Uh.

         (*Silence*)

SARA: Do you want to wait?

BRIAN: Well not out here.

SARA: Come up.

         (*It's obvious that* SARA *is not pleased.* BRIAN *enters.*)

BRIAN: Hello there.

SARA: Hi.

BRIAN: How are ya?

SARA: Fine. Is Kate expecting you?

BRIAN: (*Showing flowers*) No. This is an 'impulse' trip. (*Laughs*)

SARA: (*Doesn't laugh*) I see. Well, sit down.

BRIAN: You look great.

SARA: Thanks.

BRIAN: Are you going out?

SARA: Yes. Kate and I are going to the gallery.

BRIAN: The one where you work?

SARA: Yes.

BRIAN: Something special?

SARA: An exhibition.

BRIAN: Yeah?

SARA: A new painter. He's Irish, actually.

BRIAN: Really?

SARA: Yes. He's good, very good. I've been trying for months to get a slot for his work.

BRIAN: Well done.

SARA: Thanks.

BRIAN: This is the opening night, then?

SARA: Yes it is.

BRIAN: So what type of work does he do?

SARA: Oh it's quite abstract, there is a great focus on texture, the themes are quite urban . . . it's very interesting, quite unique.

BRIAN: I love art myself.

SARA: Really?

BRIAN: Yes, there are a few good galleries at home. I'd make the odd visit.

SARA: I see. (*She continues to get ready.*)

BRIAN: I like all sorts, everything in fact. I'm often amazed at what goes on in people's heads and how they express it, whether it's in a gallery, on film or on the pitch.

SARA: (*Short laugh*) Of course.

BRIAN: There is an elitism about galleries, though . . .

SARA: You think?

BRIAN: Yes I do. People who work with art like to surround it with a lot of crap which locks the rest of us out. Speak a language of their own.

SARA: Nonsense . . . we work hard to make it more accessible than ever. Every child can draw, every human being reacts to what is pleasing or interesting to the eye. Everyone can have an opinion on art, and must . . . I mean, it is one of the most basic human functions to draw, to sketch, to express . . . I don't know why I am getting into this, you hardly came here to discuss art.

BRIAN: No, I came to see Kate.

SARA: Of course. Kate.

BRIAN: What do ya mean?

SARA: Sorry?

BRIAN: The way you said that: 'Of course Kate'.

SARA: What?

BRIAN: Don't be so fucking facetious, Sara, you know exactly what I mean. What's your problem with my seeing Kate?

SARA: You're seeing Kate!

BRIAN: Oh for God's sake.

SARA: Well, who are you, Brian? Who are you? That's what I want to know. What does Kate know about you, or your family? You just appeared out of the blue, or green, should I say? Kate never set eyes on you before. Where were you when her mum was dying? Where were you when Kate was growing up? Not one of your great big loving family came to the funeral and now, God, now you're always popping over, like some sort of leprechaun leaping out at the most unexpected places . . .

BRIAN: Jesus. (*There is a silence.*) I don't think Kate feels that way.

SARA: No she doesn't, of course she doesn't. She's confused, you know that, she's trying to cope with this whole Mum thing and I don't know . . .You offer a lifeline, I suppose, some kind of link . . .

BRIAN: I am family.

SARA: Family, that's a laugh, is that how Irish families behave, abandoning one another?

BRIAN: I don't think –

SARA: Have you seen where they lived? Burnt out cars, windows barred . . . I don't know how her mum lived there alone and there was never any money.

BRIAN: That was her choice, Sara. I can't see why she chose it but who are we to say? I do know one thing, she'd only to lift the phone and –

SARA: So, how many of you came over, then? How many times did you all visit Nora? Come to see Kate?

BRIAN: It wasn't like that – traffic was very much one way . . . we're talking about years ago. Look, I don't have to explain myself to you.

SARA: But you do. Why are you always around? What are you looking for, Brian?

BRIAN: I'm not always around.

SARA: On the phone, on the e-mail . . .

BRIAN: Jesus, you make it sound so sinister. She's a friend and a cousin. I don't *want* anything. I came . . . because I was curious, I suppose. I'd heard about Nora –

SARA: And *now*?

BRIAN: Now? I like her. Is that all right? I like her, she's a nice woman, she's nice and she's lonely.

SARA: She is not lonely. Kate has plenty of friends –

BRIAN: I'm sure she does but she's not happy, she –

SARA: She just lost her mother, Brian, of course she's not happy and she thinks you'll help her find her again.

(KATE *enters.*)

KATE: Hi, Sara.

SARA: Oh hi.

KATE: Sorry I'm late. I actually bumped into Julie. She won't be able to make it tonight. *Brian!* What are you doing here?

BRIAN: I thought I'd pop over . . .

KATE: I didn't know there was a match on.

SARA: She actually studies the fixtures.

BRIAN: No there isn't, this is an 'impulse' trip (*Produces the bunch of flowers but the zip has been taken out of the joke.* KATE *smiles;* SARA *cringes.*)

KATE: What a nice surprise. Would you like a drink; did Sara get you a drink?

SARA: Well no, I didn't, Kate, because we're going out to the gallery. I can't be late, you know.

BRIAN: We've plenty of time. So how are you, Brian? How is everyone at home?

BRIAN: Grand, and how are you doing?

KATE: Good. Well, a bit odd really. I've just sold Mum's house.

BRIAN: So soon?

SARA: You sold it?

KATE: Yes I did, Sara. I shut the door. Time to move on.

SARA: Well done. (*Goes over and puts an arm around her*)

BRIAN: So who bought it?

KATE: No one yet, I just left it to the solicitor; the whole affair's been getting me down.

BRIAN: Sure it's bound to, the ma was only saying –

SARA: Well, are we going, Kate? Sorry, Brian, but it is an important night.

BRIAN: Of course, no problem. I'll head on up to me mates.

KATE: No, stay a while. I'll follow you on, Sara. I'll only be in the way during the speeches. I'll come around for nine.

SARA: (*Stunned*) What? This is important, Kate.

KATE: I know. I'll follow, honestly, maybe Brian will come. Will you, Brian?

BRIAN: (*Smiling at* SARA) Sure, I'd love to.

KATE: Great. We'll see you there, then.

SARA: Fine. Great. (*Takes her bag and coat and leaves*)

BRIAN: Don't think she was too happy.

KATE: Oh she'll be fine. She's been great. I must be driving her mad, I've been so morose.

BRIAN: Well you're entitled.

KATE: Mmm, I don't know. (*Getting drinks*) I went to the Irish club today, when I left Mum's.

BRIAN: Good woman, visit all the old haunts, I told you. It'll help you purge.

KATE: I know and I think you're right.

BRIAN: Great, you'll be in Dublin before you know it.

KATE: (*Pouring wine*) Maybe.

BRIAN: You will of course, everyone's mad to see you. So was it packed?

KATE: What?

BRIAN: The Irish club, I'm sure it's jammed on a Friday night.

KATE: God no. Not now, just a few old dears getting ready for bingo.

BRIAN: Go away.

KATE: No one goes there now. I'd say it will close soon, they all will. I suppose things are a lot different now, people are different . . .

BRIAN: Yeah.

KATE: I remember when I was little, the place would be packed. Big men just off the sites, buying pints; they'd seemed so much larger than life – you know, when you're a child? Big rough-red hands lifting me up and tossing out coins for lemonade. I used to love their smells; it would help me picture Dad. I'd pretend he was standing there amidst the open shirts. So many voices danced around that hall but it's quiet now they've all gone. I wonder where, Brian, where have they slipped off to? It's like a whole world has disappeared, swallowed by time.

BRIAN: Yeah. They were a different generation. Like your da – did you really never know him, Kate?

KATE: No, he died before I was born.

BRIAN: Ah that's right. I remember hearing that now. God help ya.

KATE: (*Laughs*) See, I *am* morose; I've got you all depressed now.

BRIAN: Not a bit; give us another drop of that wine.

KATE: Help yourself, I'll just go in and change.

         (KATE *exits.*)

BRIAN: About the gallery. Thanks, Kate, but I don't think I'll go.

KATE: (*Offstage*) Why?

BRIAN: Ah, not my scene and I don't think your pal is too keen.

KATE: Don't be daft, Sara thinks you're great.

BRIAN: That's not exactly my impression. How long are yiz together?

KATE: (*Coming back and pouring another glass of wine*) Four years, well almost five, we've been living together since '98.

BRIAN: Yeah. Is that the norm, like, to be together for that long?

KATE: 'The Norm'?! Of course. We're no different, Brian, we fall in love like everyone else.

BRIAN: Yeah, of course. Sorry. I don't mean to be nosy, you know. I suppose I just don't know anything about it.

KATE: There's nothing to know. We just like women, that's all.

BRIAN: Well I can relate to that.

KATE: (*Laughs*) You're great, Brian. I mean it. I'm really glad I got to know you, I always enjoy when you are around. You feel close. You're solid, aren't you, confident that you belong, Brian? I wish I had it . . . your *you-ness.*

BRIAN: Christ, sounds serious.

KATE: Don't you consider anything serious?

BRIAN: Plenty.

KATE: Like what?

BRIAN: Football.

KATE: Of course.

BRIAN: Here, ya better put these in the fridge.

KATE: What are they?

BRIAN: Sausages.

KATE: What?

BRIAN: Me ma sent them.

KATE: But . . .

BRIAN: Don't try and make sense of it, you won't, it's tradition.

KATE: But I'm vegetarian. (BRIAN *shrugs.*) Thanks, I suppose.

BRIAN: You're welcome.

KATE: (*Pouring another drink*) I bet your mum's lovely. Bet you're her little pet.

BRIAN: I am and she is. She's great.

KATE: Would she talk much about my mum, Brian? Were they close before Mum left?

BRIAN: Don't see how they could have been. You're ma would have gone to England when mine was still fairly young.

KATE: Yes. They'd have hardly known each other, really. But the other sisters – Mum mentioned Joan a lot – they were around the same age, they must have been close.

BRIAN: I'm sure they would have been. You should come over Kate, meet them all for yourself.

KATE: God, I'd be terrified, what would they think of me. (*Drinking a lot now*)

BRIAN: They'd think you were great.

KATE: I don't know. I've thought about it, you know, on and off. I would like to meet everyone but . . .

BRIAN: But what? This is crazy, Kate, it's gone on for far too long; you need family. We all do.

KATE: I suppose. I can't help feeling nervous, though, you know? My relationship with Mum (BRIAN *misses this reference to* KATE's *mum because he is topping up the vino.*) . . . things have been different here. I'm different.

BRIAN: Different, how do ya mean? (*Then it dawns on him. He thinks that she is talking about being gay.*) Ah. Look, don't worry about that, no one needs to know.

KATE: (*Talking about how she fought with her mother*) Really? Have you not told anyone, then?

BRIAN: Of course not.

KATE   (*Relieved*) Thanks, Brian, I really appreciate that. I've been really worried about what people might think. It's not something I'm proud of, you know, in fact I think it's been the greatest mistake of my life.

BRIAN: (*Aghast*) Really?

KATE: Yes.

BRIAN: Jesus, Kate, have you discussed this with Sara?

KATE: Of course I have. She's been really supportive but there is only so much she can do to help. I suppose it's you I need now.

BRIAN: Me!

KATE: Yes. Well, in a way, if you don't mind.

BRIAN: No, no. Why would I mind?

KATE: Great. I thought you might just ease me in gently.

BRIAN: (*Nearly chokes*) Jesus, you have it all worked out.

KATE: Do I? Well, I suppose I've been thinking of little else since we met.

BRIAN: Christ. Me too.

KATE: What?

BRIAN: I mean, I've been the same.

KATE: (*She misses this revelation.*) I should never have let it go on for so long – five years, I think, since I last saw her, it's just . . . once there's a stand-off, well, it's hard to find an end, call a ceasefire. (BRIAN *is mystified.*) I so regret not talking to her, Brian. I'd hate for your family to get a bad impression of me. So thanks, thanks for never mentioning the rift.

BRIAN: (*Dumbfounded*) No problem.

KATE: You really are sweet. (*Pouring more wine*)

BRIAN: Aren't you going to the, eh . . .?

KATE: Gallery. Oh God. I should, but no, not now. I'm too tired.

BRIAN: Well listen. I'll be heading.

KATE: (*Getting slightly pissed*) No, don't go, this is really nice. I'm glad you're here. You've been good to me.

BRIAN: Ah well.

KATE: No, it's true. It's been miserable since she died. I should never have gone back, you know, back to that bloody house; as soon as I walked in, Brian, I could feel it, the guilt, coming out to throttle me. It's like a fog descending and she's dead, the woman's dead, and still I feel the guilt. I should have moved country, you know? Changed my name.

BRIAN: It'd still follow.

KATE: What?

BRIAN: The guilt. All Irish are born with it.

KATE: But I'm not Irish, that's the thing, and she knew it, hated it, hated me for it, hated my accent, my walk, my life . . . I should never have been Katie Dunne. (*More wine*)

BRIAN: Who then?

KATE: I don't know, you tell me; a new identity – that's what I need, to be someone else.

BRIAN: Right, the old ones are the best. What's your favourite pet?

KATE: What?

BRIAN: Your favourite pet!

KATE: OK, how about on the tit!

BRIAN: (*Laughs*) Steady! You know what I mean – animal pet?

KATE: I never had one. She'd never allow it.

BRIAN: Jaysus, leave the auld one out of it; give us a friend's then, a friend's pet.

KATE: Mitzi. My friend had a poodle called Mitzi.

BRIAN: There you go, then, Mitzi Dunne.

KATE: Sounds like a stripper. (*Laughs and gets another bottle, studies* BRIAN *for a while*) Why don't you have a girlfriend?

BRIAN: What?

KATE: I'd say you are quite popular.

BRIAN: Where'd that come out of?

KATE: Just wondered. Do you like men maybe?!

BRIAN: No, I'm with you on that one. A dedicated feline fan.

KATE: Really . . .

BRIAN: Final answer.

KATE: Prove it!

BRIAN: What?

KATE: (*Coming close*) Prove that you are not gay.

BRIAN: Ah go on, Kate, you're just a bit pissed.

KATE: Mooching Mitzi. (BRIAN *laughs.*) Mitzi's on the make! (*They start kissing.* KATE *pulls back, playful.*) God, this is mad – I'm gay and you're my first cousin.

BRIAN: I'm straight and you're gorgeous.
         (*They kiss again.*)

KATE: Don't we need some kind of dispensation?

BRIAN: From who?

KATE: The pope.

BRIAN: I'll call him tomorrow. (KATE *looks at him.*) First thing, honest.

         They keep kissing as the lights fade.

Scene Six

The mirrorball is swirling. The young woman stands alone in silhouette. She blows a kiss and hugs herself as the third letter is read.

Dear Brendan,

How are you keeping? There was no note from Connolly, so I take it you can't get down. Our weekend seems so long ago now, wasn't it like a dream? I keep living it over and over in my head. Supper at the Paradiso on Friday and Saturday at the Four P's. My favourite part is Howth on Sunday before you caught the train, the two of us gazing out to the sea.

C says we make a lovely couple, said you couldn't keep your eyes off me. Could you not, Bren? Do you really love me? I keep imagining your eyes, your arms and big strong hands. I've never felt this way before. When will I see you again, Bren? Surely there'll be work here soon.

I was thinking, Bren, if you can't get down, sure couldn't I come up on the bus? I'm due some holidays from the shop and C says Ballintra is near Bundoran, which is gorgeous. Maybe we could sneak off there for the weekend, stay in a little hotel. I would say I was going with C, she'd never tell. Will you think about it, Bren? Write me as soon as you get this and we can plan the whole trip.

Love you lots.

Hugs and kisses,

Nora

Scene Seven

The flat. KATE *is sitting on the couch, hung-over and tense. She is drinking a vodka and tonic.* SARA *enters.*

KATE: Sara.

SARA: Has he gone?

KATE: Yes, he's gone ages. He went first thing.

SARA: (*Walking off towards bedroom*) Marvellous.

KATE: Sara, please talk to me, please, have a drink and we can talk.

SARA: Kate, just piss off! Piss off and leave me alone.

KATE: Look, Sara, that's not the attitude, we have to –

SARA: It's not the attitude, is it, Kate?!

KATE: Please, I'm sorry. I'm trying to talk to you, I want to talk, we've just got to talk.

SARA: About what, Kate? About what?

(KATE *is silent.*)

SARA: About your bloody mother, your fucking cousin?

(KATE *has no reply.*)

SARA: I've had enough of it, Kate, this crisis. Look at the state of you, pissed for God's sake.

KATE: I'm not pissed.

SARA: You are, and what about work? You never used to miss work . . . You're a mess. Just look at yourself, you and that . . . that prrraat. I'd have thought you'd enough Irish in you without that . . . kissin' cousin.

KATE: Stop it, Sara, please. I was drunk. It didn't mean anything, you know it didn't mean anything. God, he's just a man, for God's sake.

SARA: And that makes it all right, does it? He's just a man?

KATE: Of course not. But, I mean, it's nothing, it wasn't even sex . . .
Oh God. I don't know what it was, I don't know what I was
doing, it's crazy, I can't believe it happened.

SARA: *You* can't believe it!

KATE: Oh Sara, please, please. (*Starts to laugh nervously*) I haven't been
with a man since, since I was about sixteen, it seems ridiculous.

SARA: I don't believe you. You're laughing! I'm watching *our* life go
down the tube and you're laughing . . .

(KATE *cannot stop laughing.*)

SARA: I waited all night at the gallery, Kate. I spent the whole night
looking at the door, but you'd no intention of coming, had you?
You were too busy screwing that . . .

(KATE *is now in fits of laughter.*)

SARA: I can't believe you, Kate. I really can't. (*She goes to get her bag.*)

KATE: Sara. Sara. I'll stop. I'm sorry . . .

SARA: (*Returning with gear*) It's not just last night, Kate, that was just the
last straw. You have been impossible of late, a self-pitying bitch.

KATE   I know, Sara.

SARA: It's always all about you, isn't it? This grief, it's about you, not
your mum. You never cared about her, like you never cared
about me.

KATE: That's not true.

SARA: You walked out on her, Kate, like you walk out on everyone,
everything; work, relationships, the lot. You left your mum to
rot in a lonely hell-hole. You left her there and then, when she
had the affront to die, well it's poor me, poor Kate. You weren't
even there, Kate. That woman cried, she twisted as her lungs
caved in and you weren't there. Who did she have to cry out to,
Kate? Well, I bet she got on with it, on with life, on with death.
She had to, didn't she, Kate? We all do. Now I'm going to Julie's,
I've had enough of this.

KATE: (*Quietly*) Sara, Sara please don't go like this. I'm not walking
out, that's just it. I'm trying not to walk away –

SARA: I can't take any more of it. I just can't.

KATE: But you're my best friend, my family, you're all I've got.

SARA: I can't stay now. I won't. It's not even last night, it's you, you've
locked me out. You don't come out any more, don't talk, well

not about anything real, you keep raking back over the past. I'm not a part of that.

KATE: I'm sorry.

SARA: When was the last time we went to the cinema together, to the theatre? You've no interest, have you, Kate? You're lost somewhere.

KATE: I know. I am lost; I feel so lost.

SARA: And I can't help you any more

KATE: Maybe if I go to Dublin, Sara, I could find Mum. See her sisters and find her. Find her and Dad.

SARA: But they're dead, Kate, they're gone.

KATE: (*Tears falling*) I know.

SARA *leaves.*

Act Two

Scene One

In the kitchen of a small Cabra corporation house in Dublin. MARGARET, *a vibrant woman, is setting the table for tea.* KATE *and* BRIAN *enter in great form.*

MARGARET: Well, how'd you get on?

KATE: Fabulous, Margaret. It's been a really wonderful day.

MARGARET: Did you show her George's Street where Nora worked?

KATE: He did. Cassidy's is gone now but he took me into a pub which is years old.

BRIAN: The Long Hall. (*He sits and reads a newspaper.*)

KATE: Do you think Mum drank there?

MARGARET: She could well have done. (*Offering* KATE *a chair and pouring out tea*)

KATE: The city is beautiful, much brighter than I'd imagined, and the shops look fantastic. I'm going to go mad in Grafton Street before I go home.

MARGARET: Yes, it's lovely. Your mother loved Grafton Street, by all accounts. I'm sure she'd pop into the shops herself on her lunch.

KATE: Yes, I was thinking that. I was trying to picture her, turning a corner, crossing the street. Brian is taking me to Howth tomorrow; he says you all used to go there when you were young.

MARGARET: Oh we did, we used to get the tram. It was wonderful, like a roller coaster twisting around the summit.

KATE: Did Mum like it there?

MARGARET: Oh she did. She used to bring me when I was a child. Ma would insist she brought the younger ones, even if she was on a date. We'd love it. Sure we'd be given a penny to buy sweets so they could spend a few precious moments on their own.

KATE: (*Laughs*) Did she have many boyfriends, then?

MARGARET: Loads. She was gorgeous, Kate. She used to model clothes, you know, for the shop. I'll show you the photos. I rooted out a few for you when you were out.

KATE: That would be fantastic, Margaret. I found so little when she died.

MARGARET: She was a real beauty. Daddy always said she was the Queen of Cabra. He loved her, you know. The eldest daughter – oh nothing was ever good enough for Nora. He wrote to her in London religiously every week. He'd have loved you too, Kate, to see you sitting here, large as life.

KATE: I wish I'd met him. I know so little, even about my own dad, and I want to know everything; suddenly it all seems so vital.

MARGARET: Yes, well.

KATE: What about my gran, your own mum, what was she like?

MARGARET: Oh Mammy was a great woman. She loved us all. She'd a fair family to watch over, five girls. But she got us all jobs and watched us marry and have lives of our own.

KATE: How did she and Mum get on?

MARGARET: Great. Nora would have done a lot of work in the house; she was expected to, being the oldest. It was hard on her, really, when I think of it – she had to mind us a lot too.

KATE: Do you think that's why she left?

MARGARET: I don't know, really. Mam never wanted her to go to London, she'd a good job in Cassidy's, but I'm sure Nora wanted the adventure, wanted to be with her pals.

KATE: Did she have friends in London, then?

MARGARET: She did.

KATE: They can't have stayed in touch. I never met anyone from Dublin that I can remember.

MARGARET: I'd always thought she'd gone over to friends. I'm sure she did, but sure it was a long time ago, I can't remember it all.

KATE: Of course. I'm sorry to bombard you with questions. I just want to take it all in. Today was wonderful, I feel happy. Happy. This is the happiest I've felt for a long time.

MARGARET: Sure isn't it marvellous you've come! Brian is delighted. He's been talking about you non-stop. (BRIAN *is squirming*.) I'll show you those photos. (*She hands them down to* KATE.) Did you phone Bob about tonight, he'd love to meet his cousin.

BRIAN: Yeah. Yeah, I did. I'm going to head home soon and call Dermot and a few of the lads. (*Goes back to his paper*)

KATE: (*Examining the old photographs*) These are fabulous. Look, Brian . . . God she was stunning, wasn't she? And look at the clothes. They must have been going to a dance. Who's the other girl?

MARGARET: That was her friend Celia Carroll, they were inseparable.

KATE: Look at them, they look smashing all dressed up. Do you have any of her and Dad?

MARGARET: No, no I don't think so, love; there's a lovely one, though, of you as a child.

KATE: Oh, it's great. Doesn't Mum look happy, when was that? Nineteen sixty-two. Isn't it funny to look at a photo of your-self and have no memory of it, no memory of that bond – and we both look so happy.

MARGARET: Keep it, Kate.

KATE: Really? Thanks, Margaret. It means a lot.

BRIAN: Don't you have any?

KATE: No, not one. Mum never kept photos about the house. She'd rarely talk about things, not even about Dad. I was so hungry for information. You know what kids are like. I still am.

MARGARET: Sure wasn't she right? They just clutter up the place. Gather dust.

BRIAN: Would you listen to her. The sitting room is like a gallery. A bloody shrine.

MARGARET: And I should get rid of the lot . . . I hardly need them as mementoes, sure amn't I looking at you every mealtime?

KATE: (*Still looking at the photos*) Doesn't she look so young? I'd hardly know her. What was she really like, I wonder? What were her hopes, her dreams?

MARGARET: Well, didn't she do well for herself? A nice home. A lovely family.

KATE: And Dad, what do remember of Dad? Was he kind, Margaret? Did he play sport? I've pictured him so many different ways. Mum always said he was handsome but that's not enough. I want to know. I want to know his hands. Their texture, their talents.

MARGARET: Oh a great man . . .

KATE: But what did he say? He'd have had his own expressions. His own gestures. Was he a big man? What did he play? What did he sing? Was he funny? What was his laugh? Did he love her, did he love me or the thought of me, word of me? I just need so much to know.

(MARGARET *is a bit shaken by this.*)

BRIAN: Did you ever meet him, Mam?

MARGARET: No. No, love, I never did. (*Getting a bit addled,* MARGARET *starts fussing with tea things.*)

KATE: Did none of you meet him?

MARGARET: No. Unfortunately, you see, it was a whirlwind romance. Our Nora was swept off her feet. They were married in London and he died so soon after, the poor man. (*Pause. Both are hanging on her every word.*) I'm sure he was a lovely lad, though. Poor Nora was heartbroken, that I do know; sure that poor girl would have had no time for photographs. She had to get a job, Kate, and make ends meet.

BRIAN: Why on earth did she not come home?

MARGARET: To Dublin?

BRIAN: Yeah, sure you'd all have helped out.

KATE: She must have been so lonely; it doesn't make sense.

MARGARET: Well, she had a new baby, Kate. Where would she stay? Where would they sleep? There were still six of us here. Poor Ma had enough to feed. Your mother was a great woman. She got herself a job and raised you with no help from anyone.

BRIAN: Couldn't have been easy – a woman on her own in those days.

KATE: Oh they totally exploited her; she worked all hours at the launderette and she used to take in ironing, I remember that.

MARGARET: Things were a lot harder those times.

BRIAN: (*To* KATE) Well listen, will we go? I need to pick up the lads. (KATE *is studying* MARGARET.) Do you want to come now, Kate, or will I collect you on the way out?

KATE: On the way back would be great – if you don't mind, Margaret?

MARGARET: No, not at all, love, sure I'm enjoying the chat. I'll make another cup of tea.

The lights fade, but MARGARET *and* KATE *are still visible as the young woman in silhouette approaches the table and sits to write a letter.*

Dear Brendan,

Why don't you write? I keep thinking you might be sick and I wouldn't know about it. I went to the site to find Mick Connolly but the foreman said he'd got work back home; have you seen him at all? I'm sure you're awful busy, Bren, but I'd love to get some word.

Have you thought about our trip or my coming to Donegal? I'm so lonely here without you, I can't keep living on our last weekend. I need to see you, Bren, and hold you to know that it's all real, not just a lovely dream.

I've been busy in the shop and going to dances a lot with C. I'm putting a few bob by, in the hope that you'll write soon. C sends her love.

Write soon, won't you, Bren?

Love and kisses,

Nora

The lights fade back up to KATE *and* MARGARET *and the young woman exits.*

KATE: Do you know where he's buried, Margaret? I'd like to visit his grave.

MARGARET: Your father's grave?

KATE: Yes.

MARGARET: I don't, Kate.

KATE: It's in Donegal, that's all I know. Mum said they took him back to Donegal.

MARGARET: I see.

KATE: Do you know anything about the accident?

MARGARET: No. (*Starting to get upset*)

KATE: Is everything all right? I'm sorry, Margaret, am I upsetting

	you talking about Mum? I forget that she was your sister, I –
MARGARET:	Oh Jesus, this is dreadful.
KATE:	What is? Are you OK?
MARGARET:	I can't believe she never told you, pet. I mean, we kept it up, but dear God, I'd have thought she'd have told you.
KATE:	Told me what? Kept what up? What, Margaret? What's wrong?
MARGARET:	(*Pause*) Your mother went to London in 1959 . . .
KATE:	Yes?
MARGARET:	She said she was going over to pals.
KATE:	Yes.
MARGARET:	Oh God help us, after all these years.
KATE:	What?
MARGARET:	She said she'd be getting some work in a fancy London shop; she was so pretty, you see, and full of life . . .
KATE:	Yes?
MARGARET:	She was pregnant, Kate.
KATE:	Before she went?
MARGARET:	Yes.
KATE:	But I thought she met Dad . . .
MARGARET:	In London. No. Oh God, when I think about it, all the lies. It never seemed so bad until now; we just buried it, I suppose. I suppose we came to believe it ourselves; sure it was easier that way but now with you here, oh God, it seems so wrong.
KATE:	What does? Margaret . . . What? Mum was pregnant before they were married? . . . Why the fuss, what does it matter, why care about that?
MARGARET:	But they never were married, Kate, you see – poor Nora went to London alone.
KATE:	Alone? I don't understand. Will you please tell me what went on?
MARGARET:	Your mother left for London. That was all we knew. We thought she was getting on fine and then Celia Carroll called in to see Ma.
KATE:	Her friend.
MARGARET:	Her best friend. Celia was worried sick about Nora. She was the only one knew the secret, the pregnancy, and she couldn't bare it any longer. She thought if she told Ma, well Ma might be able to help.

KATE: I don't understand . . . Mum was alone, and Dad . . . Dad was?!

MARGARET: Nora fell in love with a lad from Donegal; he worked on the sites in Dublin and they'd been together for over a year. She hadn't brought him home 'cause he was older and she thought Ma wouldn't approve. Anyway, he left her with her baby. I was here the night Celia called; Jesus I'll never forget it, the others were out at a dance. Ma and I were in the kitchen. God, I can remember it like it was yesterday. Ma was livid, Kate, she let rip at Celia Carroll, as much as blamed her for the whole affair. It was such a disgrace in those days; it seems so silly now but a pregnancy like that brought such shame. Ma threatened poor Celia and made her swear not to breathe a word. The child would be adopted in London and no one would be the wiser; that was her decision, Kate, and Ma's word was law.

KATE: Adopted? Who? Me?

MARGARET: Nora loved you, Kate, she couldn't give you up, so she let on that she got married in London, to a man from Donegal.

KATE: God.

MARGARET: She wrote a letter and everything . . . all about the wedding, the whirlwind romance. Nora never knew that Celia had told Ma. Ma never said a word, said 'It would break your father's heart.' She went along with the whole thing. I was the only one who knew and sure I couldn't say anything. I had to do what I was told.

KATE: My God.

MARGARET: I know. Isn't it awful? For years we went on pretending, believing, and now when I see you sitting here asking about your da . . . well, it just never seemed so wrong before. We saved face. Da never knew, and life, it just went on. Nora seemed to get on in London; she got a house and she had her job. She wrote to say her husband was killed and that she'd had a little girl.

KATE: I can't believe it . . .

MARGARET: I'm sorry, love.

KATE: She created her whole world.

MARGARET: I suppose.

KATE: No wonder she was always shifting, never let anyone get too close. She was afraid they'd find out . . . and your mother never said?

MARGARET: No. She'd never mention Celia's visit, she just took on Nora's story and pretended it was the truth. We both did.

KATE: So what about Dad? Who is my dad?

MARGARET: Brendan, Brendan Dunne from Ballintra. That's all I know; he's the man she said she married. (*Takes her hand*) She was a good woman, Kate, she tried to make it all right, to make it easy for you and the family. She didn't want to hurt anyone or to bring on any shame . . .

KATE: Shame? Shame! You're the one who should feel shame, you and your mother. What kind of a woman, to lie, to pretend for years? To leave Mum all alone and she always spoke so highly of you, of home. She was the one betrayed, by everyone.

MARGARET: I know. You're right, but they were different times, Kate. You just couldn't break the code. Sure there were many like poor Nora – they had to take the boat and no one would breathe a word. The country was just cursed with silence . . .

KATE: I can't take it all in. Mum.

MARGARET: She loved you, Kate. She couldn't give you up. It's something you'll understand when you have a child of your own.

KATE: But Brendan Dunne, my father, what happened to him . . . did he just desert her?

MARGARET: I don't know. I don't know what happened there, Kate.

KATE: And Celia, where's she?

MARGARET: Australia. She married soon after. I've not seen her since.

KATE: I can't believe this.

MARGARET: I know, love. Don't think about it now, it must be a bit of a shock.

KATE: Shock! (*Almost laughing*) My whole life, it's been a lie. Phantoms and fairytales. So many things she wouldn't speak of and you were all the same. Pretending. Not speaking . . .

MARGARET: I know . . . I'm sorry, love. I really am.

MARGARET *comforts* KATE *as the lights fade.*

Scene Two

KATE *is alone at the kitchen table in* MARGARET's *house finishing some tea, and* BRIAN *walks in. It is the next day.*

BRIAN: Hiya, Kate.

KATE: Hi.

BRIAN: How are you feeling?

KATE: OK. God, Brian. I don't know. I'm just reeling from it all, really.

BRIAN: I can imagine. I'm, I'm . . . what can I say?

KATE: I know. Isn't it crazy? The years of collusion. Bitterness . . .

BRIAN: I know.

KATE: Had you no idea?

BRIAN: Are ya mad? Jesus, sure why would I think it'd be anything different? All I knew is what I was told. I'd never have even thought about it, only . . .

KATE: Only what?

BRIAN: Only, well, getting to know you and that. I'll tell ya, I can't get over Ma not saying anything.

KATE: For years she just pretended it didn't happen.

BRIAN: I suppose it seemed better just to leave it.

KATE: Do you think so?

BRIAN: What?

KATE: Think she was right to leave it?

BRIAN: I don't know. I don't see what she could have done. I think it's fuckin' incredible, though. Incredible to keep something like that in, when there were so many reminders. I mean, your ma didn't disappear, there was always contact. None of the others know the real story, you know, they think she got married and all that.

KATE: Your gran must have been a right bitch.

BRIAN: She was a tough woman all right. I never had much time for her, though that was more to do with her stew than anything else. It's just all comin' out now, isn't it? Incest, child abuse, selling babies, mad stuff . . . It'd rock ya . . . and now we're a part of it.

KATE: (*Frustrated sigh*) I thought by coming here I could get closer to Mum, but she's slipping away, all the time; soon I'll lose sight of her. And now I no longer have a dad.

BRIAN: But sure you never knew him anyway.

KATE: Of course I did. In my head, I did. I knew what fragments I could catch, glimpses I could muster. I stored them up, fitted the picture, but now, well now it's all blown sky high, isn't it? I mean, was it this Brendan Dunne? How could Mum, my own mum, spin me such lies?

BRIAN: (*Goes close to comfort her*) Try not to think about it.

KATE: But I have to, what else can I think of?

BRIAN: It'll be OK. We'll find out, we'll sort it all out.

KATE: Oh Brian. Thanks, thanks for being such a great guy. I don't know how I'd have got through this without you. (*He attempts to kiss her, but she moves away.*) I'm sorry, sorry, not like that. I don't feel like that, I've messed you about. I've not been thinking straight. I'm not interested, Brian, not at all, not that way. I love, Sara; we both know that that's who I am . . .

BRIAN: (*Embarrassed, but trying to appear indifferent*) Oh grand.

KATE: But it isn't. I know it isn't grand.

BRIAN: No, no. It is. It's fine.

KATE: I'm sorry.

BRIAN: Don't be; you're right.

KATE: Oh come on, don't be like that, please.

BRIAN: I'm not. I'm fine. You're upset. It's a bad time.

KATE: No, Brian.

BRIAN: What?

KATE: It's not a bad time. It will never be a good time. I'm not. We're not.

BRIAN: You're upset.

KATE: I know I'm upset. I'll be even more upset if you continue to misunderstand me . . .

BRIAN: What?

KATE: That you and I are friends. Good friends, but that's all.

BRIAN: Grand.

KATE: Brian . . .

BRIAN: I said it's fine. I know – you have your own life, with Sara. I just, I just fell for ya, fall for ya, I'm fairly fond of ya.

KATE: I know. Thanks. I'm very grateful, really.

BRIAN: Right.

KATE: I'm going home.

BRIAN: To London.

KATE: Yes. I'll book the flight . . . but I want to see if anyone knows or remembers Brendan Dunne. I think I'll go to Donegal.

BRIAN: Bit of a long shot. I mean, what do we know?

KATE: Ballintra.

BRIAN: It's not a lot.

KATE: I know, but I want to go there, see how it feels.

BRIAN: I'll go with you.

KATE: No. Thanks, Brian, but I need to go alone.

Lights fade.

Scene Three

The mirrorball is swirling. The young woman stands alone in silhouette.

Dear Brendan,

I don't know why you don't write, I can only imagine that something terrible has happened, so I'm coming up to see you myself. There is a bus from Dublin on Saturday which arrives at four in Donegal station – will you meet me there? I just have to see you. I know how much you love me and know in my heart that you want us to be together. I have waited and waited, Brendan. Every day I go to the site in the hope that there might be word. I just wish to God we could sit down and talk this out together. I'd love to see your big country smile; I know it would give me strength. I'm going to have our baby, Brendan. I've been waiting for you to come to Dublin to tell you. I know it's too important to put in a letter but what can I do? I am coming up to Ballintra, Brendan, I know you'll be so happy too when I tell you my plan. A baby is such a beautiful gift. I feel so important with this little life inside me, so proud for the two of us. I know that sounds mad, people will say different, but I don't care. I love you, Brendan, I couldn't wait. Our love came in snatched weekends and little white paper notes, we had to grab it while we could but it's all different now – we can be together always. I have enough savings to buy us two boat tickets to London. Úna and Carmel have a place there; I'm sure they'd put us up until we got sorted out. Please don't be frightened, Brendan, this is really a blessing. We can marry quiet in London and set up our own home. I'm sure Ma will come around in time. I'll not breathe a word to a living soul until we decide on Saturday. I love you, Bren, can't wait to see you.

Love, hugs and kisses,

Nora

Scene Four

A bus station in Dublin. KATE *enters and sits on a bench, putting her bag at her feet. She has a bunch of letters. She looks out front. There is a silence.* MARGARET *enters.*

MARGARET: I can't think where Brian's got to, how hard can it be to find

	parking? Isn't it typical the bus was early. We were just saying they're always late, and you sitting here.
KATE:	It was the timetable. There was a change.
MARGARET:	It's Iarnród Éireann . . . there's always something. Sure listen, love, wasn't I relying on buses for years? Useless . . . standing for hours in the rain, hail and snow. Always something.
KATE:	I didn't mind. It's only half an hour. I'm fine. Please don't fuss.
MARGARET:	Am I fussing? Sorry, love, I am. You hardly want to talk about the journey after the day you've had.
KATE:	I'm fine. It was nice.
MARGARET:	The village, was it? I'm glad.
KATE:	No, the day, the day was nice.
MARGARET:	(*Straining as she looks for* BRIAN) Well, isn't that marvellous?
KATE:	Ballintra is empty; it's quite an empty place. Even the shops were empty. Empty shelves, the butcher was standing in his white coat with little or no meat on the counter. What an eerie little street . . . it looked broken, cut off.
MARGARET:	Lots of those little places are like that – the emigration would have torn strips out of them.
KATE:	There was hardly a soul.
MARGARET:	That's it, they'd all have got work in Donegal or Dublin or wherever. With no road going through any more, no one would stop; sure there'd be nothing to stop for . . .
KATE:	I know. Empty.

(*There is a silence between them.* MARGARET *tries to fill it by looking for* BRIAN.)

KATE:	I found him, you know, Margaret. Brendan Dunne.
MARGARET:	I know. Brian said when you phoned, well he said you found his . . .
KATE:	Wife, yes, a lovely lady.
MARGARET:	God.
KATE:	Do you know, she wasn't a bit surprised?
MARGARET:	No?!
KATE:	She knew, Margaret. She knew all about me, well knew there was a baby. She said she'd wondered for years, waited, dreaded the day I'd call . . . but then he died.
MARGARET:	Her husband.

KATE: Yes. Her husband and my dad, So she'd no more reason to fear, to wait in dread for that call.

MARGARET: God help us.

KATE: She gave me these, Margaret (*She shows her the bunch of letters.*) They're all from Mum. From Mum to Brendan Dunne.

MARGARET: Dear God.

KATE: I know.

MARGARET: And how did she . . . ?

KATE: He never got them. She kept them all, his wife, he never knew a thing.

MARGARET: About Nora?

KATE: About me. She never gave him the letters.

MARGARET: He was already married?!

KATE: Yes.

MARGARET: Jesus, Nora couldn't have known.

KATE: No. That's it. He was married with two sons. That's why he didn't marry Mum. Why he didn't come.

MARGARET: Dear God.

KATE: He died four years ago. His wife never told him about the baby or about Mum coming to Donegal.

MARGARET: Nora met her?!

KATE: Yes. She came one day just like I did . . . Mrs. Dunne said she met her at the station and told her to stay away from her husband.

MARGARET: And she told you all this? This woman?

KATE: Yes. She said that Mum was stunned. Said she'll never forget her face; she was terrified for years that Mum would come back, but she never did and never wrote. She'd often wondered about her and the child . . . about me.

MARGARET: But she never told him?

KATE: No.

MARGARET: Poor Nora. Jesus, what could she do? She had no choice, you know, she could never have stayed at home.

KATE: No.

MARGARET: God help us. I can just picture her, the shock of it. Jesus, she must have sat in the station for hours, nowhere to go, no one to tell.

KATE: I know, and you should read the letters. She loved him. She loved him so much.

(*They are silent again.*)

MARGARET: And you never even met him.

KATE: No.

MARGARET: Are you sorry?

KATE: No.

MARGARET: Well. What'll you do now, love?

KATE: Go home, Margaret. Go back to London, to Sara, to my life. I don't like it here. I don't belong.

MARGARET: Like Nora.

KATE: Yes. Like Mum.

KATE *and* MARGARET *are left sitting on the bench. The young woman appears in silhouette behind them and sits next to* KATE.

A Cure for Homosexuality

NEIL WATKINS

A Cure for Homosexuality was first presented at Centre Stage Café, Dublin, on 4 May 2005 as part of the International Dublin Gay Theatre Festival, by Gentle Giant Theatre Company.

CAST

Paddy Doyle   Neil Watkins

PRODUCTION TEAM

Director	John O'Brien
Producer	Phillip McMahon
Lighting designer	Kevin Smith
Costume designer	Peter O'Brien and Orla Bass
Choreography	Muirne Bloomer

CHARACTER

Paddy Doyle, *twenty-seven, attractive, tall and fair-haired, with a military style haircut.*

Prologue

The play is set in a café. The audience is its customers. The figure of PADDY DOYLE *emerges from the gloom. He is dressed in a leather Nazi uniform. He addresses the audience.*

Berlin. Fuck.

It's 8 p.m. I've on/off slept for an hour. I don't believe I've ever felt so much at one with myself as I do now. The fact is, I collected a bespoke

111

leather uniform today. 'Bespoke' means it was made for me. And I had my hair cut. I look and feel like the person I want to be.

Leather and a masculine haircut are mine. And the freedom of the city of Berlin. Tension from work and sickness from working too hard have left my body. I feel beautiful.

It amazes me that it has taken me this long to reach this feeling in my life. Leather is what brings me to my truth. I don't say these words lightly. Seriously, don't laugh.

Fucking dying for tonight. This feeling is my own. And I resist the old instinct to text-message the lads in Ireland about my excitement.

I'll savour the taste. I'll enhance any moment necessary with poppers, grass, whatever comes my way. In leather I will be held in the arms of my leather master. In the darkness I'll commit myself into his gloved hand. His whiskers bristling at my mouth. Encouraging me and assuring me without words. I'll chow down on him and all the while the intoxicating and beautiful leather will unite us in infinity's warmth.

I'm twenty-seven and I feel like I'm alive with the angels on the earth. After all my questioning of faith, this feels like my religion. I must continue to tend to, and fulfil, my needs.

Sieg Heil. Tonight I will serve the German SS officer I have dreamed of. I am perfect for him. Amen.

Act One

Ask yourself: 'Is it something that I really like? Or is it just a fantasy?' Anything in S & M slash Sado-Masochistic sex can be broken down into three categories:

1. I'm ready for it.
2. I certainly do do that.
3. I certainly don't do that.

The list is long and I leave no stone unturned. Erotic Abrasion, TT (Tit Torture), CP (Corporal Punishment), CBT (Cock and Ball Torture), Electro (self-explanatory), Domination, Role Play, Master and Slave, and Fisting.

Now some people drop out at this point. Usually they are accompanied by a boyfriend. One of them will be into the lark more than the other fella. If anyone wants to leave, now would be a good time to do so. Good.

We will also be looking at the importance of negotiation in the S & M scene. Self-awareness is key. You have to know what you're ready to do. S & M is not just about beating the shit out of each other. Although it can be. It's about soft stuff as well. It's nearly like massage, actually. Mull that over. When you're on the receiving end of it, its so pleasurable. You think it must be boring for your Master. But it's far from bored your Master is. He loves watching you abandoned to him. The level of his mental stimualtion is something shocking. He has such power and responsibility over you.

There is nothing hornier than the Master shaving the Slave. The act, however, does have a practical outcome. It's not just sexual. Blade 1 on the head and blade 0 everywhere else keeps the slave's body neat and visible. It also acts as a deterrent to the infestation of crabs.

Just look around the home and marvel at the abundace of S & M appliances already at your disposal. A simple fork could spice things up. Please turn your attention to the wrapped cutlery sets on your tables. You can ignore the knives for the moment. Pick up the fork. Look at it. It's just a boring old fork. Or is it? In S & M we must always test everything on ourselves first.

Rub the fork against your body to test it. Do it. Shove it down your shirt. Cold, isn't it! You could try heating it using hot water. A cup of tea can come in handy. The heat stings, doesn't it? Jab yourself with the fork. That could get painful, couldn't it? Try scraping yourself with the fork. Use it as a dental device. The fork is versatile. Try long sustained insertions with the fork tips around the sensitive nipple area. Test the fork on your cock and balls, your anus. What will you discover? Remember, always practise on yourself first. You regulate the pressure. They feel the pleasure.

Always commence each Master and Slave scene by inserting a butt-plug of suitable size up the Slave's hole. This is horny. It lets the Slave know his place. And the practical outcome is that he'll be ready to be fucked when his Master wants him.

Choosing the right butt-plug for your Slave couldn't be easier. It is always the one that has been sterilized in Milton, preferably the tablets. It's excellent for dildos, as well as babies' bottles. But don't get the two confused.

A good Master is someone who permanently has Milton on his shopping list. But Milton can't protect you against everything.

The point is, gentlemen, not all venereal diseases are as easy to treat as crabs.

What is safe sex? In actual fact very little we do is safe. And before you, sir, yes you, sir, before you pipe up about how safe you think fisting is, don't bother.

Safe fisting? What's that? Playing with someone small of hand?

Out of all the play you can get up to, lads, only one act is considered safe. And that's water sports. Water sports. Does everyone know what water sports is? Does anyone not know what water sports is?

Piss. I'm talking about piss. Pissing on each other. Pissing into someone else's mouth, hole, all over someone's face, in someone's ear. Piss is sterile. It's safe. Kissing isn't as safe as pissing. Hepatitis may be acquired through kissing. But like everything else going around these days, it's all treatable. There's never been a better time to catch HIV.

(*A telephone rings.* PADDY *answers it.*)

Hello? Centre Stage, Paddy Doyle speaking. How may I help you? Who's this? Sorry? You're going to have to call back. I'm a bit busy at the moment. Where the fuck have you been? Where are you? (Aside to the audience) *Excuse me. Keep working away with those forks. I'll be with yiz in a minute.* (Back to phone call) *I don't believe this. What part are you in? Of course, you had to be in San Francisco. You couldn't have said somewhere crap like Utah or Kansas or fucking poxville DC. What do you mean, you have to go? Your friends are waiting for you? Fuck off. Tell them I said fuck off. Did you meet someone nice? Did you? What's his name? Tell us. Tell us before I get on a fucking plane, come over there and smack the fucking poxy face off you. Rick? Chip? Buck? Brad? Cunt? You're some cunt. Some fucking cunt for leaving me here to run the business. I don't know how I'm still standing. There's hardly a hair left in my head. The doctor has me taking mad shit. Well put more money in, you thick. Anyway, I know you made this call on your credit card. You've a fucking black belt in it.*

Listen. You tell Chuck, Kurt, Burt, Bradley, Kip, or whatever the fuck his name is, to hang on to fuck, till I have me fucking say. All right!

Did you know this, pox bottle? The solicitors were round. They said you've ten days to make this business work, Mr. Doyle, or 'Scarper!' Turn it around? It's a fucking goldmine, so it is. No fucking thanks to you but, shite bag. Yeah, it is packed, as a matter of fact. All the hardcore American queers are here and they fucking love it. I can't help it if they've got a better quality of gay life here. Do you know what's happening to their friends in America? You must be mad hanging around over there. If you go missing, I won't be responsible. God only knows what happened to those boys. Don't say I didn't fucking warn you.

Are you there? Say something if you're there, you fucking eejit. Don't keep me hanging on like a fucking spare. Do you hear me? Are you crying? What are you crying for? You're the one who legged it. I'm the one who should be crying. Fuck sake, give over the whingeing, will you? Kill it. Just . . . Ah . . . I'm sorry.

Da.

I'm sorry. I said, I'm sorry for being horrible to you. You're not a failure. The business was good when you ran it. It was lovely. Thanks to you, cruising was alive and well in Dublin. All your regulars love you. And your staff. You gave me a fantastic upbringing. You brought me on the best holidays. Not to America, I know. But to deadly places like Courtown and Trabolgan, and other nice places around Ireland.

Da, please come home to me. It's not safe for gays in America. Not any more. Don't mind what the president says. Visa restrictions abolished for gays! Visa restrictions abolished for people with HIV. It's all just Pleasure Island bullshit. They're only trying to lure us in. In the end Pinocchio and all the other little boys only turn into donkeys. And there ain't no Blue Fairy coming to help you.

You should see the men I'm looking at, Da, the ones who got away. Beautiful men, with sad faces. Very sad-looking. Come home, Da. I love you. I need you here with me. You're my hero. Do you know that? Come on, Da! I want you to book a ticket and come home to me. Well, if you don't come home, I'll bring you back myself. Da. Da?

(*End of phone call.* PADDY *addresses the audience again.*)

Excuse me, gentlemen. America must be great. The films, mostly the films, make me want to go there. I'd love to drive across it like in *Thelma & Louise*. And go ape-shit.

I'd love my car to break down in the middle of nowhere, Texas or somewhere. And this cowboy on horseback, or a cop on a motorbike, would have to rescue me. I'm not sure which yet. I don't know which one I like more. And he'd try to fix my car. But it wouldn't work. So I'd have to climb on board behind him, on the horse or the bike. Both would be nice. And we'd drive off into the sunset together. And that'd be the beginning of the rest of our lives together in America. But that'd be what I'd want.

There comes a time in every Slave's life . . . a time of grave disappointment. That's when the Slave realizes that there's no man alive man enough to force him into a sling and keep him there against his will. Show me the man with the physical might. The sex appeal and the proper equipment to truly dominate me. He doesn't exist.

I thought Berlin would hold all the answers. All I got was a new wardrobe. I met this man. It seemed great on the Internet. Initially, as I choked on his fat cock, I thought, yeah yeah yeah. I'll call you Boss. He insisted that I call him Boss. I felt there was something a bit eighties about this request. But I did well to just put it to the back of my mind. 'You like sucking that fat cock, don't you, boy?' 'Yes, Boss,' I would say. And he'd stare down while I licked his boots clean for him. 'Good boy,' he'd say . . . to which I'd always reply . . . 'Thank you, Boss.' I had to thank Boss for fucking everything. For putting the poxy lock and chain around my neck. 'And you'll wear that all day?' 'Yes, Boss.' 'And when Boss's boyfriend comes home, you will say to him, "Hello, Pin, I am Boss's new slave boy"?' 'Yes, Boss. Thank you, Boss.' That was supposed to be all part of the humiliation. Well, do you know what? It was humiliating. That's all grand for a wank. But I had to keep this performance up all day in all the gay gaffs in Berlin. Everywhere we went . . . Bruno's, the gay bookshop . . . where I stocked up on copies of *Tom of Finland*, *Bound & Gagged* magazine, work by the Hun and a new edition of *Spartacus International Gay Guide*. And of course the military store, where I bought a German biker police uniform and a sailor's suit for scandalously low prices. And Mask World . . . wig and costume store, where I stocked up on a few bits and pieces for Lavinia . . . she's my drag act . . . he had to stake his claim over me in front of everyone. Me fucking nut was done in.

There I was in VK79 leather workshop in East Berlin. I was picking up this. I'd ordered it over the net. As usual, the guy serving was a fucking hottee. Tall, dark and fucking handsome. Beat into the leather cacks. He was Australian and was flirting the hole off me. Any chance I had with him was permanently obliterated when Boss pulls the lock and chain outside of my shirt. The fucking prick's jealousy was blatant. He starts to get off with me in front of your man. Now I love kissing, but not with that cretin. But I was staying in his gaff. So I had to keep him sweet.

Boss announces that he wants me to buy a custom-made chastity belt. So into the changing room wih me, strip naked . . . wait to be measured by fucking Lash. Looking at my hairless body in the mirror, I look like a twelve-year-old. I'd already had the full body shave. I felt naked without the hair. And pathetic with the chain and lock around my neck. Lash arrives in to measure me.

Down he gets and starts to suck me off. He touches me all over like he likes me. He calls me a real man. I could easily spray all over him. But Boss appears. My cock flops out of the beauty's mouth and I take in the cunt that is Boss. Says he to me, 'That wig you bought today for your drag act, you will wear it for Boss in the leather bar tonight.' I was devastated. Goodbye any chance I had of impressing your man. Good luck. Boss may as well have castrated me and eaten the prize. I was no longer eligible for such a hunk of Australian Thuggery. Totally humiliated.

Just as Hot Fucker is packing up our purchases, Boss repeats his command. 'You will wear the wig for your Boss tonight.' I just look at him. His hand is on my neck and he squeezes it to check me for a reply. I manage to say, 'Huh?'

With increased irritation he repeats the question. I stare at him. I can smell and taste his breath. 'No,' I protest. 'No? You don't say no to your Boss. You do what Boss tells you to do. I thought you understood that.' 'No!' I insist. 'No what?' he scolds. 'Just no!' He clatters me across the face. The leather workshop goes silent. Poor Hotcakes doesn't know where to look. Forcing a smile, he presents the bill. 'That'll be €1200, please.' In my great shame I hand over the last of my cash. I gather my purchases and run out into snowy Berlin, ignoring Boss completely. Didn't have a fucking clue where I was. So I hung on for him. As he approached I saw him for what he was. A five foot eight control freak with intimacy issues, mincing around in leather drag. 'You know why I had to do that, don't you?' 'Fuck up,' I tell him. 'You know why I'm pissed off with you. You're a dickhead. We've been on the go all day. I'm tired and I'm hungry. I can't keep up the fucking charade. I can't keep acting.' Says he, 'I'm not acting. Ask any of my Devil's Boys. They will be able to tell you that I'm like this 24/7.' I allow him to kiss me on the lips. It fabricates the illusion that we're friends again.

Fuck it. I needed a place to kip . . . so . . . We get back to his place and I introduce myself to the boyfriend. Pin. He's not long home from work; he's a history lecturer . . . actually cute and sprawled on the couch in a shirt and tie, sucking on a beer and watching a German soap opera. It looks fucking mental. I stand by the side of the television and I say to him, 'Hi, I'm Boss's new Slave.' And he just looks at me as though to pity me. Then he says, 'Welcome to your new home, you, you useless eater, you homosexual weakling.'

At Mutchmann's later that evening, an excellent leather cruising bar in the Schöneberg district, I look excellent in my VK79 leather uniform.

It's an exact replica of a German Nazi uniform, except it's leather. They wouldn't give the insignias.

Boss's boyfriend Pin returns from the bar with a beer for each of us. He's well on. He's been hard at the drinking since finishing work early. He kind of has a go at me for wearing the Nazi uniform. I tell him to chill out. Get over himself. I'm only wearing it for the craic. It makes me look sexy.

Boss warns Pin not to be ruining anyone's fun. They both laugh as they move in on me for a kiss. Kissing Pin is so much easier than kissing Boss. And from nowhere he throws me against a wall. Prostrate against the cold brickwork, he spreads my legs for me with a kick from the inside of his boot. One hand gags me and the other cups my groin. He purrs into my ear. 'Under Paragraph 175 of the criminal code, homosexuality is illegal in Nazi Germany.' My cock responds accordingly. 'You're a pervert, aren't you? We saw you walking home through the Tiergarten. You like spying on young lovers?' 'Yes, sir.' 'You paid too much attention to the actions of the man. Had you paid more attention to the actions of the woman, we might not have arrested you.' He turns me to face him. Keeping me at an arm's length, still gagging my mouth, he proceeds to pull me off. I notice that he's wearing glasses. I feel like I'm doing something very dirty with Hair Flick from *'Allo 'Allo!*

Jealous cunt Boss interrupts the proceedings and directs Pin's mouth down to his cock. I'm left with me dick going ninety but all I get is the spectacle of Boss chucking one into Pin's hungry mouth.

We leave Mutchmann's only having had a beer each. I mourn all the hot German Masters that I have to pass on, due to my accommodation restrictions. In the cab to their place Boss teases my cock with mean gropes. Meanwhile Hair Flick spews his dirty talk into my ear. 'Your cleansing starts now. Welcome to Sachsenhausen Concentration Camp. When your name is called, step forward, give your name and mention Paragraph 175. I'll greet you with the words, "Hello you filthy queer, get over here you butt-fucker." I will kick you several times. Then I will transfer you to Boss, who will be the SS sergeant in charge of your block. The first thing you get from him is a blow to your face. You will fall to the ground. He will knee you in the groin, so that you double over with pain. That's your entrance fee, you filthy Irish swine. Understood?' 'Yes, sir.' He sits back and cracks himself open a fresh bottle of poppers. He takes a sniff. Boss takes a sniff. We all take a sniff. I'm enjoying the buzz with a bit of guilt mixed in. We pull up at their place with my hard-on raging. I take another deep breath from the Bruder's amyl nitrite and I step out into the biggest kicking of my life.

Not long after that, I'm upstairs in the sling being fucked by Boss. Pin waits for his go. He's worked up and fidgety. Boss has a very determined look on his face. He's making a concerted effort to stay in character. It's all very Jodie Foster. Me on my back enduring a cold fuck. Pin's poppers are the only thing making this bearable. I just don't fancy the Boss at all. My legs high in stirrups, I stare up at the bearded mongrel ploughin' my hole. He orders me to thank my Boss.

Pin hovers in the shadows. He's taking the poppers through his mouth now. With one gloved hand, he chokes me and with another he beats himself off. He pushes the Hair Flick routine to the next level. 'You're guilty of playing with yourself under the bedclothes. We perform several checks per night. Two SS officers masturbate into your face. We force-feed you our cum. But you resist. We know that you're a cum-hungry bitch. So what's the problem? Your punishment is one hour outside in the freezing cold. We throw buckets of water over you and rape you. Your body will freeze.' He puts the icing on the cake and fucks a pint of beer in my face.

Boss sneers as he gets into a rhythm up my hole. Pin's lost in his performance. He waves a knife like a deranged conductor. 'We will take you to sick bay. We will cut off your penis. We will insert an artificial gland into your groin. It will release testosterone in an effort to cure your homosexuality. But it will not work. You are the lowest of the low. The Jews and the Nazis alike despise you because you are a pervert. You think of nothing but your pathetic sexual desire.'

They must twig that I'm not hard any more. Everything slows down. Pin looks concerned. Boss looks angry.

Boss spits a greener in my face and I rub it about ten times to clear it. The phlegm blurs my vision. Boss tells me to leave my hands down. 'There's fucking snot in my eye.' 'Don't you like it, boy?' 'No, I don't fucking like it. Now get the fuck out of me.' 'Your Boss will fuck you until he decides to stop.'

I fucking lost it. I wasn't into having someone treat me like this.

Pin was too wasted to stop me. In the sling I was naked apart from my motorcyle boots. So I boot-stomped Boss in the face, and pushed him out of me, carefully gripping around his cock to keep the condom on him. I threw him into his shelves of pervy toys . . . and . . . I just kept punching him, and kicking him, until the blood flowed out of him . . . and from me.

I think that's how I caught HIV.

Act Two

PADDY *is dressed like an all-American boy-next-door. He addresses the audience.*

Praise Jesus. He's here. He's not queer. Put up with him. Gentlemen and gentlemen, straight from the United States of America. Fully straight and author of *Hard for Jesus* . . . it's Paddy Doyle.

If homosexuality is OK, then why wasn't Jesus queer?

I used to be just like you. A homosexual, a victim, vulnerable to attack, terrified to cross Parliament Street Bridge at four in the morning. There are people out there who want you dead because you choose to be gay. But I stopped living in fear. I made a sacrifice and I was rewarded. You can be rewarded, too, my brothers. I'm here to help you, my brothers. Do you want my help or not? Let me heal you, my brothers. Praise Jesus. Amen, brothers. Jesus is present and powerful in this room.

The Church of Christ and the Burning Bush permits no drinking and no dancing. They frown on caffeine consumption. That's why we turned off the coffee machine here, folks. But instead of your usual fix of caffeine to get you through the day, why don't you take all the energy you need from Jesus?

In the United States of America, I live in a beautiful house. Wouldn't you like that? It's a beautiful wooden frame house. It's nestled in among a load of apricot trees. Wouldn't you like that? In the shade of those apricot trees I watched my baby girl take her first steps. Soon she'll be big enough to help me chase the local kids from stealing my apricots. My wife charms them into the most delicious pie. That's right. My wife! Wouldn't you like that? Yes siree, Bob, you would. Heaven on earth. You would like that. Well, we can give you that. All the way from America, we have some of that straight cake for you.

You know, my wife is amazing. She's never sick. Wouldn't you like that? She's never even been to the doctor. Wouldn't you like that? Can you imagine that? You probably can't. She comes from very strong stock. I guess you could say she redefines 'tough cookie'. Her father, who eveyone refers to as Uncle Gene, and I mean everyone, could pick up an anvil by the nose and toss it right across the street. Wouldn't you like that?

My wife is conservative. My wife is a Christian and she has no credit card debts. My wife is a pillar of the community. No matter where we are, she will always see to it that we find a Church of Christ and the Burning Bush. And no matter what, we will always be driven there by a negro chauffeur.

(*Phone rings*)

Praise Jesus. Minister Bush says everytime a bell rings a homosexual is cured.

(PADDY *answers the phone.*)

Hello? Centre Stage. Paddy speaking, how may I help you? Pop. How are you? It's so good to hear you. I'm back in the motherland. Nothing much changed. Although I may as well be in the States. Starbucks is here, at last. I seem to be able to have my decaf caramel macchiato wherever I am these days. Oh yes, but who'd want to go to the Middle East?

But enough about me. Tell me. How is she? I got your message. Uh-huh. Uh-huh. Well, you just go up to Duane Eddie's pharmacy on Lafayette and Howard and you tell them to repeat the prescription for Paddy Doyle's little girl. Explain to the man who you are. Bernard. He's very helpful. The Ralph Lauren sweaters. Polo uh-huh. I know the one you mean. Cable knit, figure hugging, but flattering. Yes, but he also works out. You can tell. He has huge arms. Well, it also sits well on him because his stomach is flat and he's got a bubble butt in his Levi's. He's perfectly proportioned. Oh you could so. Please, I've never seen you looking so well in all your life. Your hair and everything! Why do you think we've hitched such pretty ladies to look after us and keep nice homes for us? Of course I know. I'll tell you what. Why don't you and I have a boy's day out. We can leave things for the women to look after when I get back there and just hot the shops. They've still got that wonderful Century 21 down at Ground Zero. It'll be a hoot. Give her two spoonfuls and she'll sleep like a baby. And the mommy? Of course she is. It's Sunday. And my, my. You and Marianne are taking up ballroom dancing this evening. That's awesome, Dad. I'm so proud of you. It's fantastic to see you so involved and enthusiastic for life. I want you to hear it from me. You're my hero, Dad. I mean that. And Marianne too. You guys are the bomb!

They're in for something a little different this time round. A lot of customers in . . . I'm kind of in the middle of a healing now. OK. Bye, Dad, love to Marianne. Bye-bye. Bye-bye. Bye-bye.

(*End of phone call.* PADDY *addresses audience again.*)

I've been in the States now ten years this fall. I find it hard to believe I was once such a creature. And I look at Dad and I just don't see him in

Ibiza off his face in some unexceptional bar, bobbying away like a little faggot to a Whitney Houston remix.

I have permission from my minister, George W. Bush, to swear a little on my mission here in Dublin, just to bring the point home to you people. It's shite being gay. Let's be fucking honest. It's fucking difficult. Isn't it? Huh? Don't you think so? You're into guys, for fuck's sake. That has just never fitted in with the way of the world. And don't you know it. Don't I know it. Fuck me.

Only the physical presence of another man could satisfy your craving. You've fantasized that you're a woman, a beautiful woman. You've considered sex change just because you are so in love with the straight boy next door. He's beautiful. He's healthy. He makes an honest living. He's got a strong, amazing body. His hair is perfect. He always wears clean white trainers, jeans that show his package in a cheeky, slutty manner. His T-shirts accentuate his strong torso, pecs, and massive arms. He's boy and man in one neat faded brown leather bomber jacket.

Poor homosexuals. Always after something they can't get. You think, yeah I've tried wishing it away. And wishing just didn't work. Well, how about changing your vocabulary? Instead of the word 'wish', insert the word 'pray'. Have you ever tried prayer? I have. And brothers . . . prayer works.

And my dear brothers, fear not. It's not too late for anyone. Miracles galore lie in store for all here tonight. You only have to want it. Don't block the energy of God's love. Reject Satan's message. It will only confuse you. It will lull you into false hope. It will tell you that you are being true to yourself if you exorcise your gay instincts by yourself. But you must allow them to be exorcised from you.

In the olden days, my boyfriend, Paul, and I enjoyed nothing more than our Thursday night TV crashes. We'd get home from work. We'd finish some chores. Then he would put on a big pot of coffee. And I would make us a super-size bowl of popcorn. Heck, we'd even bring blankets into the living room. Then we would veg out and watch *Will and Grace, Sex and the City, Desperate Housewives* . . . and sometimes reruns of *Charlie's Angels* and *Hart to Hart*. Until usually about two in the morning. It was a real treat.

Sorry. There's just something I have to do . . . sometimes . . . when I'm reminded of those days. It's a visualization thing.

We thought we were so happy.

But now . . . when I kiss my little girl goodnight, I thank God that he sent his angels to take me out of the self-indulgent hell that is homosexuality.

Are you a militant gay who is against a cure for homosexuality? If silence equals death why are you trying to silence a cure for homosexuality? Is it because you want to destroy the cure? Satan is too alive in you. I see him in your glassy eyes. You are the ones who steal hope from the gay teenagers who commit suicide. Gays will always ask God for a family like their mom and dad.

Prayer will help you fix the abnormality. Prayer has already cured me. Prayer will cure you. The cure will save you from dying from AIDS. You can have a normal life and family just like your mom and dad. Just like the one you always wanted and prayed to God every night for. To you gays who want the cure for homosexuality, tell those that would stop you, that you have a right to want a normal family. Tell them you have a right to become straight. Tell them you want children like your parents. Tell them you want a family like your brothers and sisters. Stand tall. Be open about a cure. Be positive. Be expectant. Tell them God is with you.

If you are Christian, God has already answered your prayers. You only need tell him you are ready to receive the cure. Homosexuality is simply a mental deficiency caused by hating the world. Let me show you how beautiful the world is. Forgive your parents for not loving that feminine boy. Only forgiveness can liberate you to find the cure. Stop depending on the half strength of another homosexual male to make one whole man of two. Only you alone can become the full man. You can do it. Be brave. Be a man. Assert your masculinity.

The people who murdered my . . . Paul . . . just Paul . . . he's not my Paul. His killers, anyway . . . are still serving time. All of them were caught. With the new laws . . . however . . . they will be released. Praise Jesus. They will be released.

We stumbled out of this nightclub . . . the Pachanga . . . at . . . it was about three, three thirty in the morning. We were giggling like schoolgirls on the pavement. I had to hold Paul up. Because he kept on collapsing . . . into convulsions . . . of laughter. We were just so high on life and champagne . . . Paul was wearing flip-flop shoes. Got them in Gap. They're for the beach. But he wanted to wear them out. He couldn't have run. Even if he was sober.

A few cars pulled up. We didn't see them coming. They were just there. And I knew to just run. Paul howled with laughter, coiled up around a trash can. I ran because I could. I wanted him to learn that you're not supposed to wear those shoes out. But gays are always selfish creatures. They live only for themselves.

I tried to hail a cab at the far end of the street. But they just were not stopping. So I hid behind a dumpster. And I watched them use two-by-fours on Paul. Just animals, using regular two-by-fours. You could pick them up from a hardware store. I was too scared to help my friend. He wasn't laughing anymore, anyway. He wasn't doing anything much. They had nails in the ends of the two-by-fours. That was it. No more laughing.

There is such evil in the world. Children killed Paul. Not thirty-year-olds. They were teenagers. An evil act. They didn't know Paul. There was no confrontation. No vendetta. All they knew was to take alcohol, some LSD . . . and go down to Montrose district to kill some faggots. And they got Paul.

Act Three

PADDY *appears in full glamour drag. He sings a seductive show tune that enthuses and titillates the audience. He sits on their laps and touches their faces, etc. They applaud accordingly.*

Thank you, thank you.

My wife's clothes did prove too much of a temptation for me. I think it was, no it was . . . the third Sunday of every month, I would feel unwell and stay at home while everyone else was at church. It was just me and her wardrobe. And I would dig out some of our forbidden music . . . I could have been executed for its possession. And I'd sing along to the Barbra Streisand hits of Broadway collection. Trimming the fat, I'd go straight for all the big numbers from *Funny Girl*. 'I'm the Greatest Star', 'His Love Makes Me Beautiful', 'People', and 'Don't Rain on My Parade'. And I'd wear my wife's wedding dress and pour my heart out into a curling hairbrush. I'd fantasize that I was pregnant . . . I was just like Fanny Brice in the hit Barbra Streisand movie . . . *Funny Girl*.

It's funny, but that's what my wife had to do, after we got married . . . pretend she was pregnant. But that wasn't for a laugh. That was for us to stay alive. We tried to wash my sperm but it just wouldn't work. There's something tricky about my HIV, even though its undetectable. You have to understand that only the authorities knew about my ex-homosexuality. It's important to give as little cause for concern as possible, for the sake of the community. So we kept the whole process of adopting Julianna a secret.

Steadily, over nine months my wife's bump blossomed. Many thanks to our friends in the CIA costume department. My wife even ate extra. We invented cravings for her. We had a ball filling our shopping cart with all flavours of ice cream and unusual fare, like olives, cucumbers and gravel. My wife even faked lower back pain and walked funny. It was just as much work as a regular pregnancy. My wife acted the pregnant damsel right up until the moment we adopted Julianna. The birth was performed at 01.00 hours on the 16th of March 2010.

We lit the lights all over the house and made such a racket. The neighbours soon gathered. The women prepared hot milk and cookies in the kitchen. The children chased the fairies in the shadows of our apricot wood. The men played gospel music on the porch. It was beautiful.

When the house was busy enough, my wife's contractions intensified. The ghetto blaster in the bedroom boomed an audio clip of Julianna's actual birth, which had only happened the day before. The house was filled with the sound of screaming.

The CIA make-up team smeared my wife in L'Oréal's Blood'n'Shit application. Her physicality was that of a cobweb, thanks to her acting coach, Matt Damon's love interest in *Good Will Hunting*, Minnie Driver. And just when the screaming got loudest, and everyone looked up . . . nobody noticed the special agent sneak through the window with Julianna. As soon as the picture was complete we threw open the door and welcomed our community. Everyone said how she looked just like me. And how healthy she looked. I was never so proud in all my life. Family.

We had wanted a boy but the authorities decided it best not to give a boy to an ex-homosexual. And so there we were. But I just couldn't keep away from my wife's wardrobe.

All that religion and George W's choo-choo train obviously didn't cure our homosexuality. My wife and I just weren't having sex. She was happy to use condoms. We had to. But she just could not make me hard. We didn't even argue about it. Oh, she knew I didn't like her. It wasn't her fault. I needed steak and she had a rasher. Needless to say, I was well tuned into the places a man could go to relieve himself.

Although I was never caught, and Father did truly seem happy with Marianne, official policy changed quietly and without fuss and we both found ourselves on that disgusting train to Santa Fe . . . quietly and without fuss.

The first time I saw my Angel was at the far end of the platform in Santa Fe train station. Father was crying and crying and held on to me for dear life. I could feel the warm trickle of his urine on my legs. I told him God would save us. And I gently pushed him off me. When I looked to see my Angel again, he was gone. The guards laughed at Father and ordered us into the truck for Camp Tesuque.

It was hot and men were howling. The smell made some of them vomit. Some of the men around me were having sex. Luckily I was by the truck wall. Hints of air rushed in through the cracks and I peeped through. It was just like one of those *Thelma & Louise* roads I'd been dreaming about. At last here I was; the plains of New Mexico stretched out before me. Juniper bushes clawed at the dry air and tornadoes danced on the roadside. All around lightning flickered on the horizon. Once we stopped to view the Rio Grande. Giant yellow butterflies made their flight path along this vital American artery. How I thirsted for it. This was the real America. This is where the cowboys lived. This is where broken-down cars were tended to by strong and wild sun-cooked men in heavy plaid shirts.

When we passed through the camp gates at Tesuque, a military band played Gershwin, 'Some day he'll come along, the man I love'. We were herded off the truck and paraded in the main square. Father and I were asked to step forward, away from all the queens. I could see Him looking at us.

My Angel told his staff to put us somewhere comfortable, no matter the expense. I felt the way I might have felt in the Backstreet in London, or in the Argos in Amsterdam, or the Keller in Paris, or the Eagle in New York when it used to be good, the way I felt when a very powerful-looking gentleman would signal that he was planning a move on me. How he made me shudder.

Father and I were kept in luxurious living quarters. We had our favourite movies and TV shows. Like life with Paul. We'd write grocery lists. People say hollyhocks don't smell. But I love the smell of hollyhocks. We'd always have hollyhocks. They are absolutely my favourite flower. And every morning even Father used to say, 'I do so love the aroma of a hollyhock.'

I remember after a few weeks in our air-conditioned condo, Father and I looked out the window at all the queens. They weren't so dandy-looking any more without their finery. Bald as coots, the lot, they boiled under the relentless desert sun. This was no Georgia O'Keeffe painting.

And just then, like the woman in the woods, three loud knocks came a-knocking at the door. And it was the Angel.

I approached him, my Angel, 40 per cent of the way and no more. He advanced towards me and took my hand and told me what a pleasure it was to finally formally make my acquaintance. He owned me and there was nothing I could do. I prepared him a chicken salad with a side of low calorie potato salad. He devoured it and left.

Father wouldn't even speak to me. His jealousy flared up like an angry cold sore. When we took our nightcap on the veranda that evening, he asked me if ever I wondered what had happened to our wives and Julianna. I had to be honest, they just weren't on my mind. I was thinking only of my Angel. My father said he wished I'd never come to America. So I firmly reminded him: 'If it wasn't for my looks and my charm, we'd already be dead.'

The visitations became more frequent. Father became less helpful. One evening I was busting to proclaim my love to my Angel. I seized the opportunity when Father went to the little boy's room. My Angel took me in his arms and whispered, 'You're mine and I'm not going to let anything bad happen to you.' Just one kiss, I begged him. 'I can't,' he replied. 'Not in front of your father.' 'Then get rid of him,' I implored.

Father was flushing the lavatory and my Angel took a syringe and vial from his breast pocket. 'Take this and we can be together, my beautiful one.' I was putty in his hands. I wasn't sure of the nature of this elixir but I trusted my Angel. I rolled up my shirtsleeve, careful not to crease the linen, and he drove his miracle home. All I could do was cry. 'All better now,' he told me. 'All better now.'

The following month Father and I found ourselves in the examination room. We weren't talking. My Angel and I were now regular lovers and this drove Father insane.

The examination started at the head. Details of every inch were taken. This took days. Next we were completely X-rayed. Then they forced tubes in through our noses and into our lungs. We were ventilated with a gas which caused us to cough so severely we had to be restrained. But my Angel penetrated me with his gaze. This fortified me with the strength to endure it. When he came to collect the sputum from my lungs, I whispered, 'I love you.'

The next few days were somewhat easier but by no means a walk in the park. At my Angel's command we had to stand, bend and kneel in many different positions as they photographed our hair patterns. It was a very classy affair. They used black-and-white film. Just like in dreams. I was concerned that my weight had ballooned. My Angel said the photos would be beautiful because I had the figure of Michelangelo's *David*.

It was a Tuesday morning, I recall. Father and I were carried into a room with tables and a vat of very hot water. We had to sit in that water until we were ready to pass out. From there we were strapped to a table where our hairs were plucked out. The boys were very careful to save the root. We were put back into that vat several times. When they had collected enough hair, they shaved us until we were smooth all over. We were then, once again, extensively photographed . . . bending, kneeling, sitting.

Exhausted after the photo shoot, I admired Father's hair-free torso. We had our usual nightcap on the veranda. And when Father retired to bed, my Angel appeared. Backlit by a full pale moon, he touched my face and told me to be strong. What lay ahead would be difficult. But it would lead to our happiness together. He told me that he wasn't going to let anything bad happen to me. 'You do know I love you, don't you?' he enquired. 'Yes,' I replied.

The following morning, back in the examination room, Father and I both received two-litre enemas. On alternative days, we were strapped on a bench table, our rectums hyper-distended. We received an extensive lower gastric intestinal examination . . . without any anaesthesia. Father cried so loud that my Angel ordered him to be gagged. I didn't cry. I just allowed my Angel's gaze to penetrate me. He was so clever to put us in there on alternate days. It was fabulous having the house to myself. While Father got worked on, I was recovering. I could sing without interruption.

But at night Father wouldn't stop whingeing. I couldn't hear the television. I had to send out for earphones. In the end I told my Angel to put Father in alternative accommodation. It was just my Angel and me now. Alone in our house in the middle of America. I'd never dreamed it. He kissed me hard on the cheek and told me if I survived tomorrow, I would become his entirely. I thanked him for loving me and called him my Saviour.

Tomorrow came. Father and I received a urological examination. Tissue samples were taken from the kidneys, prostate and testicles. Several semen samples were forcibly taken over two days. I yearned for my Angel to carry out this procedure. But he didn't.

After three weeks of this, we were wheeled to the dissection laboratory. We were each to receive an injection of chloroform to the heart. The doctors were waiting for us. They stood by our beds with syringes raised and . . . then my Angel appeared. He stood by my bed and shook his head. My doctor lowered his syringe and I breathed a sigh of relief. I turned to Father just in time to see the syringe disappear into his chest.

It was for the best. He wouldn't have been good for much else. His mind seemed to be gone since the crying started. I waved to Father as they started the dissection. Still strapped into the operating table, my Angel wheeled me into a private operating room. He had arranged the most spectacular display of hollyhocks. I do so love the aroma of a hollyhock.

When I awoke, I was in great pain. But my Angel was at my side, holding my hand. The first thing he told me was that I'd been asleep for four days. The second thing he told me was that the work done on me was a great success. And that we had to be patient. And the third thing he told me was that I was healthy again. America had found a cure for HIV. He'd checked my bloods and the injection had worked.

It's been a year and I love my new body. My Angel made it for me. He made me perfect for HIM. I am HIS. I am HIS servant. I thanked my Angel for taking me as his property each and every day. I loved my Angel taking me. I loved him. He was a real man and I was a real woman.

We came to Ireland on diplomatic business. I had to get a new passport. My name is Lavinia Swanson. And I flew business class. At last. I was just like Julia Roberts in *Pretty Woman*.

My Angel said we had no real need to go back to the States. After all, Ireland was practically another state. Well Bush had already added Canada and South America to the Stars and Stripes. Why shouldn't he choose Ireland next? Americans love Ireland.

My Angel said there was going to be a lot of reinforced bonds between Europe and the United States.

He's coming back from a business trip soon. There's something wrong with his phone. It's nice to be home.

Act Four

PADDY *wears an outrageously camp outfit. He addresses the audience.*

Shut the fuck up, by the way. You won't be laughing when you've nowhere to drink. I do not want to be raided. Right? All clear?

Continue drinking.

Now . . . David. Mmm. She's supposed to be the perfect man. Sure she's tiny. Did you see it? You probably didn't. It's tiny. Its little nodger. What's she carrying? Her handbag? No, it's a sling. No now, not the kind of sling that you're thinking of love. The kind of sling for slinging a pebble into some giant's eye. Yeah! That's David. From David and Goliath. No, they're not a band, sister. It's a bible story. Who let you out, sister?

So Goliath is fucking huge. Jaysus. I wouldn't mind that big scary fucker coming to get me on Parliament Street Bridge at four in the morning. You wouldn't stand a chance. You see, that's what it's all about. Goliath is the ultimate alpha-male. Who's going to be able to tame that massive hairy hunk with the shaved head? A good-looking girl like David. Sure, only David can get to Goliath's Achilles' heel. She lashed that pebble into his eye and tamed herself a beast, baby. Once she got her gentle giant, ain't nobody going to mess with her.

I miss Internet porn. I had my credit card driven demented, I was on so many sites. Wanking just isn't the same without it. I miss my visual stimulus, sisters. By the way, I was once arrested for wanking in an Internet café. Oh nowadays you're arrested for wanking in private. I had so many beautiful men, sisters, from all over the world, I just wanted to devour. Beautiful, fine-looking yokes. Rides! Our relationships could be very intense sometimes.

Oh, it's all very well for you. I'm at work. I'm here all the fucking time. Sure I'm home then and I've to do the accounts. I'm in here at five in the morning doing prep and orders. There's no fucking life in it. But that's not forever. I'll get someone eventually. You see having me da was great. He could run this place blind. Even with his arms tied.

I swear to fucking Jesus, if your man comes in here again looking for his blueberry muffin. I can't keep enough in stock for him. I have to say . . . your man and his muffins. I never saw anyone more inbred-looking in my life. Her eyes were so close together I thought she was a Cyclops. And her from the fucking hairdresser's for her latte with no foam! And the businessman who wants her tea, her toast and the full Irish all at exactly the same time. She'd never fucking dream of tipping.

Oh the morning – now, it's a different story to the evening. Oh different set-up, by the way. We have respectable people during the day. I'd love to say to them all: 'Fuck off with yourselves to the Four Seasons.' This is one gay winter. We serve gays. If you're not gay, then at least dress

up as one. Or tip. Or sing along when Barbra's on. Look at her. She
minds this place. She's a fucking legend. I fucking love you, Barbra. I
have to say . . . she was the last of the great belters.

'Memory' . . . I forget it.

I have to say there's an element out there on that street. You can't be
too careful. I do feel lonely when everyone's gone after closing.

The truth is . . . I get scared at night, particularly if I'm working here
by myself. And that's why I need someone else here with me. I'm not
making a profit. But I am making a living. I have to say I am. Well
everywhere else has been raided, so I am getting a lot of business. Yes I
am. The few of you who are still left still want somewhere to go. You
have to get on with your life. It's gotten to that stage, you know?

I'm not as bad if I keep some music on. It relaxes me. It distracts me.
I don't have to acknowledge my thoughts. I always leave the music to the
very last to turn off. And it's only then the café is in total darkness. I hate
it. I sense the demons all around me, sister. When I used to get that
feeling, I'd tell meself that me da was somewhere in the world. Or that
he'd be in, in the morning. And I just felt that as long as there were good
people like my da in the world, then it was a safe place. It was a good
place and I was safe in it. But now there's nobody left. All we have is each
other, girls. It's true. Isn't it, sisters?

I do so love the aroma of a hollyhock.

(*Holds up picture of his father*)

This is Da. I keep forgetting to put his picture up. He's a handsome man,
isn't he? We were very close. We both loved Barbra Streisand.

I was only twelve and my mother wouldn't let me watch *Yentl*. She
said it was too controversial for a young boy. I protested and I told her I
was twelve and I wanted to see it. She said it's about Jewish people in
history and you're not watching it. Sure she hadn't seen it herself. My
mother was mad, sure. She loved us, but I have to say, she was mad out
of it. That's being honest with you. Now.

Oh yes, but little Paddy did watch *Yentl*. Oh yes. I'd mitched off
school one day when I knew we were holding a Barbra concert at my
Aunty Bridie's. See, I knew I had to do something special to top Bridie's
ever-popular 'I'd Rather be Blue'.

I knew as I belted out the second line of 'Papa, Can You Hear Me?' I
had them in the palm of my hand. I have to be honest, everyone was
gobsmacked. Bridie herself said it was the most beautiful thing she'd

ever heard. Me mother was locked, sure, and she started bawling. She collapsed and fell into the fire. We were used to her. Me da went spare when the hot ashes went everywhere. Ma didn't harm herself too much. She was grand. But the suite of furniture was destroyed.

So if anyone's looking for a job, let me know. We'll have a little chat.

Who want's a cappuccino? My first cappuccino tonight is on the house. I'm celebrating. I'm turing that machine back on. Who wants one? Or I'll do you one of my speciality lattes. They are fucking beautiful. I've me own knack to it. I only ever give half the shot of coffee. It's instantly milkier than any other latte in town. Someone said to me it was like something they got on holiday.

I just threw those posters up there. Everyone thinks I went to some big mad effort. They were bought in fifteen minutes in a junk poster shop in Barcelona. I was running to get a train. And I just saw the shop. My one regret is I put Nicole Kidman in the *Moulin Rouge* up there behind the telly. You see, I didn't know the telly was going to go there. That was more me da's idea. You wouldn't notice Nicole. It's one of the more important posters.

I've HIV again, by the way. Well, they got rid of it in America. The bastards, sure weren't they the ones who invented it in the first place to get rid of us. Sure, isn't it what the president calls a cure for homosexuality. Well sure, AIDS is rife now. It's great to know there's a cure for it. But it's getting your hands on it. That's the trick. My supplier finds that very hard to get hold of. I mean, Bush wants us all to fucking die. The heroin addicts have all the heroin they want. Isn't it gas? They've all the luck. If it wasn't for my friend in the embassy, we'd all be fucked. His life is on the line, so I wouldn't go boasting about what I'm doing for you all. I can only look after regular customers, anyway.

I'll be doing vaccines on Mondays. Say nothing. All right? Six until nine.

You look like you're still itchy. The scabies are a fucker to get rid of. That stuff didn't work, no? I'll get you something stronger. Now, just let it take its effect. I want you to scrub yourself stupid. Sit in the bath. Make sure there's a shit load of salt in there. Sometimes you can see them worm their way out of you. They go ballistic with the salt. Fucking cunts.

What's wrong with you? What was it you said you had? Genital warts, was it? Well, leave that with me and I'll get you this brilliant stuff for them. They can be very hard to get rid of. They'd do your head in, wouldn't they?

By the way, you'd miss the services, wouldn't you? I mean, if you need medication for anything, look no further than Centre Stage. I can get you the stuff. I have connections.

I'd always imagined what it would be like to be cured. I thought the world would break into song. If only people had stood up together. Thank God I got a back-up supply of it in New Mexico just in case. I have to say, it came in handy, it did, when Bush banned condoms. Sure, no one gives a fuck do they?

They're trying to get rid of us. They need to try harder.

Somebody from *The Irish Times* newspaper is calling by in the morning. Will everyone try to get some of their straight friends to be here, please? Wait, no. This is a gay bar. *The Times* newspaper is going to know that it's a gay bar.

Who fucking comes in this morning? I have to say, I nearly died. Full of smiles and the joys of spring . . . Dr. Collins . . . my plastic surgeon. He got rid of my tits for me and built the cock for me after me being a woman and all in the concentration camp. Well, God forgive me. I don't know what happened to the professional code of silence. In he storms in front of all these solicitors . . . my regulars. They've just put in their order for the full Irish. And he says to me at the top of his voice, 'How are you feeling since the operation? Didn't I tell you I'd make a man of you!' Well I nearly fucking died. 'Thanks very much,' I said. 'What can I get you?' And do you think he'd shut up? No. Says he to his friend with a perverted degree of pride, 'Paddy is a man who used to be a woman who used to be a man. Gas, isn't it?' And he breaks his shite laughing, and I have to skip in and do his eggs sunny side up. Do you know what I wanted to do with his fucking eggs? That operation cost me a fortune, by the way.

George Bush. Cunt. Cunt.

Oh never put someone with an addicitve personality into a position of power.

I dared to dream the American dream but all I do now is scream. By the way George Bush, fuck off. How long will this experiment go on?

I'm gee-eyed. I'm talking shite. By the way, I know I shouldn't drink and drive at work. Some people don't like it. Look, I said to this one. We open late, love. I'm doing you the favour. All fur coat and no knickers, her. Get out, I said. You're barred. Five euro!

She didn't like my attitude, she said. She came in the next day to tell me. How she could even stand was beyond me. She'd been twisted the night previous. If you saw the cuntitude of her. I went ballistic. Get out of my café, I said to her. You're barred, bitch. If I throw you out, it means you're gone. She said I snatched her beer bottle out of her paw before she was finished. I said, it's part of the charm of Centre Stage. She said she wanted her money back for the bottle of Stella. I said, if you were any sort of a lady you'd be in bed at 4 a.m. on a Saturday night. Least of all, you wouldn't be drinking beer from a bottle. We do wine, champagne and spritzers, I said to her. I said, you're badly in need of a make-over, sister. There's a hairdresser's next door, go in and see if they trim dogs.

Fuck off, by the way. You just have to keep going. The angels are looking after us. I don't know why the regime didn't come for us in Centre Stage. We may as well be ourselves. I want to drink a toast. To our sisters who died. May the love in our hearts shine them to heaven and may they rest in peace. Amen.

Listen, do you remember the Pride marches? Ah Dublin was great for the Pride. The families on the streets only delighted to be experiencing the bit of gay. Sure it was like St. Patrick's Day for sisters but in summer. Our numbers were strong then, by the way. Untainted by crystal meth and AIDS. We thought there was no need for us to march.

I was there in the George the night they raided it. I saw the senator's rallying of who he called his gay brothers. I saw our beloved drag queen Panti scream at the boys to get out of the building. I saw the men push into the doorways trying to escape the gas. Luckily I had a gas mask with me. I was on my way to a fetish night. I was able to take it out of my bag just in time. I never thought I'd use it for this. I hid beneath my friends' dead bodies. Like a gay rugby team in a morbid scrum.

It was Madonna night in the George. Our queen sang her boys to sleep. And my favourite song was destroyed forever. 'Vogue'.

I waited for the silence. The roaring stopped. Then finally the music. And dead flesh cocooned me. And the face of an older man pressed into mine. I wrestled a bottle of poppers from my shirt pocket and made love to the dead. The gas mask was healing every wound I'd ever had and I wanted to cry for everything. I felt loved. And I had enough love for everyone here. The poppers brought me to New Mexico. And we were all white-water rafting together down the Rio Grande. And my greatest love of my life, a cowboy who was also a cop, kissed me hard on the mouth and filled my soul. And the autumn leaves fell down on us. And the giant yellow butterflies fluttered like fairies and sang, 'When you wish upon a star, your dreams come true.'

And my song flies out of me, 'Oh Daddy, my Daddy, I love you, Daddy. Thank you, Daddy. I'm Daddy's child. I'm Daddy's child. I'm Daddy's child.'

Lights fade.

The Drowning Room

VERITY-ALICIA MAVENAWITZ

The Drowning Room was first presented at Andrews Lane Studio on 1 May 2006 as part of the International Dublin Gay Theatre Festival, by Three Wise Women Theatre Company.

CAST

Cillian	Patrick McGrann
Bob	Simon Fogarty
Maura	Elaine Reddy
Leo	Declan Gillick
Kevin	Gordon Mahon
Conor	Bren Barnett
Breno	Eamonn Doyle

PRODUCTION TEAM

Nuala Kelly, with cast

Director	Nuala Kelly

CHARACTERS

Cillian,	*mid-twenties, a junior doctor, brother of Seán (deceased)*
Bob,	*early thirties, gay, an architect, Seán's ex-partner*
Maura,	*thirties, attractive, nicely spoken, friend of Seán's and mother of his son, Cian*
Leo,	*early twenties, outrageously camp, Conor's partner*
Kevin,	*mid-thirties, a bit of an anorak, but a good sort and strong when he has to be, old school friend of Seán's*
Conor,	*forties, working class, a builder, Leo's partner*
Breno,	*early forties, working class, decent, father of one of Seán's killers*

NOTES FOR STAGING

CILLIAN *should be seated centre stage.* BOB *should be seated to his right, then* KEVIN, *then* BRENO. *To* CILLIAN'*s left,* CONOR, LEO, MAURA *should sit. Ideally the characters should be spaced out as much as possible, with empty seats between some of them. The characters should also move about the stage as much as possible during the play.*

A deserted army-style obstacle course in a clearing in a wood. Several tree stumps and logs are laid out on the ground, tyres hang from ropes and there is some camouflage. This is a Scout camp on a hill overlooking Dublin city. It is dark and the city lights can be seen in the distance.

Music plays – Paddy Casey's 'Bend Down Low'.

CILLIAN *enters; he is a handsome young man. He is listening to his MP3 player and sings along to some parts of the song. He has a sports bag and takes some candles from it, lights them and lays them in a line downstage. He takes an urn from the bag and places it downstage behind the candles. Then he sits on a log centre stage, takes a bottle of Jack Daniel's from his bag and a glass and pours himself a drink, then adds some soda. He sits until he hears something offstage.*

CILLIAN: Hello?

BOB: It's me, Bob!

CILLIAN: Bob! (BOB *enters*) Good to see you, will you have a drink?

BOB: No, I'm grand, I have one here myself . . . Seán brought this bottle of brandy back from Paris for me . . . I couldn't face opening it before . . . so, to Seán! (*Takes a swig from the bottle*)

CILLIAN: To Seán. It's great you showed up; I was sort of thinking no one would.

BOB: Of course I was going to turn up. You don't think I'd let you send him off without me, do you?

CILLIAN: I didn't know if anyone would remember.

BOB: Ah Cillian, of course people would remember . . . but maybe they thought they would be intruding.

CILLIAN: Maybe. I didn't call or text anyone . . . I suppose I should have . . . but it's been a bad day, if you know what I mean.

BOB: 'Course I do . . . and besides you don't want a load of eejits sitting around saying crap like, 'I can't believe it's been a whole year'.

CILLIAN: I haven't even turned my phone on since lunchtime . . . there's probably about a million messages and texts waiting for me . . . but I just can't face it.

BOB: Maura is coming.

CILLIAN: Yeah? Were you talking to her?

BOB: Not since last week, but she's bound to come. I mean, she's bound to. Conor said he was coming as well. You remember, Conor? He rents our basement flat. Well . . . Seán's basement flat . . .

CILLIAN: The builder?

BOB: Yeah, he worked with Seán for years. He's a really nice guy . . . and that's enough, isn't it? To have us here . . . the ones he was closest to . . . the ones that loved him?

CILLIAN: Sure. You, me, Maura, Conor . . . and Seán. That's enough to have a party, right?

BOB: (*Noticing the urn that contains Seán's ashes*) Shit . . . I just saw it now . . . I don't think it's a good idea to have it there, Cillian.

CILLIAN: Why?

BOB: I don't know. Maybe it's . . . I don't know. I just think it's not a good idea to have it . . . on display, you might say. It's . . .

CILLIAN: Creepy?

BOB: Sort of. No . . . intimidating, that's it. It draws your eye to it . . .

CILLIAN: You didn't even bleeding see it till now.

BOB: But now that I have seen it, I can't take my eyes off it.

(CILLIAN *takes the urn and puts it back in his bag.*)

CILLIAN: You're probably right . . . I was in two minds about it myself

BOB: What a moon!

CILLIAN: I know – 'La Bella Luna'.

BOB: God it's hot! I can't believe it's so hot for half four in the morning. I thought it would be freezing. I even brought my fleece.

CILLIAN: It's going to be a real scorcher today.

BOB: I'm not able for all this hot weather. It's the humidity that gets me. It's not like this on the Greek Islands or in Turkey or even Spain.

CILLIAN: Man, you'd want to go to somewhere like Atlanta for humidity, it's something else. Or Israel – my God, the heat in some parts would fuckin' kill you.

BOB: There's lots of things in some parts of Israel that would fuckin' kill ya! Bullets, suicide bombers . . . cockroaches that fly, I've read about that.

CILLIAN: Kosher McDonald's.

BOB: They do not have kosher McDonald's?

CILLIAN: They do, I swear.

BOB: God, what will they think of next?

(*Awkward silence*)

CILLIAN: So, what did you think of the sentencing?

BOB: I thought the same as everybody else, Cillian. I thought it was a bloody disgrace. Wait until you see today's papers, they'll be full of it. I was listening to some skanger FM station on the way up here and that's all they were talking about; everyone's pissed off about it; they had some TD on calling for a major overhaul of the judicial system.

CILLIAN: Ah, sure they're always feckin' looking for that, and nothing ever happens.

BOB: Were your mam and dad inundated with reporters?

CILLIAN: They've gone to stay with Gráinne in London. My dad just left a letter with the barrister. Did you see him read it out on the news?

BOB: Yeah, I did; it was class.

CILLIAN: It says everything, nothing more to add. We've been let down by the courts. We're not the first and we won't be the last. End of story.

BOB: He did a good job, though, that barrister. I mean, I thought there for a time that they weren't going to be able to convict them on anything. But he just kept on at it, little by little, chipping away. And he used the evidence of the Fanta bottle very cleverly. Everyone said that.

CILLIAN: He's a pedantic fuck, though!

BOB: I thought he was splendid! (*Impersonating the barrister*) 'Do you mean to tell me Mr. . . . O'Connor, that just because someone is wearing '*poncy fucking boots*' that it's therefore justifiable to kick their head in, what? . . . Why, if that were the case, then we could all just go around kicking in the heads of anybody whose dress sense we didn't like . . . I tell you, no skanger in a tracksuit would ever be safe again walking through the doors of this court. We would have total anarchy!' It was brilliant! And then the judge, bang, bang, bang with the hammer: 'Mr. Sullivan, Mr. Sullivan, this courtroom is not an amphitheatre for you to amuse the citizens of Dublin, stick to the facts of the case.'

CILLIAN: Well, I'm glad it all amused you.

BOB: Now that's not fair, Cillian.

CILLIAN: I know it's not . . . I know . . . and I'm sorry. It's just everyone is talking about it all the time. In every pub, every shop you go into, every taxi driver . . . and I know they all sympathize with us. But now it's like they own it . . . like it's their story . . . and they seem to forget that it's not a bit of gossip from Hollywood . . . it's here, in Dublin. It's about a real person who has a family that are still grieving for him . . . and they keep going on about the fact that he was an architect . . . 'Oh, a brilliant young architect', as if it wouldn't have been as bad if he'd just been a butcher or a binman or something. It's become entertainment and we can't control it.

BOB: People are just riled up about it, Cillian, they don't mean any disrespect.

CILLIAN: But it hurts . . .

BOB: I know. I know it does. I think I hear a car! Yeah . . . it must be Maura . . .

CILLIAN: Good.

          (CILLIAN *gets up on the tallest log to see who is coming.*)

BOB: Do you know what you should do? You should write to the council or the parks department or whoever and see if we could sponsor a bench dedicated to Seán up here.

CILLIAN: That's a good idea.

BOB: I have seen them sometimes. Or if not that, maybe plant a tree in his name, or even both.

CILLIAN: I'll mention it to the folks. I think they'll love the idea. I'm heading over there on Sunday.

BOB: Give them my love.

CILLIAN: Of course I will.

BOB: Are you still sharing the house with the Canadians?

CILLIAN: Yeah, still with the same two. They're great and all, but I wish I had the place to myself. But I won't be able to afford it for a while.

BOB: I thought doctors got paid a fortune?

CILLIAN: Not for a few years yet. I still have the junior tag on me. All the same, it was good having people around me after Seán was murdered. Better than rattling around a big empty place night after night on my own; it would do my head in.

BOB: Like me?

CILLIAN: I didn't mean that.

BOB: I like solitude. I need it for my work. (*Startled*) Did you hear that?

CILLIAN: Yes, that's definitely someone coming. Hello? Over here by the clearing . . . follow the path!

     (*Some noises offstage. Three people enter –* MAURA, LEO *and* CONOR. *They are all carrying food and drink in plastic bags.* BOB *stands up when they enter the clearing.*)

CILLIAN: Hey, good to see you.

MAURA: Hi, how are you doing?

     (*They all greet each other.*)

BOB: Cillian you remember Conor . . . and Leo!

CILLIAN: I do indeed.

LEO: Oh Mammy. I hope there are no snakes here. This is like being in the fuckin' jungle: 'I'm a drag queen get me out of here!' It's a good job I didn't wear me expensive Manolo Blahniks or they'd be wrecked.

BOB: Get lost, will ya, you don't own a pair of Manolo Blahniks.

LEO: I do so, bitch!

BOB: The best shoes you have are cheap wannabes that you got in Turkey for about €40! Don't forget, I've seen your act.

LEO: And I'm sure it was just brilliant as usual.

BOB: I wouldn't use the word 'brilliant' to describe it.

LEO: Sheena Ribena doesn't like people saying derogatory things about her act . . . or her shoes. So shut your face. Oh Jesus, I need to go for a piss. All that champagne is not good for me bladder.

BOB: Have you all been drinking?

CONOR: Yeah . . . is that OK with you, Bob?

BOB: I was only asking.

LEO: Someone come with me.

BOB: Get lost!

LEO: I'm not going on me own.

BOB: Just go behind a tree.

MAURA: Not one of these trees! (*Pointing*) Go out there somewhere.

BOB: Yeah, go way out there and don't come back.

LEO: Fuck off you! Come on . . . Conor?

CONOR: I'm not bringing you to the toilet like you were a five-year-old
          – go yourself.

          (MAURA *starts taking out sandwiches, drinks, napkins and so on
          from a bag.*)

MAURA: Anyone want anything?

LEO: Yeah me! I want someone to come with me, so I can take a piss.
          Come on, I'm bursting!

BOB: (*To* CONOR) What did you bring that screaming queen for?

LEO: I heard that, Bob Kennelly.

CONOR: He wanted to come. He liked Seán.

BOB: (*Under his breath*) Well, Seán couldn't stand the feckin' prancer.
          And he's pissed.

LEO: What are you saying about me?

CONOR: He's not saying anything, Leo. Look, we had a few cans on the
          way up here. Nobody's pissed, so keep your knickers on, Bob.

LEO: Yeah, keep your big ugly knickers on, Bob. I'm going to piss my
          good DKNYs in a minute. I'm in a bad way.

BOB: Is it from all the cans of champagne you drank?

CILLIAN: (*Trying to change the subject*) Thanks for coming. I thought
          there for a while no one would show.

LEO: Come on, someone. Maura? Help me out, my lovely?

MAURA: Leo, just go to the toilet by yourself . . . there's nothing out
          there to be scared of.

          (LEO *looks at* CONOR.)

CONOR: I said I'm not bringing you.

CILLIAN: Don't even look my way.

LEO: Then I'm not going. I'll just hold it in till I blow up . . . and it
          will be all your fault then, so it will . . . You do be all really
          mean, the lot of ye!

          (LEO *sits down but looks like he is in some discomfort.*)

BOB: Why . . . what splendid grammar you have, my dear.

LEO: Shut up, you snobby bastard. At least I have style!

BOB: Piss off. Oh no, wait. You can't, can you? 'Cause you're too
          scared.

CILLIAN: (*Takes a sandwich from* MAURA) Oh these are nice, thanks,
          Maura.

          (*They sit and begin to make a big show of eating to tease* LEO.
          They also begin to drink.)

CONOR: (*To* MAURA) Yeah, great.

BOB: Mmm, and the relish is lovely. (*To* MAURA) Did you make it yourself?

MAURA: I did, with my own lily-white hands.

CILLIAN: It's better than Ballymaloe.

BOB: Oh much better than Ballymaloe.

(*Pause as they eat*)

CONOR: And the bread . . . mmm.

LEO: *I have to go!*

CONOR: All right, come on, for fuck sake!

(*As* CONOR *and* LEO *exit the others burst out laughing.*)

BOB: What does Conor see in him?

MAURA: I have not got a clue, but don't give him a hard time about it.

BOB: I'm not.

CILLIAN: He is a real attention-seeker, though.

(*Noises offstage*)

LEO: (*Shouting offstage*) Oh the relief! It's good to be alive.

MAURA: Oh God . . . you'd want to have him living downstairs from you. He'd drive you mad. I can hear him through the floor practising his drag act.

CILLIAN: He hasn't moved him into the flat?

MAURA: About six months ago. He must have been lonely, I suppose.

CILLIAN: You'd want to be really, really lonely to end up with that. I mean, I've nothing against him or anything, but . . . he is what he is.

BOB: Nothing better than a fuckin' rent boy.

MAURA: Well . . . I wouldn't go that far . . . but as you say, he is what he is. Then again, they seem fairly happy. And Conor's been around long enough to know what he's getting into.

BOB: You should put the rent up; it might make that little fucker pay his share.

MAURA: No, he does; he has a job and all now. Anyway, Cian likes him.

BOB: You don't let him babysit, do you?

MAURA: Do I what? As if I'd entrust the most precious thing in my life . . . to that!

CILLIAN: Good, 'cause if you'd said yes, Uncle Cillian was going to bring you to get your head examined.

MAURA: No, he just plays with him in the back garden . . . and I have to say, he's very good with him.

BOB: That's because he only has the mentality of a two-year-old himself.

CILLIAN: Someone's coming . . .

BOB: We're not expecting anyone else are we?

MAURA: It better not be reporters.

BOB: They wouldn't have known where you meant, would they, Cillian?

CILLIAN: No, not unless someone told them. I'll go and have a look.

           (CONOR *and* LEO *come back as* CILLIAN *exits.*)

CONOR: What's going on?

MAURA: Someone is coming. We're hoping it's not reporters.

CONOR: If it is, they better not start flashing cameras at us.

LEO: The paparazzi give you no peace, so they don't.

BOB: This is a private matter . . . it's none of their business.

           (CILLIAN *returns with* KEVIN, *who is all kitted out with a knapsack, flashlight, hiking boots, walking pole and water bottle.*)

CILLIAN: Everyone, this is Kevin, an old school friend of Seán's. Sit down there, Kevin, and have a rest for yourself.

ALL: Hi, hello, hello, Kevin . . .

MAURA: We thought you were a reporter.

KEVIN: Oh no . . . just a civil servant.

           (*No one laughs.*)

CILLIAN: Kevin, this is Maura . . . who Seán had a baby with. I think you met her at the funeral.

KEVIN: Oh I did indeed, Maura, nice to see you again. (*Looking at the cans of drink*) So did you drive up?

MAURA: Oh no, my sister gave us a lift up as far as the car park.

           (LEO *sits beside* CONOR, *linking him.*)

LEO: And we hiked the rest of the way. It was like finding your way through the feckin' Amazon. I can't believe we found it at all.

BOB: Yes, it must have been very hard following the signs that said: TO THE PICNIC AREA.

KEVIN: Ah, I nearly got lost there, myself. If I had kept going, I would probably have ended up in Avoca or somewhere like that. Good job it's a full moon or I could have broken my neck, 'cause this flashlight's not the best.

CILLIAN: I thought you would know this place well, having spent so much time sitting around the camp fire here singing, 'Ging gang goolie goolie goolie goolie, watcha ging gang goo, ging gang goo . . .'

KEVIN: Yeah, about eighteen years ago when I was a kid. My own kids aren't interested in the Scouts. Apparently, it's '*très* uncool'. So it's been a while. I didn't know if anyone would be here. I was getting a bit nervous.

BOB: Hi, I'm Bob.

KEVIN: Hi, nice to meet you.

CILLIAN: Bob was Seán's partner.

KEVIN: Oh yes, I heard about you.

CILLIAN: Kevin was Seán's best friend at school.

BOB: I heard about you too.

KEVIN: Oh right. I'm . . . I'm not gay myself.

BOB: I know.

CILLIAN: And, this is Conor, who used to work with Seán.

CONOR: Nice to meet you.

KEVIN: Likewise, Conor.

CILLIAN: This is Leo, Conor's . . . partner.

(LEO *puts his hand out as if he wants* KEVIN *to kiss it.* KEVIN *awkwardly shakes it.*)

BOB: Kevin doesn't want to meet Sheena Ribena at any time tonight, Leo.

LEO: Hi, Kevin. But if you were gay, would I be your type?

KEVIN: Well . . .

BOB: That's enough, Leo. Don't mind him, Kevin, he's a bit of a prat at times.

LEO: Oooh, you're in a right mood. It must be that time of the month.

CONOR: OK, that's enough, Leo; you're embarrassing the man.

LEO: I just wanted to know his type, that's all. Jesus, I was only asking.

BOB: Well, you're definitely not his type. I'm surprised you'd be anyone's.

LEO: I'd be lots of people's type, Bob. You *would* be fuckin' surprised!

CONOR: What are you going on about?

LEO: Nothing . . . just saying.

KEVIN: Like Cillian said, I'm just an old school friend. I'm not gay myself . . . but I've nothing against it, if you know what I mean –

> (*To save* KEVIN *from any more embarrassment,* CILLIAN *interjects.*)

CILLIAN: Can I get you a drink, Kevin?

KEVIN: No, it's OK. I have my trusty water bottle here.

CILLIAN: Well, have a sambo or something.

> (KEVIN *takes a sandwich just to be polite but is surprised at how nice the relish is.*)

KEVIN: Mmmm, this is lovely.

CILLIAN: It's the relish; Maura made it.

KEVIN: It's very good . . . does anyone else find it bloody hot? I thought it was going to be freezing this time of the morning, so I brought my fleece, but after walking up here from the car park, I'm sweating.

BOB: Yes, we were saying that ourselves, that it's hot. I brought my fleece too.

CILLIAN: So did I.

KEVIN: The fleece brothers, what? (*The others only smile politely at Kevin's joke.*) I can't believe it's been a whole year. Sorry, what am I saying . . . I'm always like this when I'm outside 'my own environment', as they say.

CILLIAN: Relax, Kevin, you're grand.

MAURA: I get like that, too, Kevin. I'm always making a eejit of myself . . . not that I'm saying you're making an eejit of yourself or anything . . . just that I get all . . . you know? . . . awkward . . . at times too.

KEVIN: That's how Seán and I became friends, you know? When I was about eight. We had just moved house and I was starting at St. Alban's College and I was such a wet rag back then, my God. Anyway, I was sitting in the back of my mam's car, balling my eyes out 'cause I didn't want to go to that school and definitely there was no way I was going in on my own. (*To* CILLIAN) So then your dad drives past and my mam recognizes him from living on our road. So she says, 'Look, there's a boy from our road, maybe you can go into school with him?' And I'm there all boo hoo, hoo, hoo, hoo, not even listening to her. So my mam gets out and goes and has a chat with your dad, and the next thing, Seán is standing looking at me through the window. 'Are you coming in or what?' says he. But I still wasn't budging from the back seat. So he opens the door and says, 'Come on, you, or we'll be late.' Then he just pulls me out of the car and grabs me in a sort of head lock, like we had been friends forever and he walked me in, sat me down at a desk beside him and minded me for the whole day . . . and then . . . I was fine.

CILLIAN: He was always confident, I'll give him that.

KEVIN: It would be the same on the first day back to school every year – the stomach would be churning, the old legs would be like jelly. Just the thought of it would have me in a panic almost, you know? New classroom, new teacher, new desk, sometimes new kids even, I'd just hide behind him for an hour or so and then I'd be OK. And do you know, he never betrayed me . . . he never made fun of me . . . or told anyone I was a scaredy-cat or anything like that?

BOB: No, Seán would never make fun of anybody. He was kind.

CONOR: Always tried to help people . . .

MAURA: Yeah, he never liked to see people being left out.

KEVIN: The first dance we went to, I was nearly shiting myself . . . but he was all cool and calm. He pointed at this girl and said, 'Go over and ask her to dance and she'll say yes', so I did. And do you know what? She did say yes. I even got a snog. Seán could handle any situation, he just had that knack. The girls used to go mad for him, you know! . . . I'm just saying. (*Becoming awkward again for a moment*)

CILLIAN: I know they did, Kevin.

KEVIN: That was crap today, what? The sentencing . . . three years each and one year suspended. They'll be out in two for . . . good bloody behaviour and all that! And then that one fucker got off with six months . . . four of them suspended. What in the name of Jaysus do you have to do in this country to get put in jail for any length of time? It's disgraceful you know. If it wasn't for the fingerprints and the saliva on the Fanta bottle, they would have probably got off scot-free, the lot of them. I wrote a letter to *The Irish Times* about it. Well, Isabel typed it out, but I signed it. All about that intimidation of witnesses and all . . . and then there was nothing done about it. I posted it off just before I came up here . . . and a copy to your mam and dad, Cillian . . . 'cause it's disgraceful.

CILLIAN: Thanks, Kevin. Are you sure you won't have a beer or anything?

KEVIN: No, no I'm grand here with my water. (*Pause*) So what do we do?

BOB: How do you mean?

KEVIN: I mean . . . what do we do? Do we just scatter his ashes into the wind? . . . Well, figuratively speaking, as there's no wind right now. Or do we have sort of a Druid ritual or something? Or do we just have a prayer, or what?

CILLIAN: I'm all for a piss-up, and when the sun comes up on the horizon, I'll just scatter his ashes onto the ground and say a few words. Anyone can say what they like; I'm just sort of busking it here, you know?

   (*Awkward pause*)

LEO: I know, we could have a seance like they do on that show *Haunted House*.

BOB: Would you show a bit of respect here?

CONOR: Maybe that was a little inappropriate there, Leo.

MAURA: We could sing something . . . like a hymn . . . like 'Abide with Me' or 'Nearer My God to Thee'. Seán loved those.

LEO: (*Jumping up*) I could sing something. I could do the 'Pie Jesu'. Oh I do do that lovely, don't I, Conor?

CONOR: Well . . . er . . .

BOB: I said no Sheena Ribena, OK!

LEO: But I sing it lovely!

BOB: Conor, tell him.

CONOR: (*Gently*) No Sheena Ribena, Leo.

LEO: I can't promise anything. When she wants to sing, she just sings. (*Starts to sing 'Bootylicious'*) See . . . I have no control over that diva.

CILLIAN: And I have no control over that baseball bat I have in my bag, Leo!

LEO: Jesus, I was just having a bit of craic. You'd swear we were at a funeral.

BOB: Leo!

LEO: What? Seán wouldn't have wanted everyone sitting around po-faced.

BOB: You better start behaving yourself. You have no right being here in the first place, as far as I'm concerned.

CONOR: OK, that's enough you two.

LEO:	Huh? Have so! In fact . . . I have as much right to be here as *you* have, Bob. You're not the only one who was close to Seán, you know.
CONOR:	What are you going on about?
LEO:	Nothing. I was just saying . . .
CONOR:	Saying what, Leo?
MAURA:	He's saying nothing, Conor. He's just trying to stir things.
LEO:	That's right, I was saying nothing . . .
BOB:	Well, you seem to be saying something. So why don't you tell Conor what you're making your little quips about?
CONOR:	Tell me what?
LEO:	Nothing . . . OK! I'm just saying, Seán would have liked a bit of craic, not everyone sitting around with a po-face . . . like Bob.
BOB:	Tell him what you meant by 'You're not the only one who was close to Seán, you know'. Go on, tell him . . . in fact, tell everyone what you meant. Because you seem to be just waiting for the opportunity to let it all spill out.
LEO:	No I'm not!
BOB:	Yes you are. Well, I know all about the dirty little deed, Leo. Seán told me.
LEO:	He did not.
BOB:	He did so, so there.
CONOR:	What are you talking about?
BOB:	See, you don't care who you hurt, do you?
LEO:	You're the one that's after feckin' saying it!
CONOR:	What are you on about?
BOB:	Nothing, Conor; don't worry about it.
CONOR:	What's he on about?
LEO:	(*To* CONOR) It was before you and me!
BOB:	No it wasn't!
LEO:	Well, it was before we got serious, then.
CONOR:	(*Incredulous*) I don't believe it.
LEO:	It didn't mean anything, Conor.
CONOR:	When did it happen?
LEO:	It doesn't matter . . . 'cause it didn't mean anything!
CONOR:	When – did – it – happen!
LEO:	I didn't mean to say anything; he was just pissing me off, being all pompous and everything!
CONOR:	*When?!*

LEO: After Tom Webb's fiftieth birthday party . . . OK?

CONOR: You fuckin' shit head (*Gets up to leave*)

LEO: No don't go, Conor . . . it didn't mean anything!

CONOR: Then why did you do it?

LEO: Because . . . well, you know how it is.

CONOR: No, I don't know how it is . . . that seems to be my problem . . . I don't know how anything is . . . I just trust people, I take them at face value . . . I must be the biggest fuckin' eejit on the planet . . .

MAURA: No you're not, Conor.

LEO: It didn't mean anything . . . I keep telling you.

CONOR: Was it just that one time?

MAURA: Conor, don't do this to yourself.

CONOR: (*To* MAURA) Did you know?

MAURA: Sort of . . .

CONOR: (*To* LEO) But we said we'd tell each other everything.

LEO: Well, I'm telling you now, Jesus! Some people want jam on it! It happened . . . these things happen . . . it didn't mean anything.

CONOR: And you all knew?

MAURA: Didn't you guess there was something going on when you saw how upset he got when Seán was killed?

CILLIAN: He wasn't killed, Maura, he was murdered!

MAURA: I know, I know, sorry! Look, Conor, don't go now . . . you and Seán were good friends . . . he'd want you here . . . it's only a little stumble along the way . . . you know that . . . you've got to know that . . . look, why don't you have another drink . . . and –

CONOR: I'm going for a piss.

          (*Conor exits.*)

LEO: Will I come with you?

CONOR: (*Offstage*) No!

LEO: What did you have to go and say that for, Bob?

MAURA: Because you couldn't leave well enough alone, that's why . . . And I hope you're happy with yourself, you've been dropping hints about you and Seán for ages now and doing it in front of poor Conor is the meanest thing I've seen in years. I just can't believe you at times.

LEO: I was just saying.

MAURA: Well in future, keep your trap shut about your conquests!

          (*A tense silence*)

KEVIN: (*Changing the subject*) Does anyone remember Seán and the bloody lipgloss?

BOB: Oh my God! That damn stuff. He always had it on and it used to drive me mad. I know it was clear but it just had a hint of colour, just enough to make you wonder. He always said it was lip balm but it wasn't, it was one of those cheap greasy lipsticks out of the pound shop.

MAURA: I found them all over the house when I was clearing the place out. There was one in every drawer.

BOB: And in every pocket. I can't tell you the amount of times one of them went into the washing machine.

CILLIAN: I lay all the blame on my mother. When we were kids, she always put Vaseline on our lips in the morning so they wouldn't get chapped, and then she bought this pot of strawberry-flavoured lip balm for herself and he decided he liked the taste of it. So he took it and started wearing it and everybody used to call him a girl or a queer or a puff, but he didn't care, he just always had it on.

LEO: (*Sheepishly joining in*) Like he was addicted to it . . . that can happen, you know.

KEVIN: I remember one day in class when we were in third year he had this really sort of pink stuff on and the teacher said, 'Roche, are you wearing lipstick?' And he says 'No, sir! Just because I'm gay doesn't mean I wear lipstick', and the teacher didn't know where to put his face and everyone in the class started laughing and jeering.

MAURA: He just said it straight out like that?

KEVIN: Straight out . . . and then he quietly went on doing his maths. I'm sure everyone thought he was joking at first. Then they just all shut up one by one 'cause they were embarrassed, because it had just hit them, that he wasn't messing. And everyone sort of sat there and you could feel the tension.

MAURA: God, how brave was that!

KEVIN: When we were walking home after school, he told me if I didn't want to be friends with him any more, that would be OK, he'd understand. I mean, I was in shock, so I just said no, no of course, I wanted to still be friends with him and all that sort of thing . . . but I felt a bit . . . you know? uneasy. So I told my mam and she said Seán would need his friends to be his friends right now and so . . . that was that. I mean, I knew he didn't fancy me or anything, so it didn't bother me and you know? I was glad I could do something for him for a change.

(CONOR *has returned and has heard the last bit of the conversation.*)

CONOR: That was nice.

MAURA: Are you OK?

CONOR: Yeah, I'll survive.

KEVIN: But after that he wore the clear stuff.

BOB: But I'll bet it had just a touch of pink.

(*They all laugh.*)

KEVIN: So I just thought, seeing as everyone remembered . . .

LEO: That's a condition, you know, Kevin.

KEVIN: What is?

LEO: Not liking to have dry lips. You can look it up. There's a name for it, but I can't remember what it's called. I heard about it on the radio . . . it's being addicted to lip balm . . . but there's a name for it but I can't remember . . . What's it called? Does anyone know? Oh that's driving me mad!

BOB: Oh, oh . . . wait a minute, I think I know, is it called . . . um . . . I-don't-like-dry-lips-so-I'm-going-to-fuck-off-to-the-pound-shop-and-get-a-cheap-lipstick?

(*Everyone tries not to laugh but they do and* CONOR *feels a bit sorry for* LEO.)

LEO: Yea, that's it! Ha ha, very funny! It is a condition, you know. I heard it on the radio.

CONOR: You'll think of it in a bit.

KEVIN: Well, as I was saying . . .

BOB: Did he fancy anyone at school, Kevin? 'Cause he never would say . . .

KEVIN: Oh yes. He had a big crush on one of the rugby players, you know? A big tall blond guy. . . . And I remember one day Seán was out on the pitch watching him practise, and some of the guys, big ignorant fuckers, started to jostle him around just for the fun of it, ya know? Now, I knew I couldn't fend them off if they started getting nasty and I was just about to run and get the coach or somebody when Seán says, 'Are we going to have a big fight, guys? 'Cause if we are, just be darlings and give me a second to put my face on and then I'll be right with you', and he takes out the lipstick and very carefully applies it and then smacks his lips together, the way women do, and says, 'Now, who's first, oh and by the way . . . I like to be on top' (*Everyone bursts out laughing*) and they all backed off and walked away . . . 'cause they were scarlet. But I saw the blond looking over at him . . . and I knew . . .

(*Everyone is listening to the story in amazement but* KEVIN *just takes another sandwich and begins to eat.*)

KEVIN: Mmm, this really is good relish . . .

BOB: Well?

KEVIN: Well what?

MAURA: Well, what the fuck did you know from the look?

KEVIN: Ooooh . . . If the guys had beaten Seán up, he wouldn't have defended him and Seán knew it, because he was scared shitless someone would find out about him. That look between them was sort of 'Will you ever show the world how you feel about me?' And I knew. I knew that he and the blond were in love. I mean really . . . truly . . . in love . . .

CILLIAN: (*Sceptical*) And you could tell all this . . . from one look?

KEVIN: No. I could tell it from watching the big blond head of him jumping over your back wall every Sunday when you and your folks were all gone up to Newry for the day to your grandma's. Remember all that 'I have to stay here and study' crap?

CILLIAN: The little fecker!

KEVIN: I used to see him hopping that wall every time Seán had the place to himself and it went on right up until the blonde went to university in the States.

BOB: My God . . . I always knew there was someone from his past that he never got over! He used to say little things . . . and I always knew, but I also knew not to ask questions.

CILLIAN: Who was it?

KEVIN: Now, if Seán wanted any of you to know, he would have told you.

CILLIAN: Ah come on!

KEVIN: All I'll say is that his wedding was in *VIP* in 2007. I nearly fell over when I saw it . . . Isabel gets all those crap magazines.

LEO: Brian O'Driscoll. Oh Mammy!

BOB: One, Brian O'Driscoll didn't go to Seán's school; two, he didn't

go to university in America; and three, he didn't get married in
2007.

LEO: I'd fuckin' marry him any day.

CONOR: You shouldn't have got him started on Brian O'Driscoll.

LEO: I'd be his slave, chained to the kitchen sink with me Cillit Bang
. . . or is it Oxi Action? Well, whatever it's called . . . and I'd be
scrubbing away till me fingers bled just to make sure them
shorts were washed whiter than white, so I could send him out
on the pitch . . . looking like . . . an angel.

CILLIAN: He's got a very pretty girlfriend, Leo.

MAURA: He sure has.

LEO: Have you ever noticed how smooth Brian's thighs are? I
wonder does he wax?

CILLIAN: No, I've never noticed it, Leo.

BOB: Well . . . I have to confess that I have taken note of it once or
twice . . . and his chest.

LEO: Oh Mammy, that chest!

KEVIN: Ah now, lads . . . give it over.

CONOR: (*Teasing* LEO) I don't think Brian O'Driscoll is that good-
looking . . . I think he looks a bit like a blown-up jelly baby.

LEO: He does not and you're just jealous. Oh God . . . do you
remember when those two All Blacks, mother-fuckers, bashed
into him and dislocated his shoulder and he was lying there on
the pitch in agony. Well, I never seen anything so beautiful in
all me whole life. If I'd have been there, I'd have ran in and
saved him.

MAURA: I'm sure he would have loved that, Leo, and in front of the
whole world.

LEO: He would so!

CILLIAN: So you're not going to tell us who it was, Kevin?

KEVIN: No way.

MAURA: Some things are better left unsaid or better off not being known
at all – that man is married now and he could have kids.

BOB: But he's living a lie.

MAURA: Well, that's something for his own conscience.

BOB: Yeah, until in a few years' time, when it all gets too much for
him and he leaves the wife and the kids and it's all one big
fuckin' mess . . . because he now realizes that he would have
been far better off in the first place admitting to himself, and

everyone else, what he is and not have been such a poxy coward all along!

CONOR: That's easier said than done, Bob; sometimes you just don't understand these things.

BOB: Ah come on, Conor, for fuck's sake, you knew you were gay and you still went ahead and got married and got a mortgage and had kids and then five years on you come clean and you're still . . . ten years later . . . feeling the repercussions.

CONOR: My kids are the most precious thing in the world to me and I wouldn't be without them. I know things are a bit of a mess but I don't regret getting married because I had them, and anyway, things aren't that bad.

BOB: You lost your house, lost your car, you didn't see your kids for three years, your family are still not speaking to you, and you're living in a rented basement flat.

LEO: It's decorated very nice, so there!

BOB: (*Aside to* LEO) Shut up, you! (*To* CONOR) They wouldn't even let you coach the football team any more, Conor. Everyone got hurt – you, your wife, your kids, your family and your friends. The guy that was your best man gave you a black eye, for Christ's sake . . . at least I have always been honest about who I am and what I am and if people don't like it, then that's just too bad.

LEO: They can just all fuck off, that's my motto.

BOB: Shut up, Leo! Now, I'm not in favour of outing people or any-thing like that . . . but you are what you are . . . and that's what you are and you have to own it . . . and by hiding in the closet, you're just conforming to what society wants.

LEO: So far in the closet, he was almost in Narnia.

BOB: Society wants everything to look nice and smooth on the surface. Have the funny little queen mincing around on the TV for everyone's amusement. But we have to face things head on and say, we exist here in everyday society not just in the books and the songs and the films and in soap operas.

LEO: Oh, give us a drink . . . he's off on one of his politicals . . .

BOB: We're your postman . . . your teacher . . . your nurse . . . your bank manager and . . . your binman.

LEO: Ugh! You'd never get a gay binman.

BOB: Leo, I swear I'll do you in a minute. We are people and we have rights and we have the right to be what we are!

CONOR: It's not always that easy for people, Bob. You don't understand how hard it is when you come from where I come from.

BOB: Oh don't give me all that crap about been working class or uneducated or coming from a small town . . . it doesn't matter what your background is, it's hard to come out and tell the truth . . . but you just have to hope that people respect you for being you . . . and not for what you are.

CONOR: I'm just saying, it's not that easy for some people.

LEO: Well, at least he came out and admitted it in the end and that's what counts! Now stop talking about it, 'cause it's very boring! So let's talk about something else . . . Kevin, are you absolutely sure you're not gay?

KEVIN: 'Course I'm not gay, sure I'm married.

LEO: Conor was married . . .

KEVIN: You'd know if you were . . . and I know I'm not.

(*Everyone starts to laugh at* KEVIN.)

CONOR: Relax, Kevin, he's only winding you up 'cause he's being stupid. Leo, behave yourself or we're going.

LEO: I am behaving myself.

KEVIN: (*To* CONOR, *embarrassed*) I knew that.

CONOR: (*To* LEO) No, you're not.

LEO: I am.

KEVIN: (*To everyone*) I knew that.

CONOR: You're being very bold, Leo, and if you don't give it up, I'm going to dump your stuff outside the door when we get back.

LEO: I was only defending you . . . against Bob. He looks down on people who don't have as much as he has, so he does.

BOB: I do not!

LEO: Yes you do.

BOB: How do I?

LEO: You do be always making snippy remarks to me, saying I'm a gobshite and an eejit.

BOB: Well you are.

LEO: I am not!

MAURA: Shut up the pair of you.

LEO: (*To* CONOR) You should be standing up for me.

CONOR: Why the fuck should I?

LEO: Right then . . . I won't say one more word.

BOB: Great, there is a God.

LEO: You're a gobshite yourself.

BOB: That was four words, by the way.

MAURA: Will you give it a rest, the pair of you? You're starting to piss me off . . . it's like listening to kids in the playground. Does anyone know what time the sun will be coming up at?

CILLIAN: Well . . .

KEVIN: Well, according to my calculations, it's 5.21 a.m. in Tralee and 4.58 a.m. in Belfast, so seeing as we are in the middle and a little bit more north, I reckon it should be approximately 5.10 a.m., or thereabouts.

MAURA: Will we wait until there is a good bit of sun up, or will we do it when we just see a glimmer?

CILLIAN: We'll just know when the time is right.

KEVIN: Well, because I didn't know what we would be doing today and I wasn't even sure if anyone would be here, I just thought I'd bring something that was significant to Seán. Something that made him who he was, and so earlier on I went to the –

MAURA: Is there someone out there? (*She stands up.*)

CONOR: It's probably only a bird or something.

MAURA: No, I thought I saw something moving.

CONOR: Or . . . a rat!

          (CONOR *grabs* MAURA, *who jumps up on a log.* LEO *also jumps onto a log.*)

MAURA: Stop, I hate rats. But really, guys . . . I saw something . . . Could it be reporters?

CILLIAN: Hello? . . . Hello? If there's someone there, just show yourself . . .

LEO: We have a gun!

CILLIAN: No we don't! What are you trying to do, Leo? . . . I don't think there's anyone . . . it could have been a deer.

LEO: Oh Jesus, they could gore you. I seen that on a wildlife programme once . . . or was that a gazelle I'm thinking of?

MAURA: Sorry, Cillian, I just thought I saw someone.

LEO: We are taking our life in our hands coming up here at this time, there could be anything out there. There could be vampires and we don't even have Buffy's number –

          (*A noise offstage*)

KEVIN: Now, I heard something there.

CONOR: Me too.

(*A man comes into the clearing. He is tall and is dressed casually. He looks around uneasily.*)

BRENO: Hi . . . sorry for butting in, I know I'm intruding . . . I didn't mean to alarm anyone.

MAURA: I knew there was someone!

CILLIAN: No, no come on in, the more the merrier. You're not a reporter or anything, are you?

BRENO: No, no, honest to God . . . I just wanted to come to pay my respects.

CILLIAN: Right, well thanks. Were you a friend of Seán's?

BRENO: No . . . not exactly – as I said, I just wanted to come to pay my respects.

CILLIAN: Thanks . . . but obviously you weren't just passing by?

BRENO: I read in the papers what you said at the funeral, about, you know, that you would scatter the ashes of your brother when the people responsible for his murder were sent to jail . . . And I knew where this place was because I used to be in the Scouts myself when I was a kid . . . I wasn't sure if you meant today when they were sentenced or last week when they were convicted but I didn't come up here last week . . . I just did tonight on the off-chance.

CILLIAN: You're sure you're not a reporter?

BRENO: No, no I swear.

CILLIAN: We don't want anyone spying on us.

BRENO: I promise you, I'm not a reporter . . . I just came up here on the off-chance.

KEVIN: (*To* CILLIAN) I was going to come up here last week myself as well, but seeing as it was pissing rain, I reckoned you would leave it until the sentencing . . . and, I mean, I know that's what you said all along but it could be a bit confusing because things like that are open to interpretation . . . sometimes. (*To* BRENO) Hi, I'm Kevin . . . I'm not gay myself, just an old school friend of Seán's.

BRENO: I'm Breno. I know I'm probably not welcome but I just had to come up here 'cause . . .

CILLIAN: No, really, you're welcome. I just had to check things out, you know?

BRENO: My name is Brendan O'Shea. I'm just called Breno.

CILLIAN: Hi, Breno. (*Goes to shake* BRENO's *hand*)

BRENO: I'm Dillon O'Shea's father . . . I just wanted to pay my respects.

(*Everyone is silent and looks at* BRENO.)

BOB: Well that's very kind of you, thanks, but this is a gathering for friends and family and I don't think you fit into any of those categories.

BRENO: I understand . . . I do, but . . . I just wanted to say –

CILLIAN: Yes, well we appreciate the gesture and everything, but if you don't mind pissing off now.

MAURA: No, don't go. Come in and sit down.

BOB: No, Maura.

MAURA: Yes, Bob! Let the man say what he came to say.

BOB: It's up to Cillian!

MAURA: No, it's not. My child doesn't have a father because of his son and his friends, so I would like to hear what he has to say.

KEVIN: Yes, let him say what he came to say.

LEO: Jesus, I have to go for a piss again.

CILLIAN: (*To* BRENO) So do I . . . so make it quick.

MAURA: (*To* CILLIAN) No, not like this . . . you go and do what you have to do. (*She takes* BRENO *by the arm and brings him over to an empty place.*) Sit down here; will you have a can?

BRENO: No, I'm fine.

MAURA: No, do – here, there's loads. ·

(CILLIAN *exits.* LEO *runs after him.*)

BRENO: I just came to say, well . . . I just wanted to pay my respects to you all. I recognize Cillian from the funeral but I don't know who yous all are.

MAURA: You were at the funeral?

BRENO: Yes, but I stayed at the back.

MAURA: You just said that you read it in the paper.

BRENO: I know . . . I did read it in the paper but I also heard him say it at the funeral.

MAURA: I can't believe you went.

BRENO: I tried to be as inconspicuous as possible. I didn't want to be upsetting anyone.

MAURA: But why did you go?

BRENO: Because . . . it didn't seem real until then. It was all just this one big mess of things . . . police coming to the house, the press, gawkers just standin' outside for hours, solicitors, everything just sort of buzzing around. I had to go and see the coffin and see the family to make it real. Do you understand?

MAURA: Yeah I think I do . . . (*Holding out her hand*) Maura. As I said, I'm Seán's son's mother.

BRENO: I seen in the papers that he had a baby son; I was surprised.

MAURA: It can happen.

BRENO: I didn't mean anything by it. It's just that he was gay and all . . .

MAURA: It's OK . . . this is Conor, Seán's tenant. And you've met Kevin.

BRENO: Oh right. I thought maybe Seán's mother and father would be here?

BOB: They have gone to England to be with their daughter. It's a tough time for them.

(LEO *comes back.*)

MAURA: And this is Bob, who was Seán's partner.

LEO: Well, his ex-partner, actually. Seán threw him out, then he went off with Maura and had a baby.

(*They all look in shock at* LEO.)

BOB: I better go myself. (*He exits.*)

MAURA: And this is Leo, Conor's boyfriend, who doesn't seem to be able to contain himself.

LEO: I won't shake your hand 'cause I've just had a piss.

CONOR: What did you say that for?

LEO: I forgot me wipes . . . me hands are dirty.

CONOR: You know what I'm talking about – that was a very hurtful thing to say to Bob.

LEO: Well the truth hurts . . . anyway, what do you care? . . . look at all the hurtful things he said to you.

CONOR: Bob wasn't trying to hurt me, he was just making a point.

LEO: Well the point hurt, didn't it?

MAURA: (*To* BRENO) Did you drive up here?

BRENO: No, I walked. It's a nice clear night; took me about an hour and a half, though.

LEO: You're lucky no one kicked your head in on the way.

KEVIN: Now, that's not called for at all, at all, so it's not!

LEO: I was just expressing myself! I mean, it's not like it doesn't happen, that's what happened to Seán.

CONOR: That's enough, Leo.

MAURA: Yes, that's enough. He's not responsible for what his son did.

CILLIAN: (*Coming back*) Then who is? Is anyone? Because it seems to me that no one is responsible for my brother's murder, or no, sorry, sorry, it wasn't murder was it, Breno? It was violent disorder! Did you ever hear the like of that? He was 'violently disordered' to death? At two o'clock in the fuckin' morning, by a gang of skangers, who targeted him, followed him, attacked him and killed him! But . . . it doesn't seem to be anyone's fault! Even though they have the four scumbags that did it! But that's the whole crux of the matter . . . you can be responsible for killing someone by beating and kicking them to death without it being manslaughter or murder! Who was it that said the law is an ass, 'cause he was dead right! (*He takes the bottle of Jack Daniel's and begins to drink from it.*)

BRENO: I understand your pain.

CILLIAN: That's a really patronizing thing to say when you made sure that everything possible was done to protect your son.

BRENO: But he didn't set out to kill anybody, that's not why he went out that night.

CILLIAN: But how the fuck do you know that? Two of those guys already had convictions for larceny, actual bodily harm, grievous bodily harm and public disorder against them . . . You don't think they went out to help the poor and heal the sick, do you?

BRENO: We only did what we had to do, for our son.

CILLIAN: And his mates! Did you have to protect them as well? Even though you and everybody else knew full well that they were as guilty as sin?

BRENO: I know, but those other guys weren't his friends . . . not really. That's why I've come here tonight . . . to explain . . . it's complicated.

CILLIAN: What's complicated about it? They did it, and they should have been convicted of it because they are vicious thugs who have no right to be in any society.

BRENO: That's what I've come to say . . . my son Dillon wasn't like that . . . he wasn't brought up like that. He just got in with the wrong type of crowd . . . there was just something about him that was attracted to those types of guys.

LEO: Maybe he was gay?

ALL: Shut up, Leo!

KEVIN: Now, there was no call for that, Leo, this is not a joking matter.

BRENO: Like I said . . . Dillon wasn't friends with them guys . . . not really, I mean, he wanted to be . . . he wanted to be a big man . . . like he thought they were, but we always told him that they were a shower of wasters and that they would end up getting him into trouble if he hung around with them, but he wouldn't fuckin' listen . . . We never made them welcome in our home. . . not like his other friends . . . but he'd sneak out with them behind our backs . . . and then, the thing is when he did hang around with them . . . they did nothing but slag and bully him all the time . . . and he couldn't defend himself, so he just let them, because he wanted to be part of the gang. He thought they were big guys, you know? . . . hard men . . . and he wanted to be like them. He took so much crap from them because he thought it was some sort of initiation . . . that one day he'd be one of them . . . he thought they were great the way they walked around throwing shapes and acting the fuckin' heavies and they thought he was a piece of shite, but he couldn't see it . . . I'm just trying to explain the circumstances. He was bullied, so he ended up joining the bullies.

MAURA: 'He was bullied, so he ended up joining the bullies' . . . that's like some sensationalist crap you get on those bloody daytime talk shows. There is such a thing as personal responsibility. He was old enough to know that.

BRENO: I know he was . . .

MAURA: Standing up for who you are . . . being your own person. I think you're making excuses and I, for one, don't buy them.

BRENO: I'm not making excuses.

KEVIN: You are. What you're saying is, he was just a poor innocent gobshite that got dragged into it all. He was old enough to know better and when you know better, you should do better, and if you don't, then you deserve to suffer the consequences of your actions.

BRENO: It's just that . . . he thought it was all just fun. Like, when people got out of their way, he thought it was out of respect and he wanted that too.

MAURA: Then you should have told him!

BRENO: *We did!* I said to him . . . and so did my missus, time after time, that it was only because people were afraid of them that they did that and that it was a false power, because there was no respect there, but he wouldn't be told ... no, no, he just thought it was all one big fuckin' game ... I just wanted to come here and talk to you, Cillian, and say sorry and explain.

MAURA: We're not looking for explanations, we're looking for the truth – can you tell us that?

BRENO: I hoped your ma and da would be here.

KEVIN: You could always drop them a note in the post.

CILLIAN: If you wanted to say sorry, you could have come to our house. You could have said sorry to my mother and father and my sister and me. Why didn't you back then? A whole year has passed since the funeral.

BRENO: The solicitor told us not to have any contact with anyone until after the trial ... he said any type of contact could be used as evidence.

CILLIAN: But your son pleaded guilty, so what difference would it have made? Not that he pleaded guilty to much, common assault, causing an affray, damage to private property 'cause someone's car mirror got knocked off. Jesus, I'd almost plead guilty to that myself just for the craic!

BRENO: The solicitors said we still shouldn't have any contact.

CILLIAN: We would have given anything ... anything, just for an apology or even a sign that there was any sort of remorse or guilt there ... but all we got was a deafening silence.

MAURA: It's hard knowing people are laughing at you, Breno. It's hard to comprehend people laughing at your grief ... but that's just what they did to us every time they gave a smart answer in court and all their scumbag friends laughed at them and I know Dillon wasn't there and your family wasn't part of that ... but we were mocked ... and believe me, a kind word from you would have been much appreciated.

CILLIAN: He couldn't do that, Maura; he was too busy sitting at home playing the shut-your-mouth-and-say-nothing game with his son. (*He is vexed now and goes right up and gets in* BRENO's *face.*)

BOB: Cillian, take it easy (*He goes over to pull* CILLIAN *away gently.*)

BRENO: The solicitors said we still shouldn't have any contact.

BOB: Because it might prejudice the case against that other shower of shites?

BRENO: Dillon didn't try to protect them on purpose.

BOB: It was all a big accident, then?

CILLIAN: (*Very heated*) That's the only reason he got any jail time at all, because he wouldn't testify. So he could protect those other scrumbags . . . and you encouraged that . . . because I know you did!

BRENO: We weren't protecting them! We were protecting ourselves! You don't know what those fuckin' people can be like.

LEO: Hel-lo-o! Dead brother here! So I think he does know what they can be like.

CONOR: Leo!

CILLIAN: But he's right.

LEO: Yes I am!

(KEVIN *stands up; he gently but firmly sits* CILLIAN *back down.*)

KEVIN: Now calm down, everyone, the man came to apologize and to try and put things right . . . so let's hear what he has to say without us all losing the head.

BRENO: I'm talkin' intimidation here . . . I'm talkin' about having your windows smashed and shit put through your letter box and paint thrown in your garden and your tyres slashed and people threatening to firebomb your house . . . I'm talkin' about looking over your shoulder when you're just walking down the road to get a paper at the shop, in case you get a bleeding bullet in the back! Every day, afraid for your life, and all because they didn't want Dillon or anyone to testify against them, but they were ratting each other out left, right and centre. Every night, wondering if this is the one when a brick comes through your window or a petrol bomb. Will you have to carry your kids out as your home goes up in flames around you, would you make it out alive even? They had a big fancy lawyer working for them. Where do you think they got the money to pay for that? Who do you think we were dealing with here? They were even sayin' there were guys there that were in London at the time. It was all part of the smokescreen – that's how they operate. We were terrified. At one stage they even tried to pin the whole thing on Dillon and his friend Martin. And Martin hadn't even stopped that night, he just kept walkin' right by, but they said he had started the whole thing and that they were just bystanders, and that poor guy was dragged in for questioning off the street in front of his neighbours and he wanted to join the Guards, so how will that look on his application? He was the one that called 999 on the night but his name is mixed up with this for the rest of his life.

MAURA: But the eyewitnesses had an even worse time; one of them had a dead rat sent to them in the post, but they all still got up in court and said what they saw. They didn't let themselves be intimidated and they didn't owe us anything; they weren't responsible for any of it, but Dillon was. You know, if he got caught up in something, that's his own fault, and don't tell me at any time he didn't know that what he was involved with was wrong. What's this about? Are you saying your son has nothing to answer for?

BRENO: God no, no way. I'm just trying to say that we tried to bring him up properly. He wasn't a spoiled brat; he wasn't a thug; he was just . . . just a fuckin' eejit.

MAURA: Just a fuckin' eejit? You're making it sound like he did nothing.

BOB: He was there; he was with that gang. He's not being punished unfairly you know!

MAURA: He was part of them and he didn't do anything to stop them beating Seán up! If he wasn't really like them, as you say, he could have at least tried.

BRENO: But they would have turned on him, then.

MAURA: Maybe so . . . but they wouldn't have kicked him to death; he might have gotten a bruise or two and been out of the gang, but Seán would have been alive, my Cian would have his dad still . . . I point to a photo every day and say to my son, 'That's Daddy Seán'. Do you have any idea what that's like? What do I say to him when he's old enough to ask where his daddy is? Can you tell me how I am going to explain that to him?

BRENO: As I said . . . I understand your pain.

KEVIN: And I think we should leave it at that . . . We have come here to say goodbye to Seán . . . so I was thinking that we could –

CILLIAN: (*Ignoring* KEVIN; *addressing* BRENO) You're sitting there . . . making excuse after excuse for your criminal of a son. How could you possibly understand her pain?

BRENO: Because I do. My son might not be dead, but in many ways he's dead to me.

CILLIAN: Oh for fuck's sake!

BRENO: The little boy in the photographs, the little kid I loved, the chubby guy in his Cubs' uniform – that's all gone. I can hardly look at him.

MAURA: But you still have him, and he has all his life to make it up to you. That's the thing about being alive – you still have a chance to make amends.

BRENO: Cillian, your da stood up at the funeral –

CILLIAN: *You were at the funeral?!*

BRENO: Yes.

BOB: He stayed well at the back, Cillian.

CILLIAN: You knew?

CONOR: No, no. He just told us when you were having a piss.

CILLIAN: You came to our church and watched our grief and you went home and told your son to keep his mouth shut?

BRENO: No, it wasn't like that. I never told him to lie, I never would. But I'm trying to explain to you . . . that at the funeral . . . your father said that no matter what Seán ever . . . did, he was always proud of him. He could always, always look his son in the eye. Well, I can't look my son in the eye. I'm ashamed of him. I even hate him at times. I've hated my own son! I've wished he was never born; I hope none of yous ever gets to know what that's like. I hate his weakness, I hate his lack of character and I hate his inability to just fuckin' say no! No, I'm not getting off the bus now! No, I'm not following that guy home . . . he's broken his ma's heart, he's broken my heart.

KEVIN: We understand that . . . but, as Maura said, you have a lifetime to get over it.

BRENO: Look, I always thought I done well in life. I have a good job on the buses; I've never been a day out of work; we own our own home; me missus works part time in the hospital; we pay our bills; we keep out garden nice; we get on well with the neighbours; we even paid our fuckin' bin tax; and then this comes along and knocks you sideways and I don't know how to get over it. So I'm like yous in a way, only I have to live with shame as well as loss.

MAURA: Dillon will be out of jail in a few weeks; they won't make him do the full two months. And as long as he keeps his nose clean for the next few months he's home scot-free . . . I know he didn't kill Seán but he didn't stop it either. Can you understand why we're angry? If he had just told the truth, that's all! Just the truth. At least we would have known what happened.

BRENO: All I can say is I'm sorry. They had everyone lying for them, it didn't really matter what Dillon said in the end.

MAURA: But the truth is the truth and at least we would have known it.

BRENO: I am so sorry, everyone, I really am. (*Pause*) Look, I should go. I've said what I came to say. (*He stands up to go.*)

MAURA: I don't know what you wanted to get out of tonight but if it's forgiveness, then I have to say that, for me, it's too early. I can't just say it, I have to mean it. But if it helps you to know, I don't blame you or your wife. That's all I can say to you.

BRENO: Thanks.

KEVIN: I think that sounds fair enough.

CILLIAN: Is that why you came here tonight? Did you think you would be forgiven? Because I don't think you fully understand the situation here.

BRENO: Of course I do.

CILLIAN: No, I don't think you do! I don't think any of you really understand. (*He is drunk by now.*)

BOB: What are you on about, Cillian?

CILLIAN: He comes here looking for forgiveness or absolution or redemption or . . . I don't know the fuck what . . . but what he doesn't seem to understand is that we are the victims . . . not him!

CONOR: We're all victims.

CILLIAN: Yes, Conor, but victims of different things.

MAURA: Cillian, you have a few on you, so let's just forget about it now, OK? We'll wait till the sun comes up and do what we've come here to do and then we can all go home.

CILLIAN: No! No! Let's do a little bit of maths here, right? My brother was murdered and somebody did it . . . that means that somebody is responsible for it . . . but the people who were responsible for it . . . didn't own up to it . . . well, that's to be expected from a shower of scumbags like that – no offence, Breno, but I include your son in the equation. So the scumbags . . . being scumbags . . . do everything they can to get away with it . . . and they did! They did get away with it, for the most part . . . but they wouldn't have gotten away with it if your son, Dillon, had just told the truth at the beginning! Before all the shite started . . . when it would have mattered . . . he was the only one that would have been believed. You talk about . . . how well he was brought up . . . and how nice he really is . . . and how it was all . . . like this big accident that he was even there . . . with those guys . . . on that night. But Breno . . . what I want to know from you is . . . and I really want to know this . . . is . . . what did you do?

BRENO: How do you mean?

CILLIAN: Did you sit your son down and ask him what really happened?

BRENO: Of course we did!

CILLIAN: And . . . did he tell you?

(BRENO *is silent.*)

CILLIAN: Well, Breno, did he tell you?

BRENO: Yes he did.

CILLIAN: Everything?

BRENO: Yes!

BOB: Cillian, take it easy now.

CILLIAN: And did you believe him?

BRENO: Yes.

CILLIAN: And did he tell the police everything?

BRENO: No.

CILLIAN: And did you tell the police everything?

BRENO: No.

CILLIAN: (*To everyone*) You see, that is what I am talking about.

BOB: Oh right, I see . . . but Cillian, sit down now because you're making everyone nervous.

CILLIAN: Am I? Well, we don't want that, do we? We don't want our nice little picnic spoiled.

MAURA: Cillian, what's up with you?

CILLIAN: OK, I'll put it plain and simple for you, Maura –

MAURA: Don't fuckin' patronize me, Cillian.

CILLIAN: Sorry, but my brother . . . the father of your son . . . was murdered . . . somebody did it . . . somebody knew who did it . . . but they didn't tell . . . because they were afraid . . . for themselves and their family . . . and I understand that . . . I really do . . . but sometimes . . . you have to do what's right . . . and hang the consequences. Now . . . because the person who knew . . . didn't tell . . . my brother didn't get justice. We are the victims here . . . and you're right, Breno . . . you and your family are victims also. The whole of Dublin are victims . . . because they've had to suffer it for the best part of a year in the media. But because of your son's stupidity . . . and his weakness . . . and your weakness . . . and your eagerness to still look . . .

'respectable' and to make it look like your poor son . . . just got dragged into something . . . that he was . . . what was it they called him in the paper? 'An unwilling participant in the whole sordid affair' or some crap like that . . . see . . . it looks like he's a victim also . . . but he's not!

BOB: OK, Cillian.

CILLIAN: He's not! Do you know why? Do you want to know why? Because . . . he had a choice! And you . . . you had a choice . . . but Seán never did . . . and we never did . . . so now . . . we are double victims. Because we have lost Seán . . . and because we didn't get justice for him! Well . . . not the kind of justice he deserved.

BRENO: But Dillon's life is ruined now . . . he'll never get a good job here; he'll have to go to England or somewhere just to be able to walk down the street without being recognized . . . and I'm not saying he doesn't deserve it! But just because he isn't going to be in jail for the rest of his life doesn't mean he is not going to be punished for the rest of it.

BOB: A natural justice of sorts –

CILLIAN: 'An innocent bystander', right? Who saw . . . everything . . . but said he didn't, and no one could do anything about it. So he gets two months for contempt of court, big fuckin' deal! You see, Breno, the law is most definitely an ass, but most of all, the thing that you should know is, it's not enough for justice to be done. Justice has to be seen to be done . . . and because it wasn't seen to be done, you have to accept your part in that.

BRENO: But I do . . . and that's the part that's eating me up.

CILLIAN: But you don't! . . . And that's what's eating you up . . . You've answered to no one and neither has your son!

CONOR: Leave it be now, Cillian, I understand what you're getting at but that's enough.

BRENO: All I can say to yous all is that I'm sorry.

(BRENO *stands up but* MAURA *stops him again.*)

MAURA: No, no, no, don't you dare leave. I want you to stay with us. Because, whether we like it or not, you're part of this. I want you to see it through with us; maybe then you'll stop making your excuses.

CILLIAN: No, Maura, let him walk away like the fuckin' coward he is.

MAURA: Well, I want him to stay!

BRENO: I'm just upsetting everyone.

MAURA: We are upset anyway, Breno. (*She puts a can into his hand.*) And
            just because there is sandwiches doesn't make it a bleedin'
            picnic, Cillian.

CILLIAN: Oh touché. (*To* BRENO) Well, if you're staying . . . drink your
            drink.

BRENO: No, I'm fine.

MAURA: Drink your drink, for God's sake.

BRENO: Do you want me to go?

CILLIAN: No! You sit down and wait with us. (*He takes the urn out of his
            bag.*) You watch me putting the ashes of my brother in the dirt.
            That's the dust of a real human being in there. (*He makes a
            drunken dash for* BRENO.)

CONOR: Look, someone grab him.

BOB: (*Catches* CILLIAN*'s arm*) Cillian, that's enough. We all under-
            stand . . . even Breno understands . . . but there's nothing we
            can do now.

            (BRENO *opens the can and takes a good drink from it.*)

KEVIN: Life is crap, OK? . . . That's just what living is about sometimes.

CILLIAN: I just want to know what happened. I just want to know what
            really happened . . . and I want to know why.

MAURA: I know . . . I know, but it's over now.

            (CILLAN *takes another swig from the bottle.*)

KEVIN: I think you have had enough to drink, Cillian. Here, have some
            of the fizzy water.

            (KEVIN *hands* CILLIAN *some water.* CILLIAN *sits and drinks. There
            is a tense silence.*)

LEO: Maura . . .?

MAURA: What?

LEO: Can I ask you something?

MAURA: What?

LEO: I always wanted to know . . . did you and Seán . . . did yous two
            do it or did you use a turkey baster thingy?

BOB: *Oh my God!* Don't answer that! It's none of your fuckin' busi-
            ness! Jesus, what are you like?

CONOR: That's way too personal, Leo.

LEO: All right! Take a chill pill. But yous are all hypocrites 'cause yous all want to know, even you (*Pointing at* BRENO). And Bob, I'll bet you're dying to know but you just don't have the guts to ask her to her face . . . 'cause you've been saying it behind her back for long enough.

BOB: I said it once, Maura.

LEO: You said it loads . . .

MAURA: I am mortified.

BOB: Of course you are . . . I don't know what he was thinking asking you such a thing.

MAURA: It's not like I'm ashamed of anything.

BOB: Of course you're not.

MAURA: It just happened, all right!

BOB: Of course it did.

MAURA: It's not like we made a big secret of it.

BOB: Of course you didn't.

MAURA: Nothing is for certain, you know; people change.

BOB: Of course they do.

MAURA: Bob, shut the fuck up!

BOB: Sorry.

MAURA: I'm just mortified.

BOB: Of course you are . . . sorry.

MAURA: I don't possess a turkey baster, if you must know.

LEO: But he was gay and so are you . . . so how could you?

CONOR: 'Cause they needed each other, Leo . . . isn't that right, Maura?

MAURA: Yeah, we did . . . and then . . . we thought about having a baby and I had always wanted to have one but not on my own and Seán was all for it and then it just happened . . . and I felt blessed. I know that sounds mad but we both just felt blessed when Cian was born. And now here I am, I'm bringing him up all alone anyway, not that you all aren't great, Cillian, but it's still hard.

LEO: But you done very well out of it all the same – a big fuck-off house in Dublin 4.

MAURA: Seán left that to his son, not me; it's all he will ever be able to give him.

LEO: It was just an observation.

MAURA: He had a second mortgage on that house that the insurance didn't fully cover and Seán had debts, you know. If I were some sort of bloody millionaire I wouldn't have the likes of you living in my basement. No offence, Conor, I'm not talking about you.

CONOR: No offence taken, Maura.

MAURA: Seán was a great guy but he wasn't good with money. But . . . he would have been a great dad and I'll make sure that Cian knows that if his dad had lived he would never, ever, have let him down. Now if you'll excuse me, I have to go for a wee.

LEO: Do you want me to come with you?

MAURA: Feck off!

(MAURA *exits.*)

LEO: I'd say that's her hormones.

CONOR: No, Leo, it's your rudeness.

LEO: I wasn't being rude, I was only asking; she didn't have to say anything if she didn't want to. It's not like we're the Gestapo . . . or is it the SS? . . . or whatever they were called.

KEVIN: Well, I think it's great that we are all here to see this through . . . and if you don't mind me saying . . . to get all this stuff out in the open is very therapeutic . . . healing, as they say.

CILLIAN: Healing? Was it healing for you, Breno? To get it all off your chest? To try to get us to say, that's all right, Breno, you're a grand man altogether, so you are? We understand everything. Go on home now with ya and sleep well in your bed at night. Good man yourself for making the effort!

BRENO: It wasn't meant like that.

(MAURA, *who has been in earshot of the exchange, returns.*)

MAURA: Just stop this! He came here to do what's right. He's trying to make amends. As I said, I don't have forgiveness in my heart but I appreciate the gesture.

BOB: It's a bit late to be doing what's right.

MAURA: I know, but that's enough! OK? It's enough!

KEVIN: Now, let's look at it from how Seán would feel if he was here. I think he would, like Maura said, appreciate the gesture. And that's why we are here tonight. We're here for Seán. To say goodbye, to pay our respects, to honour him, if you like, and Seán was a man of honour and he had great dignity, so tonight, or this morning as it were, should be about dignity and respect, and if not forgiveness, then . . . acceptance.

CILLIAN: Oh grant me the fuckin' serenity and all that crap.

KEVIN: It may be crap, Cillian, but bitterness eats you up from the inside. It's like a worm . . . it takes away reason and hope and any glimmer of happiness that you may have left.

BOB: And did you read that somewhere, Kevin?

KEVIN: Yes, as a matter of fact I did, Bob!

CONOR: Well, it makes sense to me. Anyone for another can?

CILLIAN: Is that the sun?

KEVIN: Yes, right on time.

(*They all stand.*)

LEO: It's not fuckin' much, is it? I thought it would be like on the telly.

MAURA: I think it's lovely.

CONOR: Me too.

LEO: Charles Dickens!

BOB: What?

LEO: Charles Dickens! That's who said that 'the law is an ass', in the book *Oliver Twist*. It was Mr. Bumble that said it: 'If the law supposes that . . . then the law is an ass.' See, I do know things . . .

KEVIN: I wanted to bring something that would be especially significant to Seán, so I went to the –

CILLIAN: 'Is that the sun . . .' That was a line from a poem by . . . Emily Dickinson . . . oh shit, I can't think of it.

BOB: Emily Dickinson is a bit doom and gloom for me.

CILLIAN: No, she was great. It's something like 'Was that the sun' or 'Is that the sun' – does anyone know it?

LEO: I only know Charles Dickens!

CILLIAN: Fuck . . . that's annoying me. It's something like 'That was the sun'. That's going to bug me now. What is it? Someone must know. It's . . . something, something and 'That was the sun . . .'

BRENO: (*Reciting*)
I'll tell you how the sun rose –
A ribbon at a time.
The steeples swam in amethyst,
The news like squirrels ran.
The hills untied their bonnets,
And the bobolinks begun.
And I said softly to myself,
'That must have been the sun!' . . .

CILLIAN: 'That must have been the sun!' That's it! 'That must have been the sun!'

BRENO: . . . *But how he set, I know not.*
There seemed a purple stile
Which little yellow boys and girls
Were climbing all the while
Till they reached the other side,
A dominie in gray
Put gently up the evening bars,
And led the flock away.

MAURA: God, you have me crying again.

BRENO: We done that for our Inter Cert.

BOB: Or even, 'did it' for your Inter Cert.

CONOR: Leave the man alone, Bob. I thought that was very nice.

LEO: This would have meant a lot to Seán . . . to have had all of us here thinking about him when the sun came up. We were all special to him. Well, not you, Breno, no offence . . . but the rest of us were.

BOB: Will you just give it a rest?

CONOR: He's not saying anything wrong.

BOB: Breno, Leo had a few sordid little fucks with Seán . . . that he seems to be wearing as a badge of honour. So now, Leo, that everyone knows, just shut up about it.

LEO: You're just jealous.

BOB: I could never be jealous of you and Seán, Leo. Disgusted yes, jealous no.

CONOR: Was it why you and Seán broke up?

BOB: No way. Seán and I wouldn't break up over a weedy little fuck like that!

LEO: Watch who you are calling names, SpongeBob SquarePants!

CONOR: Then why?

BOB: We broke up because . . . we just didn't love each other any more . . . and we never did. There, I've said it!

CILLIAN: Of course you loved each other.

BOB: No we didn't . . . I mean, we did love each other but we weren't in love with each other and, really, we never were.

CILLIAN: But you were together for ten years; you were part of the family.

BOB: I know . . . and we did love each other . . . but really . . . we just needed each other, 'cause it's a hard life being alone out there, and we got on, we gelled, we were companions, we came from

the same background. You know, both going to be famous
architects one day? It was just easy being with each other, but
Seán . . . well . . . he wanted more, he wanted shooting stars or
something and I didn't have it to give . . . 'emotionally redundant', that's what he said I was.

LEO: And he was dead right.

BOB: And maybe I am, Leo. Big deal, but at least I am not a user and
I'm not a show-off. I'll bet you don't know what 'emotionally
redundant' means.

LEO: I do fuckin' so know what 'emotionally redundant' means,
bitch!

CONOR: Well?

LEO: It means . . . It's when . . . you are . . . em . . .

MAURA: Emotionally redundant, isn't that right, Leo?

LEO: Stop takin' the piss, you!

KEVIN: It's when you are not in touch with your feelings and emotions,
Leo, when you don't seem to have anything in you to give to
someone.

LEO: I knew that; no wonder he threw you out.

BOB: He didn't throw me out, ever.

CILLIAN: So what happened?

BOB: Oh God, what happened? He wanted a family, but I couldn't
be that . . . so I moved out for a while, 'cause one of my apart-
ments became vacant. Then he got depressed . . . so I moved
back in – but his mood didn't seem to change. So we called it
a day for good . . . and I moved out again . . . and then the
next thing I knew, Cian was on the way and there was such a
change in him. I'd never seen him so happy and so . . . complete . . . and you're right, Leo . . . you and him, it didn't mean
anything.

LEO: Don't say that . . . don't say Seán said that . . . he didn't say that
. . . I know he didn't.

CONOR: Did Seán really say that, Bob?

BOB: No, he never said that . . .

LEO: I loved him . . . I did . . . I knew he didn't love me . . . or even
want me . . . I knew that . . . but I loved him . . . and it did
mean something to me, Conor . . . it meant a lot, if you want to
know . . . and it was only the once . . . when he was a bit drunk
. . . and he probably was disgusted with himself afterwards. But

now and again he used to give me a little wink . . . if we were at
a party . . . or if he was in the audience when I was doing my
act . . . and I'd be so happy . . . so happy for days . . . I just
couldn't stop myself . . . say you understand, Conor.

CONOR: We'll talk about it at home.

LEO: Don't start getting huffy with me.

CONOR: Can't I have a bit of dignity?

LEO: I'm not trying to hurt you or show you up. I'm just trying to
explain to ya how I felt about Seán. I want you to understand.
It had nothing to do with us . . . that's a different thing.

CONOR: Different how? Seán was the big hero and I'm the big fool?

LEO: That's not the way it was.

KEVIN: You're making him feel like he was second best, Leo.

LEO: No, God, no way, I didn't mean to do that, honest . . . you're
one of the best, most decent guys I ever met in my life and I
feel safe with you and I'm proud to be with you.

BOB: That's probably the only sincere thing I have ever heard you say
in your miserable life, Leo.

LEO: Butt out, you, Bob the Builder!

CONOR: He's being nice to you, Leo.

LEO: Oh.

KEVIN: Jesus, if I cheated on Isabel, I'd be out on my ear. What about
you, Breno?

BRENO: I'd be back living with me ma, in two seconds flat.

KEVIN: How long have you been married?

BRENO: Eight years.

KEVIN: Oh!

BRENO: We had Dillon when we were sixteen.

KEVIN: I see.

BRENO: We were both still at school. It was a very hard time, you know?

MAURA: Did your parents go mad?

BRENO: Mine were all right but her family didn't want us to see each
other at all, like I'd raped their precious daughter or something
. . . and they kept Dillon away from me as much as possible.
They even had a barring order so I couldn't even walk down
their road.

KEVIN: My God.

BRENO: We didn't have mobiles in them days, so I couldn't get in touch
with her. I'd get her friends to drop her in notes from me. They

used to tell Dillon I wasn't his da. That a real da would be married to his ma like they were and that he didn't have a da, that he was a bastard, and that I made him that way.

CILLIAN: My heart breaks for you.

KEVIN: Ah, but you got together in the end.

BRENO: Yeah.

MAURA: Do you have any other kids now?

BRENO: We have two, a boy who is seven and a girl who is five.

KEVIN: Ah that's grand. I have two myself, an eight-year-old and a six-year-old and another on the way.

MAURA: Congratulations!

CILLIAN: (*Getting agitated*) OK, let's do this.

(*They all stand up.* CILLIAN *begins to distribute plastic glasses and pour champagne.*)

KEVIN: No thanks, Cillian, I'm driving.

CILLIAN: Have a fuckin' drink, Kevin!

KEVIN: Well, OK then, I suppose a drop won't hurt.

CILLIAN: When Seán was about thirteen, he wrote this poem called 'The Drowning Room'.

KEVIN: Oh that thing! Sorry.

BOB: I know, he read it to me the first time I went to your house, Cillian. I could hardly keep a straight face.

CILLIAN: Yeah, and although I was only eight or nine at the time, even I knew it was crap . . . but some hippy, tree-hugging, gobshite of a teacher gave him an A for it and a gold star and got the school secretary to type it out. So we had it for breakfast, dinner and tea. He even put it in a glass frame and hung it on the wall, so to shut him up we started slagging him and so everything became the 'Drowning Room'. 'Seán, will you go down to the Drowning Room and get me a pint of milk?' my mam would say. Or, 'Will we have fish and chips from the Drowning Room tonight?' Or my dad would say, 'I'm off to the Drowning Room now for a pint.' And, in the end, he did shut up about it – only just – but the slagging went on for years. If we wanted to get at him about anything, even when he was talking about having his twenty-first, my mam said we should see if we could book the Drowning Room for it. I mean, he laughed along with us about it but deep down I knew it hurt him a bit. I don't know if 'The Drowning Room' was a poem about being gay or not, or just about how a thirteen-year-old feels in general, but for some reason he was proud of it and I don't know why because it was . . . crap. I had a read of it tonight before I came up here 'cause it's still on the wall of his old bedroom. I have it here. I was going to read it all to you but I have decided to spare you and just read you this: (*Reads*)

> *In my Drowning Room*
> *I wait silently for the wave of unacceptance*
> *To sweep over me and cover me.*
> *I am about to be no more*
> *So I ask the spirits of the unknown*
> *To look kindly on me.*

I think he stole that last bit from one of the priest's sermons at church. But . . . here . . . now . . . I ask the spirits of this place to look kindly on my brother and may he rest in peace. To Seán!

ALL: To Seán.

CONOR: He was a good friend to me, despite . . . well, he was a good friend . . . and we all make mistakes and it's forgotten, Seán. Rest in peace.

ALL: Rest in peace.

BOB: Most of all he was my friend and I'll never forget him and it shouldn't have happened the way it did and wherever you are, Seán, even if it's in the Drowning Room, I hope it's a better place.

ALL: A better place.

MAURA: I'll never stop telling Cian how much he was loved and wanted by his dad – to happier times.

ALL: To happier times.

KEVIN: He was my first real friend and, as I said, I thought it would be good to do something symbolic that would mean something to those of us that knew Seán and his ways, so earlier today I went –

BRENO: I . . . I need to say . . . He called me at about half past three in the morning, Dillon did, he sounded very upset, like very upset. I immediately thought that he'd been in a fight or had an accident. So I threw my clothes on and I went to find him. He said he was in Pacific Avenue but when I got there I couldn't see him. I drove up and down the road looking but I couldn't find him. So I called his phone and then he came out from one of the gardens. He was freezing and he had been sick on himself. I had my

running gear in the boot, so I made him change into my tracksuit. I dumped his gear into a plastic shopping bag, which I later
burned. He was in bits, he was shaking, and I could tell he'd been
crying and I kept asking him, 'What's wrong, Dillon? Tell me
what happened', but he just kept saying, 'Help me, Da, help me.'
I didn't know what was going on, so I got him into the car and as
we were driving home I saw where the police had cordoned off
Darby Road and he went hysterical. I knew then that Dillon was
connected in some way with what was going on there and that's
why he was upset. (BRENO *sits down and* MAURA *goes and sits
beside him.*) Then, on the way home in the car I heard the news
and it said that a young man had been killed on Darby Road and
straight away I knew that that was what the police were there for
. . . and Dillon was involved. But I had no idea how. When we
got home, I got the missus up and we tried to talk to him but he
just kept sitting there with his head in his hands, crying, saying,
'I can't, I can't.' He couldn't face us and he was rocking back and
forth and he was scratching himself and hitting himself and he
wouldn't stop. I thought we should call the doctor or something,
'cause you should have seen him, but the missus said no and she
gave him painkillers that she had and he calmed down after that,
just a bit. I was upset, he was upset, the missus was upset. I didn't
know what to do . . . so I said to write down what had happened
and to be a hundred per cent honest, to leave absolutely nothing
out. So I got a notepad and pen and we left him to it. 'You can tell
us anything, son, we will always love you; you know that,' the
missus said to him. But I couldn't say it . . . I couldn't even look
at him, because deep down I knew. Before he started to write, he
said, 'I'm sorry Ma, I'm sorry Da.' (BRENO *takes out a letter. He
hands it to* MAURA.) You can do whatever you like with this . . . I
was going to give it to the police, but I didn't. The missus told
me to burn it . . . You're right, Cillian . . . I did tell my son to keep
his mouth shut and deny everything, because I wanted to save
him. It was all I could do for him . . . it was all I could do to show
him I loved him and that I really was his da.

MAURA: You read it.
BRENO: I can't.
MAURA: Yes you can, you owe us that much.

BRENO: I just can't.

MAURA: It will be your last chance to do right by us . . . read it!

BRENO: (*Reading*)

Me and Martin were walking down Grafton Street for the night bus when we met Justin, Stewart and Keith. They had been thrown out of some club that I had never heard of for robbing pints, so they were also going for the night bus. Keith was being a real bollox and hitting girls on the arses and all that kind of thing and he had a bit of a scrap with a boyfriend of one of the girls. We all went into a shop and bought stuff like potato wedges and breakfast rolls and drinks. Justin bought a bottle of Fanta and then we saw that the night bus was about to pull out so we all ran for it. It was full upstairs so we stood in the area where the wheelchairs are meant to be. Everybody was eating their food and Stewart was grabbing everyone's 'cause he didn't have money to get anything. He was grabbing Martin's stuff mostly 'cause he knew that Martin wouldn't do anything about it. Then he noticed this guy sitting on the single seat as you go up the stairs and he had a brown suede jacket on and a beige T-shirt and beige Chino jeans and brown suede boots. Stewart started pointing at the boots and saying to the guy, Look, look, like there was something on the bottom of the shoes and the guy started looking at the soles of the boots but couldn't find anything and then Stewart started saying, Look, look what you are fuckin' wearing, and the guy copped on that he was being slagged, so he just started ignoring him but Stewart kept on about the boots. Asking if he was gay and saying the boots were very fuckin' poncy-looking and then he started asking him had he just been to meet his boyfriend and did his boyfriend like his boots? But the guy just kept on ignoring him and then Stewart shook his bottle of Fanta and opened it and it sprayed everywhere and went on the guy's jacket and his trousers and his boots and we were all laughing and Stewart started saying, Ah sorry, man, sorry, don't get your boyfriend after me now will you? And then this big guy with tattoos all over him, that was sitting in the seat behind the guy with the boots, gave Stewart a hard shove and told him to watch where he was spilling his fuckin' drink and Stewart was pissed off 'cause the big guy did that to him in front of everyone but he knew he couldn't take on the big guy but he was raging. Then some people got off the bus that were sitting on the back seat, so we moved down there. Stewart was still slagging the guy, asking him rude stuff, and some auld one told him to shut up and so Stewart started getting into it with her and then we noticed that the guy had hopped off the bus, so Stewart ran to get off but he was too late and the driver wouldn't let him. So Keith said we should get off at the Golden Palms and double back. Martin didn't want to get off but Keith and Stewart dragged him. We walked down past the pub and down Pacific Avenue and onto Pacific Road and we saw the guy walking up Darby Road and we hid behind a van that was parked in a driveway, but Martin wouldn't come in behind the van, so Keith and Stewart grabbed him and gave him a few digs to keep him quiet. Then, when the guy walked by, they jumped out and started pushing the guy around and asking if he thought he was clever, trying to give us the slip. Then Keith started slapping him in the face. Martin took off back down the road but he had his phone out and I knew he was calling the Guards. So I said, Come on, lads, let's go! I didn't tell them that Martin was calling the Guards because they would have killed him. I was getting scared and I said, Come on, lads, someone is looking out the window, they might call the cops. But Justin started screaming, So let some fuckin' auld one call the cops, just fuckin' let her, and they were pushing the guy around between the three of them and slapping him and shouting things at him, like queer and arse bandit and things, and his nose was bleeding and his face was scratched and then the guy fell against me and some of the blood got on my jacket and that pissed me off, so I gave him a hard push back and he fell on the ground and then . . . then Justin starts kickin' him and Stewart and Keith joined in and they just went mad, they just went mad and I could feel the vibrations of the kicks in the ground and then Stewart bent down and started punching the guy, seven maybe eight times, and then Justin stamped on him, just stamped on him like you would on an empty coke can, people were opening their doors and shouting at us and I could see all the blood and a woman came out with a hurley stick and started swinging it at us. Then I saw other people coming out of their houses . . . and then we ran off . . . but Justin flung his Fanta bottle at the woman and called her a cunt and said he knew where she lived. We all ran back to the main road and then we heard the cops, so Keith said to split up, and I jumped over a wall into someone's

back garden. I sat there for a bit and then . . . I got sick and I sat
there for ages more, crying, and then . . . I called me da . . .

(BRENO *finishes reading, and speaks to the others.*)

So now you know. I came here tonight, Cillian, because I'm
eaten up with guilt. I thought I could just come here and apologize, and if you didn't accept it, then that was your hard luck
– after all, I'd made the grand gesture, as you said. I don't
know what I was thinking. And you were right, I didn't accept
my part in all of it or my son's. You could see that, 'cause it
came screaming out of me. The truth always does. Here, take
it. (*No one takes the letter.*) Please someone take it. Please . . .
please . . .

CONOR: Maybe you could get them re-tried. (CONOR *takes the letter.*)

CILLIAN: I couldn't face that all over again. I couldn't put the folks through
it. It could take years and anyway . . . sure you can strangle an
eleven-year-old child and only get four years for it. You were
right, Maura, some things are better off not being known.

CONOR: But what about fighting for justice and all that?

CILLIAN: I haven't any fight left in me. What is it they say? A good soldier
knows when to retreat! Well, I'm retreating. No one is ever to
tell my folks about that letter!

MAURA: What are you going to do with it?

CILLIAN: Burn it.

BRENO: Are you sure? I'm willing to do what needs to be done.

CILLIAN: It's too bleedin' late to be a hero! I'm off home to my bed.

KEVIN: What about the ashes?

(CILLIAN *opens the urn.*)

CILLIAN: Bye, bro, see you again sometime, OK?

KEVIN: No, no, no. Not like this. We came here to honour Seán's
memory, we don't have to send him off in a blaze of glory but
this is just disrespectful. Don't let us be embarrassed by how
degraded Seán was at the end; no one expected him to be a
fuckin' gladiator. He couldn't defend himself against them but
he died with dignity and we have to give him the respect and
honour he is due. (*He takes the letter from* CONOR *and speaks to*
CILLIAN.) Are you sure about burning this?

CILLIAN: Yes, it would destroy my mam and dad to read something like
that.

KEVIN: OK then. (*He sets the letter alight and holds it up as it burns. He then puts it on the ground and douses the flames with the ashes.*) May the spirits of this place look kindly on you, Seán. We will remember you with fondness and happiness and we won't let you be remembered as the gay guy that got kicked to death some weekend in Dublin. I'm going to make sure they know you had a name and that people loved you. You never got the chance to design a famous building like Frank Lloyd Wright or Gaudí, but we could get something built in your name . . . something to help people. Maybe a place for young gay kids that get kicked out of home or something . . . I don't know. But we'll do something grand for you. I promise you that, Seán. (*He puts the urn down and takes out a brown paper bag.*) I thought this would give us a laugh maybe . . . but now . . . Well, as I said earlier on . . . because I didn't know what we would be doing today and I wasn't even sure if anyone would be here, I just thought I'd bring something that was significant to Seán. Something that made him who he was, and so I went to the pound shop and I got this. (*He takes a lipstick from the bag.*) I was going to bury it or something, or I don't really know what, but now I'm thinking maybe it wasn't such a good idea . . . and I've put me foot it again . . .

(CILLIAN *smiles when he sees the lipstick.*)

CILLIAN: Kevin, you are all right. Do you know that?! You're an all right sort of bloke.

Paddy Casey's 'Bend Down Low' plays. CILLIAN *takes the lipstick and puts it on* KEVIN, *then puts it on* MAURA; *she takes the lipstick and puts it on* CONOR, *who takes it and puts it on* LEO *and kisses the top of his head; then* LEO *puts it on* BOB *and pops a bit on the end of* BOB's *nose just because he's* LEO. BOB *wipes it off but is only momentarily annoyed. Then* BOB *puts it on* CILLIAN. CILLIAN *sits down and puts the top on the lipstick. He plays with it in his hands, then he gets up and walks to the pile of ashes. He holds the lipstick for a moment as if he is about to put it in with the ashes, but then he turns and walks over to* BRENO. CILLIAN *puts lipstick on* BRENO, *hands him the lipstick and walks back to his seat.* CILLIAN *raises up his glass. Music fades. All raise their glasses.*

CILLIAN: To a new day.
ALL: To a new day!

          Fade lights.

Danny and Chantelle
(Still Here)

PHILLIP McMAHON

Danny and Chantelle (Still Here) was first presented at POD Nightclub, Dublin, on 18 September 2006 as part of the Dublin Fringe Festival, by Gentle Giant Productions and THISISPOPBABY.

CAST

Danny	Phillip McMahon
Chantelle	Georgina McKevitt
DJ	Sally Foran

PRODUCTION TEAM

Director	Deirdre Molloy
Producers	Louise Kiely and Phillip McMahon
Lighting designer	Sarah Jane Shiels
Stage manager	Jo Richards

CHARACTERS

Danny, *twenty, northside Dublin accent, wild boy but gentle*
Chantelle, *twenty, working class, big attitude, feisty, big-mouthed*

All other characters – Valerie (Danny's mother), Cornerstone bouncer, Tracey, Swiss-Tony, Kaco, Steo, Sinéad, Chris, the bank machine bird, the Asian doctor – are played by Danny and Chantelle.

The stage should be relatively bare, with all locations suggested. The original production used a live DJ onstage, mixing throughout. Images of the demolition of the Ballymun tower blocks were also projected.

The action takes place over one night through a mix of direct address to the audience and direct dialogue within real-time scenes. However, there are no acts and scenes as such, but rather discrete episodes, marked here by styled breaks.

DANNY *and* CHANTELLE *are onstage as the audience arrives.* DANNY *is dressed for a night out; most likely a tracksuit top and jeans.* CHANTELLE, *too, is dressed for a big night out; sovereign rings and hoop earrings. They are waiting at a bus stop – but it could be anywhere. They play ringtones on their mobile phones and take pictures of each other. The mood is light excitement for the night ahead.*

      A phone rings. DANNY *answers it.*

DANNY: Swiss-Tony! Story? . . . We're on our way now, bud . . .waitin' on a bleedin' bus . . . Tracey what? No way! . . .

CHANTELLE: What?

DANNY: (*Ignores* CHANTELLE) Ah! Hate that! (*Laughs*) So where is she now?

CHANTELLE: Who?

DANNY: Yes she will! . . . Never stopped her before!

CHANTELLE: Stopped who?

DANNY: (*Covering phone – addressing* CHANTELLE) Tracey. Stupid cunt broke her ankle, reckons she's not goin' out!

CHANTELLE: Ah! Hate that! (*Laughs*)

DANNY: (*Down the phone*) So who's with 'er?

CHANTELLE: Never stopped her before!

DANNY: Steo?

CHANTELLE: Is what?

DANNY: Is with her!

CHANTELLE: Is with Tracey?

DANNY: Yeah!

CHANTELLE: Steo?

DANNY: Isn't that what I said?! (*Down the phone*) So pal, where we headin' before POD?

CHANTELLE: Fuck, me keys!

DANNY: What about them? (*Down the phone*) No mate, I'm talkin' to Chantelle . . .

CHANTELLE: Fuckin' lost them . . . or left them . . .

DANNY: Call your ma and see . . . (*Down the phone*) And they're there now? Yes, mate, I'm talkin' to you!

CHANTELLE: (*Dials her phone*) Hello, Ma?

DANNY: What time will you make it in at?

CHANTELLE: Da, tell me ma I want her.

DANNY:　　　Right, right. We should hit the Corner Stone within the next half hour or so . . .

CHANTELLE:　Maria, tell me ma I want her.

DANNY:　　　Hang on . . .

CHANTELLE:　Ma, did I leave my keys there?

DANNY:　　　(*To* CHANTELLE) . . . How many yokes do you want?

CHANTELLE:　What, for tonight, or the weekend?

DANNY:　　　Whatever!

CHANTELLE:　(*Down the phone*) Maybe in me jacket pocket in the hall? (*To* DANNY) Whatever you're gettin'!

DANNY:　　　(*Down the phone*) I'll take ten off ya, bud!

CHANTELLE:　(*Down the phone*) They are?

BOTH:　　　Nice one!

CHANTELLE:　Thanks, Ma.

DANNY:　　　Right, see yiz in there in a while.

CHANTELLE:　No, Ma, I'm staying in Danny's . . .

DANNY:　　　Nah, it's no hassle . . . how much are they?

CHANTELLE:　Yes . . . His ma knows!

DANNY:　　　(*Surprised*) How much?

CHANTELLE:　She does!

DANNY:　　　No, no, it's cool!

CHANTELLE:　Riiiight, Maaa . . . niiiight!

DANNY:　　　Yeah, nice one . . . right, see ya . . . yeah, yeah, see ya in there . . . yeah . . . bye . . . bye.

ઝઝઝઝઝ

CHANTELLE:　(*Speaking directly to audience*) The bus bombs into town, or outta the flats more like. Running on adrenaline and fear, fuck diesel! The driver, who could use a suit of armour, looks suicidal! He obviously pissed some cunt off in Dublin Bus to be put on this shift, to be sent out this way. Before I've time to feel sorry for him a rock hits the side of the bus, scaring the shit out of the young one in front of us . . . (*To* DANNY) Ah Danny, there's Jacinta with little Shakira . . . (*Waves*) Hiyiz!

DANNY:　　　(*Directly to audience*) As the bus dips and drops, messy punters slip and slop on the back seats, hurlin' abuse at, and scabbin' smokes off, each other. They've weighty issues on their mind as they discuss the pros and cons of being joined at the hip, Siamese style. They're locked. It's only half eight, for fuck's sake. But that's OK. That'll be us in a few hours, as we blip blop our way into the morning. These back of the bus bastards are no different to us; just on a different shift . . . and different substances, of course. We pass McDonagh Tower. Wrapped in black. There's a funeral for the flats tonight. (*Pause*) We're still here.

༝༚༝༚༝༚༝༚

CHANTELLE: Jaaaaaay-son!

DANNY: (*To audience*) Walkin' up the road after swimming one day. I'd me wet togs and towel in a Crazy Prices bag. First year of the Comp, and I can hear this young one coming towards me. I take no notice 'cause she's looking for . . .

CHANTELLE: Jaaaaaaaaay-son! Waaaait for me.

DANNY: This is years ago . . . Nine or ten years ago . . .

CHANTELLE: Jaaaaaaaaaaaaay-son!

DANNY: Poor fuckin' Jason! I look back to see who's roaring, and get a schoolbag in the mush. (CHANTELLE *hits him with her bag. He falls.*) Me lip and me Crazy Prices bag busted.

CHANTELLE: Oh sorry! You've the same back as Jason!

DANNY: (*To* CHANTELLE) And you've the same face as me arse! Who the fuck is Jason?

CHANTELLE: Me cousin.

DANNY: And who are you?

CHANTELLE: Chantelle Satelle. (*She pulls him to his feet.*)

DANNY: (*To audience*) Cheeky bitch! (*To* CHANTELLE) I'm Danny Delaney.

CHANTELLE: (*To audience*) I gave him a can and a half of Bulmers to say sorry, and under a set of stairs, in some shite flats, over some fizzy apple loveliness, a friendship was forged. And that was nine years ago. Nine years buzzin'. Nine years laughin'. (*To* DANNY) Best mates, what?

DANNY: (*To audience*) She asked me for the ride when we were eighteen!

CHANTELLE: (*To* DANNY) No I didn't. (*To audience*) I didn't!

DANNY: Well, she wouldn't o' got it if she had've! But we're tight. I look out for her, and she looks out for me. (*Smiles*) Best mates!

CHANTELLE: (*Almost to herself, an afterthought*) Asked ye for the ride. Me hole!

⁓⁓⁓⁓⁓⁓

DANNY: (*To audience*) The bus empties on Parnell Square. There are gangs of smokers outside the Rotunda. Devastated aul' ones and expectant teens pull at cigarettes in the cold. A chorus of voices call over: Hiya, Chantelle.

CHANTELLE: Hiyiz!

DANNY: We cross over to the Ilac . . . where the unconscious go to shop. Where the dead, the dangerous and the depressed go to delve in discount outlets. Where the bored go to browse and the poor go to peruse.

CHANTELLE: (*To audience*) Danny's to find a hole in the wall. A drink link, he says in his best D4. It's pissin' down. I wait in the entrance to the Ilac. A bleedin' umbrella is what I lack. The fuckin' Ilac, I'm scarlet!

DANNY: Chan waits while I find a bank machine. Money for drink, money for yokes. The bastard rain is ruining the *gruaig*, and the young-one in front of me is in no hurry! (*To the stranger*) Are ye right?

CHANTELLE: (*As the bank machine bird*) Shit, didn't see you there!

(DANNY *nods, not listening.*)

CHANTELLE: (*As the bank machine bird*) This machine is only giving out fifties . . .

DANNY: Is it, yeah?

CHANTELLE: (*As the bank machine bird*) Hey, I know you!

DANNY: Do ya, yeah?

CHANTELLE: (*As the bank machine bird*) Yeah! We met at a party at Swiss-Tony's place!

DANNY: Did we, yeah?

CHANTELLE: (*As the bank machine bird*) Yeah! Don't you remember? We were all mullered and I was leading the Macarena! Is your name Daniel?

DANNY: (*To audience*) Is she for real? I look her up and down. She's fit. Annoying but! Mind wanders . . . I'd love to doggy that . . . big style! Relax, Danny, the night is young kid. But I've a horn on me now . . . (*To her*) Sorry what?

CHANTELLE: (*As the bank machine bird*) Is your name Daniel?

DANNY: Danny, yeah!

CHANTELLE: (*As the bank machine bird*) Well, Daniel, I'm going to Traffic, then to this party, minus the Macarena . . .

DANNY: (*To audience*) I'd have to kill her before I rode her!

CHANTELLE: (*As the bank machine bird*) . . . But you could come to this party, if you like? George's Street . . . South . . . cool place . . .

DANNY: Pills?

CHANTELLE: (*As the bank machine bird*) Sure! (*Beat*)

DANNY: Yeah . . . probably not . . . but give us your number anyway . . . you never know, darlin'!

ᘓᘐᘓᘐᘓᘐᘓᘐ

CHANTELLE: (*To audience*) Danny kicks rotten fruit as we stroll down Moore Street. My stomach tightens through Henry Street. Danny chats away as we cross the Ha'penny Bridge. *I'll see you at the water.* Stop in the arch. Pity the homeless pox. Genuinely do. Two euro from Danny. Poor fuck. I feel uneasy as hundreds of hens spill out of Temple bars. My stomach goes round and round. Danny buys chewing gum from Spar. On the outside, I feel lonely. As he jokes with the shopkeeper, I feel scared. I could puke right now . . . or go home. But I won't do either. This'll pass, it always does! We head up George's Street. Danny snaps me out of it. Tells me it's just pre-party nerves, and it is! Happens at this time every week. Danny, too, but not till later. I always feel like this and I always have a deadly night. Danny holds my hand.

DANNY: You look deadly, Chantelle.

CHANTELLE: (*To* DANNY) Shut up, Danny!

DANNY: (*Honestly*) You look deadly! (*To audience*) And she does. She looks deadly. She gets ready in my flat because her da doesn't like her going into town; he's overprotective or worried or something . . .

CHANTELLE: (*To audience*) . . . Or something is right! Get this . . . my da won't move out of our flat, can you believe that? We're next to be knocked and he just won't go! Sap! They've offered us a house in Balbriggan, but no! It's a house . . . like, why would you want to stay in the flats? There's something wrong with him . . .

DANNY: Chan has to lie every time she's going out. Says she's staying in my flat, where she stashes clothes, and my ma, assisted only by a GHD and an endless supply of Bacardi, does Chantelle up lovely and poses such questions as, 'That top is massive, Chantelle, where did you get it?'

CHANTELLE: I got it in London, Valerie.

DANNY: (*As Valerie*) London, Chantelle? Is that beside Japan in the Ilac?

CHANTELLE: (*To audience*) Valerie's a buzzer! She's getting ready herself tonight. There's a wake for the flats, and Christy Moore is playing. She says that she's hoping that Ian Dempsey'll sing, 'cause she's mad about him.

DANNY: Do you mean Damien Dempsey, Ma?

CHANTELLE: She does and we laugh.

DANNY: The Bacardi's kicking in and I watch the tiny hand of the clock count the seconds. Round and round. It's eight o'clock and the news is on the radio.

CHANTELLE: Valerie is shushing us to hear the stories.

DANNY: 104 leads with a story of French conjoined twins, Marie and Michelle . . .

CHANTELLE: Conjoined?

DANNY: Siamese, like. Joined at the hip.

CHANTELLE: Joined at the hoop!

DANNY: Joined at the . . . whatever. They're getting this operation tonight, to separate them. The chances of them both surviving are slim.

CHANTELLE: So why would they, then?

DANNY: (*To* CHANTELLE) Dunno. Sick of the sight of each other I 'spose. (*To his mother*) Marie and Michelle, that's their names, Ma, say a prayer for them. (*To audience*) She will, she says, and we head into the night tipsy on Bacardi and drunk on each other's company. Chantelle's phone goes and she ignores it – her da checking up on her.

CHANTELLE: (*To the audience*) My da used to be big into *Superman*. Can you believe that? The comics and the films, like. Loved them, he did; bought pictures and posters, an' all. Now he's a cunt. Grumpy cunt. Watches the new *Superman* on E4, switches over when you come into the room, pretends he wasn't watchin' it. Spa. Thought I heard him cryin' when he heard Christopher Reeve was dead.

DANNY: Your da's not a cunt, Chantelle. He's . . .

CHANTELLE: A cunt?

DANNY: . . . He's hurtin', Chan.

CHANTELLE: (*She knows this is true*) That's no excuse, Danny.

***

DANNY: (*To audience*) Camden Street and it's the same aul' shite on the door of the Cornerstone, it's the same every week. Round and fuckin' round! (*To bouncer*) We're here with Tracey.

CHANTELLE: (*As bouncer*) Tracey who?

DANNY: Her uncle owns it.

CHANTELLE: (*As bouncer*) What's his name?

DANNY: Mazzie! (*To audience*) So we get in, and he does, her uncle owns it! Cunt'd never give ya a free pint, though!

CHANTELLE: (*To audience*) Tracey, the hoo-er is looking gorgeous. She's sitting by the bar getting felt up by her Uncle Mazzie, giggling like a schoolgirl . . . her, not him! He's sweatin' buckets!

DANNY: Buckets of bleedin' lust!

CHANTELLE: It's sick.

DANNY: (*As Tracey*) Hiya, Chantelle!

CHANTELLE: (*Waves*) Hiya, Tracey . . . ye hoo-er. (*To audience*) Stools have been saved by Steo, fair play, but God love him, he looks like he's making his confo! He's delighted to see Danny. He thinks Danny's deadly, and Danny thinks Steo's deadly, too, so they're happy at the sight of each other. Steo's sister is out as well. Sinéad, she's only seventeen – sound but. She's mortified by Steo and I don't blame her. So that just leaves Swiss-Tony. No one's heard from him since Danny spoke to him on the phone.

DANNY: (*To* CHANTELLE) Sure, you could be all night waitin' on that cunt!

CHANTELLE: (*To* DANNY) He'll be here. (*To audience*) Swiss-Tony's a buzzer! Always has been!

DANNY: (*To audience*) Met him on our first E. The Temple. T-shirts off!

CHANTELLE: We were chattin' and dancin' with Swiss-Tony and his mates.

DANNY: Feedin' us pills an' all. For nothing'. Great buzz!

CHANTELLE: And there was this aul' fella . . . Mouldy, he was!

DANNY: (*To* CHANTELLE) Who?

CHANTELLE: Givin' Danny poppers an' all . . . having none of me!

DANNY: (*To* CHANTELLE) Was he?!

CHANTELLE: And Swiss-Tony butts in and warns Danny to beware of the chicken hawk.

DANNY: (*To* CHANTELLE) The what?

CHANTELLE: (*To* DANNY) That's what he said about your man. Beware of the chicken hawk. (*To audience*) Then it's outside, chewin' our faces off, and it's back to a party with Swiss-Tony. We spent the night on the couch of some hairdresser, with Swiss-Tony in between us, educating us on chickens, and chicken hawks, poppers and rimming, cock rings and anal beads! At about eight in the morning he pronounced us educated, and sent us home. He stored his number in my phone and told us to ring him the next day when our heads were wrecked, that he'd take us for a pint. We did and he did. We drank and chatted about the night before, and Swiss-Tony told us stories of other nights, in other countries; straight nights and gay nights, discos and raves. He said we were his new best friends and that he'd look after us. When we've needed looking after, he's been there, and it works both ways.

ᘔᘔᘔᘔᘔᘔᘔ

DANNY: (*To audience*) Me heart bleedin' bleeds for Steo. He can't take his eyes off Tracey, but she's busy being rubbed by Mazzie, who's the spit of your man Barry out of *EastEnders*. Dirty bastard gettin' a kick out of her cast an all, it's sick, but fair play, she's the only one who can get a drink out of him! Steo's gone, though. I'd love to say he's sick with love, but he's sick with the horn, or so he keeps saying!

CHANTELLE: (*As Steo*) I'd bang that all night, Danny!

DANNY: I know you would, pal.

CHANTELLE: (*As Steo*) No, I would, Danny, given half the chance. I'd bang her till she bled!

DANNY: That's my boy! (*To audience*) We sit and sink several pints. Did yiz hear about those Siamese twins? I say. They didn't, so I tell them, and it's great, shitin' out of us till the cows come home. There's no sign of Swiss-Tony with the yokes, but he'll be here. Cunt is probably off ridin'!

CHANTELLE: (*To audience*) I'd ride the hole off Danny, says Sinéad. I smile, but Tracey's pissing herself, a real fuckin' cuntish laugh! Gee-bag!

DANNY: (*As Tracey*) You'd have to go through Chantelle first!

CHANTELLE: What are you on about, Tracey? The painkillers must be making you talk shite! (*To audience*) Tracey laughs and Sinéad joins in, but Tracey's laugh . . . it's a fuckin' cuntish laugh!

DANNY: (*To audience*) Swiss-Tony texts with sordid details of the fuck he's just performed on some little knacker from Ballyfermot (his words, not mine). Dirty bastard! I text back with appropriate levels of disgust and admiration and suggest he wipes his dick in the curtains and meets us in POD pronto.

༄༅༄༅༄༅

CHANTELLE: (*To audience*) Camden Street's a nightmare. There are high heels hitting the Village, wankers heading to Whelan's, and pricks being refused from the Palace.

DANNY: (*As Tracey – leans in to* CHANTELLE) You know exactly what I'm on about.

CHANTELLE: Do I, Trace? (*To audience*) But I do. She's being a bitch, but yeah, I know what she's on about! The thing is, right? . . . look it . . . I was only looking out for me pal, yeah? You see, Danny used to go out with this young-one, Kaco was her name, she was a bleedin' knacker, she was, a dope. But . . . Danny liked her. No sense. In five months, I saw Danny once; keeping in mind he's to pass my block every day. Anyway, Steo told Tracey who told me that your woman, the bleedin' Kaco, wasn't too keen on Danny having friends who were girls. She was a dope; she was on a FÁS course in household maintenance. For two years. Two years to learn how to clean your bleedin' gaff? But Danny was into her for some reason. Anyway, in No-Name one day, and Tracey texts from the changing room to say that the Kaco is in the next . . . the next . . . cubicle? . . . the next . . .

DANNY: . . . Booth?

CHANTELLE: Booth! To say that the Kaco was in the next booth, and
              could I bring Tracey an 8 in the denim skirt. So I delivered
              the denim belt to Tracey, and I put my foot through the
              next curtain. Pulled the curtain back and there was the
              Kaco on a heap on the floor, all stunned, like, so I hopped a
              hanger off her head.

DANNY: (*As Chantelle*) It's like this . . .

CHANTELLE: . . . I told her.

DANNY: (*As Chantelle*) You being around is wrecking my bleedin'
              buzz, so fuck off away from Danny, right!

CHANTELLE: *Right!*

DANNY: (*As Kaco*) Right!

CHANTELLE: (*To audience*) She says all teary, little bit of snot, 'And you
              needn't go telling him about this neither, or I'll be forced to
              kick the snatch off ya! And one last thing . . . don't buy that
              bleedin' top, it looks poxy on ya!' The stupid thing is that it
              worked. She fucked off. Gave Danny no reason. He was
              gutted . . . Cross the Luas tracks now, Tracey filling Sinéad's
              head full of shite, Danny telling Steo about some bird he
              met at a bank machine . . . when did that happen?

                        ᘔᘔᘔᘔᘔ

DANNY: (*To audience*) I love telling Steo stuff, 'cause he's always full
              of admiration. That's a great feeling. Steo and me were born
              in the same hospital, and lived on the same floor of the
              same flats. Buds since babies, we are. Steo's granny croaked
              when we were nine. Good Friday, she went. Steo's da joked
              that she'd be back on Sunday, but she wasn't, and during the
              Easter holidays, Steo and Sinéad were moved to Rialto,
              where the granny's bed was still warm. I was allowed to ring
              Steo's house and when Steo was fourteen, he was allowed to
              come over our way, on the condition that my ma knew
              where he was. On his first day back, with a scissors and a
              rope, we robbed a horse. From the backfields, we took what
              wasn't ours and called her our own. It took ages to calm her,
              but once relaxed, we sat on her back, for ages, just sitting
              there. Chattin'. Talkin' a load of fourteen-year-old shite.
              Steo said we'd keep the horse in his garden in Rialto, but I

said we should sell it to a knacker. We named her Biddy, after the lovely one out of *Glenroe*. We rode her to the back of the airport and watched planes and made promises that we've kept. There were no secrets shared – I was saving them up for Chantelle – but hands were shook, and we agreed to never not be friends. I love Steo's company. I put me arm around him on the street. He flashes me a smile and calls me a faggot. I kiss him on the cheek, and run before he digs me.

☙☙☙☙

CHANTELLE: (*To audience*) No door shite at POD, lads know us. Sound.

DANNY: (*To audience*) We drop our coats in with some scorpy Chinky bird, who's having none of it when Tracey wants to put two items on one hanger, and plays her bad English card when Tracey suggests sticking the hanger up her hole. We leave the girls to it and head to the bar. It's early enough. The dance-floor is empty bar one trampy-looking yoke, giving it loads, lickin' the top of her WKD bottle every time she catches our eye. Steo says he'd ride her. You'd ride anyone, Steo! I say. But I agree! I'd ride her too. The night, my friend, I say, is young. You're a handsome man and you've plenty of time! I've me eye on Tracey, anyway, he says. (*Laughs*) I wish you luck, budster, you'll need it!

CHANTELLE: It's freezing inside, and I'd to listen to Tracey annoyin' that poor Chink in the cloakroom.

DANNY: Swiss-Tony arrives in all his gay glory, looking deadly, the cunt, he'll have young-ones dripping off him. He greets everyone with a kiss, which pisses Steo off no end.

CHANTELLE: (*As Steo*) I've warned you about *that* Swiss-Tony! . . .

DANNY: . . . says Steo.

CHANTELLE: (*As Steo*) You're makin' a show of us.

DANNY: Swiss-Tony thinks this is gas, which is why he does it, and it *is* gas. I'm laughing, the girls are laughing, and I tease Steo, suggesting that he'd only have a problem with it if there was a bit of the gay in him.

CHANTELLE: (*As Steo*) Fuck off, Danny.

DANNY: (*To Steo*) I'm serious, Steo, they've done these surveys and tests an' all that prove that homo-haters are actually homos themselves. So is there something you wanna' tell us, Steo? (*To audience*) He looks around to see everyone looking at him. We laugh and eventually this fuckin' eejit laughs. Swiss-Tony doles out the yokes and announces that the night *starts here!*

፨፨፨፨

CHANTELLE: (*To audience*) We've pills inside us and the come-up is slow; we drink our pints in silence. I hate this bit. The craic of the pub is long forgotten. We're in a limbo. Between places. Between times. It's like going on your holidays. You know where you're going is hot and colourful, but the delay at the airport is miserable. I want the heat. I want the colour.

DANNY: (*To audience*) Tracey only has to uncross her legs and lads are cummin' in their pants! It's her gift! Sinéad doesn't notice, or takes no notice, as she happily chats away to anyone willing, but I clock Chantelle looking at Tracey. If I didn't know her, I'd say it was a disapproving look, and it is, but it's fuelled by . . . it's pure fuckin' jealousy. Chan and Tracey go back years now. They swam together in St. Vincent's Swimming Club. Poxy club, if you ask me, but whatever floats your boat! Tracey is from Bertie's constituency, and well, Chantelle is not. There's no one raising a hand to claim where we live! Sleepovers were always in Tracey's gaff, and it was a rare occasion that Tracey pushed the button on a broken lift to call up to Chantelle. Nonetheless, they'd craic galore in Tracey's, doing girlie stuff, like? . . . well, you know . . . girls stuff, like . . . smelling fancy paper and fantasizing about the swimming instructor! He was only bleedin' massive apparently! I know all this because Chantelle has told me; she has shared the secrets of her heart with me. (*Pause*) Chantelle left the swimming pool one Saturday and realized at the bus stop that she'd forgotten her scrunchie. She went back, and inside the changing room, Tracey was getting rode by the instructor, the one who was bleedin' massive. Chantelle said nothing. She left her scrunchie and walked home. The following Saturday Chantelle stayed in the shower longer than anyone, making sure she was the last to get changed. Once she had waved goodbye to the last swimming clubber, she sat around in her birthday suit . . . waiting. Eventually the instructor came to clean the room.

CHANTELLE: (*As the instructor*) Chantelle . . .

DANNY: . . . he said, oblivious to her undress.

CHANTELLE: (*As the instructor*) Get dressed, petal, you'll catch a cold and miss your bus.

DANNY: She did. She got dressed. She caught a cold, and she missed her bus . . . and so a green-eyed monster was born!

CHANTELLE: (*To audience*) The come-up is slow and Danny's edgy. Pre-party nerves.

DANNY: Those fuckin' yokes tasted like hairspray. I've to keep swallowing to keep the vomit down, and I've a scorp on me 'cause Swiss-Tony wants five fuckin' euro a pop for them. We're his bleedin' mates, should be sortin' us out. Three euro at most! Fuck it. Fuck it . . . I fuckin' hate this bit. All in between. I might get another pint . . . I can't be arsed . . . I'm . . . I'm . . . I don't fuckin' know what I am. The craic of the pub is well fuckin' gone. We sit and wait. (*They wait*) And wait. (*They come up*) And . . . (*To* CHANTELLE) Wait till I tell ya, Chan –

CHANTELLE: It can wait, Danny . . .

DANNY: . . . Squeezing me hand . . . pulling me to the dance-floor.

CHANTELLE: Orange light kisses me eyes.

DANNY: Fuckin' love this track!

(*Music plays – David Guetta, 'Just a Little More Love'*)

CHANTELLE: (*Sings*)
Just a little more love,
Just a little more peace,
It's all it takes to live your dream,
We're walking hand in hand, you've got to understand
And one day soon we'll live in harmony.

DANNY: (*To audience*) Danny and Chantelle. Best buds. All lovely. Sweaty. Sweet. Souped up.

CHANTELLE: Eyes all half-closed an' heavy. Wrap around Danny. Face on his back. Arms around waist.

DANNY: Suck in the air, new an' fresh. Big botox gob. Smiley an' stiff. Double dropped. Impatient fuck. Double bubble.

CHANTELLE: Burnin' inside. Nice fire. Feel the beat, the base in me box.

| | Feet mixin' it up, all . . . all . . . |

DANNY: . . . Gloopy- . . .

CHANTELLE: . . . -Gloopy. Eyes wide. Chewing-gum gob. Body wakin'. Rubbin' shoulders. Danny and Chantelle, joined at the hip . . .

DANNY: Joined at the hoop . . .

CHANTELLE: Joined at the heart . . .

DANNY: All joined up and tangled . . .

CHANTELLE: Tangled in dance . . .

DANNY: Strangled by the tunes . . .

CHANTELLE: Faces mashed and mangled . . .

DANNY: Feet crashing through the air to the floor.

CHANTELLE: Sinéad arrives with water, and everyone's up on their pills. *Uisce* all round. We dance and chew to the tunes.

DANNY: Everyone looks fuckin' great. No bad buzz. Better than the pub. Fuck pints. Drink'll be the end of ya.

CHANTELLE: Steo's bleedin' mad out of it! Doesn't know where he is. Gas. Must've double dropped. Keeps trying to spell his name in the air. He's OK but. He's grand. Just away on his own little buzz.

DANNY: Sinéad is giving me proper loved-up smiles and is comin' in for more than her fair share of mad-out-of-it hugs. I'd say she wants some of the Danny boy. Cock all tingling. Not for Shinners though, sister of Steo an' all.

CHANTELLE: Danny's off on a wander. Says he'll be back with some water. Says he's grand, just going for a walk and a waffle. See ya so. Swiss-Tony is dropping circles and triangles all over the place. Little bitch loves himself. He's a bleedin' deadly dancer.

DANNY: Do a lap of the club. Love this bit. Every mad-out-of-it cunt, a friend for the night. No ice to be broken. Chat to whoever you like. Nothing better than a Bird's Eye potato waffle with a complete stranger. A fair swap of statistics: what's your name? Where you from? So on and so forth. Should be jottin' this down but, 'cause fucked if I'll remember it tomorrow!

CHANTELLE: Sinéad's tearing the head off some young fella. Fuckin' ride he is. Lovely smell off him and everything. Mad out of it. Sinéad asks him his name, but he doesn't know.

DANNY: (*As Swiss-Tony*) That's a steamer! . . .

CHANTELLE: . . . whispers Swiss-Tony. (*To Swiss-Tony*) Would you go way outta that, you're only bleedin' jealous!

DANNY: (*To audience*) Have a sit down with Tracey, who is out of action due to the gimped up leg. She's gulping a bottle of WKD, courtesy of some culchie. Says he was rude, so she told him to fuck off. (*Explains*) He bought her a drink, responding to her come-on, from Leitrim he was, up for the match. Bought her the WKD, says he'd love to see her naked! She says she'd love to sit on his face. He's getting all hot now, horny like, says he'd love to slide the WKD bottle up her hole . . . Those culchies are dirty bastards. She told him to fuck off.

CHANTELLE: (*As Tracey*) I wouldn't mind. . . .

DANNY: . . . Waving her casted leg like a finger.

CHANTELLE: (*As Tracey*) It was the fact that he didn't say please!

DANNY: That *is* a joke . . . I think.

CHANTELLE: (*To audience*) Sinéad's getting all stressed out 'cause Steo's givin' her fella dirty looks. Word in his ear and Steo promises there'll be no trouble.

DANNY: (*As Sinéad*) We had an agreement, Stephen.

CHANTELLE: (*To Steo*)Your sister's grand, Steo, she's having a good time. (*To audience*) But he's mad out of it. The young fella's name turns out to be Chris. I tell him not to worry; that Steo is just out of it, nothing personal.

DANNY: (*As Chris*) All attention welcome . . .

CHANTELLE: . . . lisps, Chris. I look to Swiss-Tony who mouths 'Steamer' behind his back. I don't bleedin' believe this!

DANNY: (*To audience*) I'm stuck with Tracey now, so it strikes me as a good idea to put in a good word for me bud, Steo. Buds, like. Tell her how lovely he is. That his tough man show is just an act. And how all anyone is looking for is love. And even though Steo, or Stephen, as I call him for the purpose of the exercise, even though Stephen seems like he's just out for a bit of gee, he's a real, sweetheart, y'know?

CHANTELLE: (*As Tracey*) Why are you telling me this?

DANNY: (*To Tracey*) 'Cause he likes you, like, y'know? Thinks you're the bee's knees, the cheese, the dog's dinner . . . nah that's . . . the dogs bollix . . . he thinks you're the (*Thinks*) . . . ace . . . of base . . . Trace!

CHANTELLE: (*As Tracey*) Danny, do you think 'cause I've a cast on me leg I'd suddenly ride you or Steo? I'm not a complete cripple! Come back to me when I've a plaster of Paris on me flaps!

DANNY: (*To Tracey*) Tracey, you smelly minge-bag. (*To audience*) I'm all hurt for me pal! (*To Tracey*) It's wheels you need on your flaps, stop them dragging off the ground! (*To audience*) She can fuck right off. Head to the bar.

CHANTELLE: (*To audience*) Sinéad is getting all fucked off with Swiss-Tony, 'cause he keeps trying to muscle in on Chris with the lisp – it's handbags at dawn.

DANNY: (*As Swiss-Tony*) It's a man-bag, Chantelle!

CHANTELLE: He's got one of those, y'know, across-the-shoulder-type yokes.

DANNY: (*As Swiss-Tony*) It's for me smokes, me yokes and me phone an' all, it's not my fault if Dolce and Ga-fuckin'- bbana are too lazy to put pockets on their jeans, chicken!

CHANTELLE: I'm enjoying the catfight, but Steo looks edgy, he's mad out of it, and I know that Swiss-Tony gets his goat at the best of times. Can't really read him. Deep breathing. Eyes open, then closed. Rub his shoulders. Comfort him.

DANNY: (*To audience*) Real bleedin' twins. Can't fuckin' believe it! Ordering water and the bar bitches are twins. Double bubble. So I get stuck into them about their mates. The French ones getting the op, or the chop, I dunno. Marie and Michelle are their names, do you know them, yeah? I say. They've no bleedin' idea what I'm on about! The conjoined, y'know? the Siamese, anyway, no worries, good luck to them, best wishes and so on! Give them my regards!

CHANTELLE: Sinéad and Chris are back on track; Swiss-Tony took the hint and dances with me. Chris is lovely; I smile for Sinéad. I close me heavy eyes, dreamin' a real light dream, clear thoughts. Swiss-Tony is massaging me neck and it's pushing me dream in a different direction every time. He squeezes tight. Eyes open, then closed, reverse blink. The dream is gas. Could have swore I just saw Steo getting stuck into his sister's steamer! *Open!* Open up! All open! Dream well fuckin' gone. Fuck me; Steo is wearing the face off . . . off fuckin' Chris! *Steo!* Trust Danny to miss this! Tracey the hoo-er's managed to catch it . . . Stunned. Steo comes up

for air. Everyone just staring. Strangers and all! Sinéad legs
it to the jacks. I fuckin' hate being a girl, means I've to go
with her. Grab Tracey.

DANNY: (*To audience*) I can't get the bank machine bird out of me
mind. It's only clicking with me now that she must've been
into me. She wouldn't have invited me to that party if she
wasn't. She was good-looking. And she fancied me! I'll text
her after the club, see if the offer's still on.

CHANTELLE: Three in a cubicle's a squeeze. Tracey's holdin' Sinéad's hair
back. (*To Tracey*) She's bleedin' crying, not puking, Trace.
(*To audience*) Mascara hoofin' down her face. Real Central
Bank lookin'. Don't know what to be sayin' . . . err . . . Steo's
just mental out of it . . . I'm sure he's not a bender, like. She
sobs and snorts some snot.

DANNY: (*As Sinéad*) He is!

CHANTELLE: She cries. Me and Tracey lean in so as to miss nothing. (*To
Sinéad*) He is what?

DANNY: (*As Sinéad*) He is 'a *gay*', but he promised he'd never go for
the same fella as me!

CHANTELLE: I look at Tracey, both knowing that we've just found the
confidential pot of gold at the end of the gossip rainbow.
Sinéad sniffles and rubs her mush, mixing mascara with
snot and tears. You look fine, I lie. The toilet bitch is roaring
at us to get out of the cubicle. I'm bursting. Get out, girls,
I've to piss.

DANNY: (*To audience*) Swiss-Tony catches me on the way to the
dance-floor. He can't wait to fill me in on 'The Adventures
of Steo the Super Queen'. Am I hearing this right? . . . Steo?
. . . fuckin' . . . bud of me whole life . . . a steamer? . . . Jesus!
Swiss-Tony says that Steo is having his first gay drama –
they're very common apparently. (*To Swiss-Tony*) Will you
give me a minute, Swiss-Tony!

CHANTELLE: I sit on the toilet for ages, but no piss comes. How do those
Siamese bints piss? I giggle, then realize, You're in a toilet,
Chantelle! Ssshh! I say. Where's Danny? Jesus, it would help,
when the squirt comes, if me knickers were down. The girl
in the next shed is having more luck than me. Not only can
I hear her loud and clear, but the smell is choking me. She's
excused, coming-up affects us all in different ways.

DANNY: (*To audience*) Find Steo in a corner. All Billy-no-mates.
              Feeling all, 'no one understands me'. Bruised ego, bruised
              pride . . . bruised bleedin' hole, for all I know! (*To Steo*)
              Snap out of it, Steo, stop feeling so bleedin' sorry for your-
              self; so you're a steamer?! You're shite with women anyway!

CHANTELLE: (*As Steo*) What's that, Danny?

DANNY: What's what? Which bit? You're a steamer . . . so what! Just
              means you might start getting on with Swiss-Tony . . . in
              fact –

CHANTELLE: (*As Steo*) Shut the fuck up, Danny, right!

DANNY: Settle, Steo, no one's putting it up to ya.

CHANTELLE: (*As Steo*) You can just fuck right off.

DANNY: Oi! I'm your fuckin' pal. I've no beef with ye being a bender.

CHANTELLE: (*As Steo*) Well, you'd be a fuckin' hypocrite if ye did.

DANNY: (*Taken aback*) Ye what?

CHANTELLE: (*As Steo*) Ye know what!

DANNY: (*To audience*) I don't know what . . . but I'm feeling great
              and nice and I was only buzzin' with me pal, and I just
              wanna sit beside him, and put me arm around him, and
              waffle . . . and just . . . sit there, you know?

CHANTELLE: (*As Steo*) The horse!

DANNY: (*To Steo*) Yeah?

CHANTELLE: (*As Steo*) Biddy!

DANNY: What?

CHANTELLE: (*As Steo*) When we had that horse, Danny. We'd sit all day
              long. God help me if I'm lying. We'd sit and talk shite, talk
              about wankin' and riding women.

DANNY: Yeah?

CHANTELLE: (*As Steo*) . . . And we kissed.

DANNY: No . . . we didn't!

CHANTELLE: (*As Steo*) Yeah we did! We fuckin' kissed –

DANNY: *Fuck off, Steo!* (*To audience*) Can't take this shit – shoving
              before I know what, don't mean it but. Makin' shit up. Fuck
              off, Steo, I say. Fist hits his mush. Fuck! Shut up. Catches me
              a nice one in the guts. All out of breath. Me bud. Can't trust
              fuckin' no one!

CHANTELLE: (*To audience*) I'm fixing me face at the mirror and this cunt
              is claiming she knows me. She's gee'd. You don't know me.
              You're mad out of it. You know everyone, I say. But she's

insistin'. This doesn't feel right. It'll come to me, she says. I do me lipgloss in the mirror and catch a look at her . . . it's come to her . . . and it's come to me too. It's the sister of the Kaco. I make for the door but she catches me by the hair. You've the wrong person. D'ye know Tracey? I say. She doesn't, and she doesn't care. I get the standard talking to about if you ever do this and that ever again, and then a punch, where a slap probably would've been enough! I'm sitting on a toilet, with your one standing over me. She's fat legs in a skirt, and she's . . . is it? She has shite on her leg! Was that you next door? You dirty bitch! I say. She holds me head up by the hair and spits in me face. Cunt. Me nose. My blood and her spit all over me face. Fuck this. No pain, though. That last half is just kicking in! I'm flying!

DANNY: Out on the street now. How did I get here? The cool air is nice on me face. Shit. Chantelle. Me phone rings and it's Swiss-Tony to say that Steo is raging. He says to switch off me phone and go after the bank machine bird. Says to find her and doggy her goodo in the name of Swiss-Tony! I can't, I say, not without Chan. He laughs. Are you gonna doggy 'er with Chantelle in the room? Go on ye sap, he says, I'll look after Chantelle. Turn off your phone or you won't hear the end of it with Steo. He's right and I will, turn off me phone but not before texting this posh bitch. Fucked if I can remember what she looks like. It's half three. How did that happen? She texts back straight away! You dirty bitch. She's already at this party. George's Street South, whatever that means. Address in me head. Phone off.

CHANTELLE: Danny, the fuckin' fuck face fucker has fucked off some-where. Stupid fuck. Fuckin' Swiss-Roll is covering for him, saying he'd a row with Steo, so he went on home. It's a lie. Danny would never let me go home on me own. An' anyway . . . we're out for the weekend! I call him, but his phone's off. Prick. Supposed to be me pal. Swiss-Tony says that he is bringing me to a party and that it'll all be fab. We'll keep trying his phone, he says. Everyone wants to know the sca about the bloodied face and before we know it I'm embel-lishing in a taxi on our way to Swiss-Tony's apartment to pick up more drugs.

DANNY:　I'm staring at Superman, getting me dick sucked. Fair play to ye, Danny. Keeping it hard on yokes. That's me boy. She hasn't said a word to me yet, which is great. Not one. It's like a porno . . . or somethin' French. Fuckin' great. In the bathroom of this party on George's Street, a poster of Superman on the wall. Two supermen squaring up to each other! One getting his dick sucked! Who's the superhero now? Chantelle's da is into Superman. He'd love this poster. The detail. I'll take it home for him. That'd be shite of me. Fuck these cunts, they can afford another one. Then I hear a voice I kind of recognize . . .

CHANTELLE:　(*As the bank machine bird*) Everything OK?

DANNY:　Fuck! It's soft. I've gone bleedin' soft in her mouth thinking of Chantelle's da. That's sick . . . I think! (*To bank machine bird*) I'm fine, the yokes, ye know? Err . . . deadly BJ, though.

CHANTELLE:　(*As the bank machine bird*) It's grand, happens all the time; wanna get a drink?

DANNY:　Er, yeah . . . (*To audience*) Happens all the time? *Slut!*

CHANTELLE:　(*To audience*) Steo's not letting up about Danny, saying what a prick he is, and how mates don't start on mates for no reason! (*To Steo*) He must've had a reason, Steo, you've the ability to be a prick yourself at the best of times. Chantelle, he says, I don't mind telling you to fuck right off. Swiss-Tony is pouring drinks and telling us all to shut the fuck up and relax. He's right, we've no reason to be fighting. If Danny was here, we'd be fine. I wink at Steo, we cheers and knock back our vodka and cokes. Tracey is rubbing Sinéad's back in the toilet. Swiss-Tony is only too happy to top up our drinks, saying he'll be making vodka and double coke, returning with full glasses and rows of white lines.

DANNY:　(*To audience*) Turns out, the sap who owns the apartment works in Forbidden Planet! I mumble something about having better things to be doing with me time, but no one's joining in, so I let it go. There are comics all over the place, *Batman* and *Superman* mostly. He's got *Planet of the Apes* figures and rows of DVDs: *Star Trek, Babylon 5, X-Men, Will and Grace*. He's a whole wall of his sitting room painted like the *Superman* symbol. Shite bag. The posh yoke brings me a vodka and coke. We chat. She's OK.

CHANTELLE: Blue WKD equals blue vomit. Makes sense. Still funny but. I've taken over from Tracey in the jacks. Sinéad's shitin' out of her between retches. She's flyin' but she's had too much to drink, and she's upset about her brother ripping her off. Hold her hair, rub her back, I must be flying too, 'cause I feel real close to Sinéad. Protective. Want everything to be OK for her, tell her that if Danny was here, he'd rub her back too.

DANNY: (*As Sinéad*) That'd be nice.

CHANTELLE: (*To Sinéad*) It's a shame that he fell out with Steo, Sinéad. Bad buzz . . . probably back in his bed nursing a bruised ego.

DANNY: (*As Sinéad*) You really haven't a clue, Chantelle, have ye? Danny's in bed all right, the bed of some yoke he met at a bank machine.

CHANTELLE: What?

DANNY: (*As Sinéad*) He can't even tell his best mate when he's scored, especially after the whole Cracker thing.

CHANTELLE: Do you mean Kaco?

DANNY: (*As Sinéad*) Whatever . . . Tracey filled me in . . . Jesus, Chantelle, talk about marking your territory. Why didn't you just piss on him?

CHANTELLE: (*To audience*) Blue spew. I carefully place her hair *in* the toilet bowl. She's wrecked. Fuck 'er . . . what bleedin' young-one at the bank machine?

DANNY: (*To audience*) The young-one's name is Oonagh, and she's deadly. She introduces me to people as Daniel, and tells them how she wooed me on the street. I turn on my phone and there's sixteen new messages, one from Chantelle saying I'm a cunt and fifteen from Steo . . . saying I'm a cunt, but I don't care, I'm having a deadly time. This gorgeous young-one is sitting between my legs and chatting to me and her mates, chatting to me like I was her boyfriend. Holdin' me hand an' all. All thoughts of doggying her to the back of me mind, making room for nice thoughts, like smelling her hair and ringing her tomorrow and stuff.

CHANTELLE: Tracey is off her gee on coke and decides that everyone should listen to her listing off the names of all the guys she's fucked. It's a long list and she's proud of it. Swiss-Tony puts his arm around her and tells her to sit down and have a drink, take the edge off the coke, but she's having none of it. She pushes him away and grabs a crutch to stand up.

DANNY: (*As Tracey*) Everyone was looking at the menu. But no one wanted to eat!

CHANTELLE: She is absolutely gee'd. She's chewing the face off herself and her cast is stained blue by WKD. Steo can't help himself, he pisses himself laughing, not just a snigger, a big bleedin' belly laugh. (*To Steo*) You bad bastard, Steo, no one was laughin' at you!

DANNY: (*As Tracey*) The only one who wanted me tonight was you Steo . . . and you turned out to be a faggot! And that's depressing on every level. But a shag is a shag, so you'll do.

CHANTELLE: (*To audience*) Steo is still and silent, like his pride has been sucked out of him. Tracey is bang out of line and no one is saying nothing. Tracey collapses onto the couch. Steo gets up and puts on his jacket. Still no one says anything. At the door now, Steo turns back as if to say goodbye, but doesn't, instead he says . . .

DANNY: (*As Steo*) . . . Yous are supposed to be my mates. You've made a cunt of me. My sister is seventeen. Seventeen! She looks up to you fuckers. Look at her, shit man, look at yous! What the fuck did I do? You can tell Danny he's a prick. I'm a fuckin' prick.

CHANTELLE: Steo helps Sinéad out the door, and there's crying. In my head I'm hoping it's Sinéad and not Steo. Swiss-Tony throws a dressing gown over Tracey, who was impolite enough to sleep through Steo's response to her kind offer. Swiss-Tony says not to let all this ruin our night, he just needs my phone to make a call and then we're off to this party. But I'm a bit over it. I'll share a taxi to town. And then some air might be good.

DANNY: (*To audience*) Turns out we've something in common. Marie and Michelle, the stuck-together twins soon to be separated. Not only does Oonagh know about them. But she knows more than the Danny Boy knows. She knows their second name and pronounces it in a French accent. The fuckin' horn! She knows how many kidneys they have between them, two, and she knows that half five is the moment of truth. *Sky News*. She has her alarm set. I tell Oonagh that they're tearing down the flats this mornin' as well. She says she doesn't know what that means . . . and neither do I! Her alarm beeps and it's not my place but I turn down the music and turn up the TV. Oonagh shushes the madouvits while I do me best to fill them in, get them up to speed on why we're watchin' *Sky News*. Marie and Michelle . . . If I've to say it one more fuckin' time! Where the fuck have I left Chantelle? She'd get great craic out of this. I call her but her phone is engaged. She'll be raging, but fuck it. Oonagh sits back in my lap and we kiss away the ads, then it's title sequence, intro, and an Asian lady in doctor's gear, looking wrecked, speaking into a hundred microphones . . .

CHANTELLE: (*As the Asian doctor*) . . . After a lengthy operation, the French conjoined twins, Marie and Michelle D'Argent, have been successfully separated, both are in good health and look forward to pursuing their separate lives.

DANNY: The room erupts, and we kiss like it's New Year's Eve and everyone is happy. I'm genuinely happy.

CHANTELLE: We're back in a taxi and Swiss-Tony won't get off me bleedin' phone. I can hear the call, waiting, going bleedin' mad. That'll be Danny the cunt telling where I've to meet him, but Swiss-Tony is chatting and repeatin' the address 'cause he's no pen. Remember this, Chantelle! he keeps saying. Right! The taximan takes us to George's Street South. He's finally off me phone, and we're at the apartment block. I'll leave you here, Swiss-Tony, I say. Kiss kiss, tight hug. A walk is what I need. Head to the water.

DANNY: When the doorbell goes, I answer it. It's none other than Swiss-Tony, ye gay bollix. Should've known that bleedin' Forbidden Planet head was a super-steamer! Great to see you and so on. Where's Chantelle?

CHANTELLE: I fix me hair in the window of Dunnes. They say all things lead to the water. The Centra on Dame Street looks worse for wear. Was it a heavy night? Cut through Temple Bar. 24hr e-mail café. Play games all night for a tenner. Why? Across the square. Street sweeper. Pity you, buddy! Probably shouldn't. Sing a little song, 'cause no one's around. Homeless pox still in the archway. Poor fuck. Breaks me bleedin' heart! Alone on the Ha'penny Bridge. River. Flowing through me.

DANNY: Corner Oonagh to tell her I'll be back, and maybe I will. Swiss-Tony's getting stuck into some mincer in the kitchen. I'll text him. Stand on George's Street South . . . 'cause it's south of the river. Stand and listen. Nothing. Disco Rick's is closed on the corner. All burgered out! Cross over Central Bank. Mascara crew are fasty wasty. She said: I'll see you at the water. Pal Joey's – Bad Ass – pizza once, bad buzz. Crown Alley, poor cunt. Have you the price of two cups of tea, buddy? – I ask him. Too bleedin' right, I gave it to him earlier. Centra for tea. Ha'penny Bridge. High tide. To do with the moon. Boardwalk. River Liffey. I see her and she sees me.

CHANTELLE: We sip tea. We sit and sip. (*Long pause. To* DANNY) It was a mad night, Danny.

DANNY: (*Smiles*) They all are, Chantelle!

CHANTELLE: (*Smiles. Pause. To audience*) We sit and sip and suck in a new day.

DANNY: (*To audience*) Danny and Chantelle.

CHANTELLE: Joined at the hip.

DANNY: Joined at the hoop!

CHANTELLE: Still here!

THE ECSTASY OF TOMORROW
1987—2010

Niall Sweeney

01. 1,000 FUTURE GENDERS powderbubble 1997

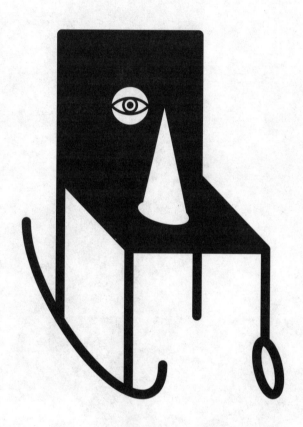

03. G.L.O.R.I.A. PANTI THE STORY OF 'O' 2007

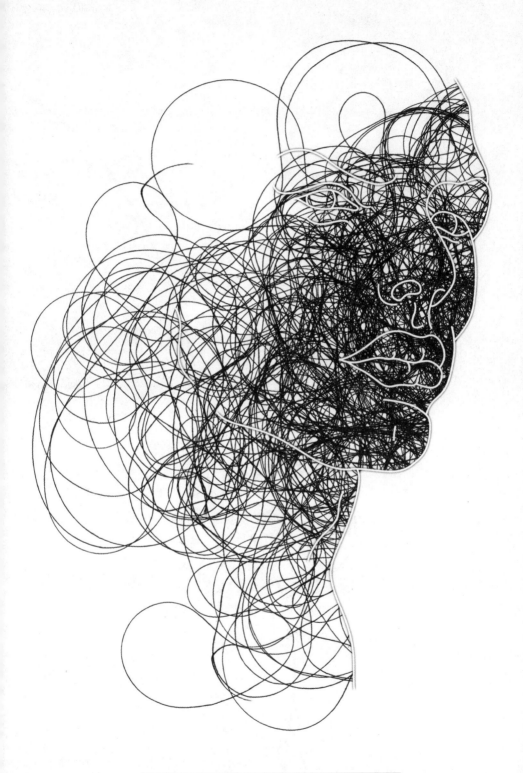

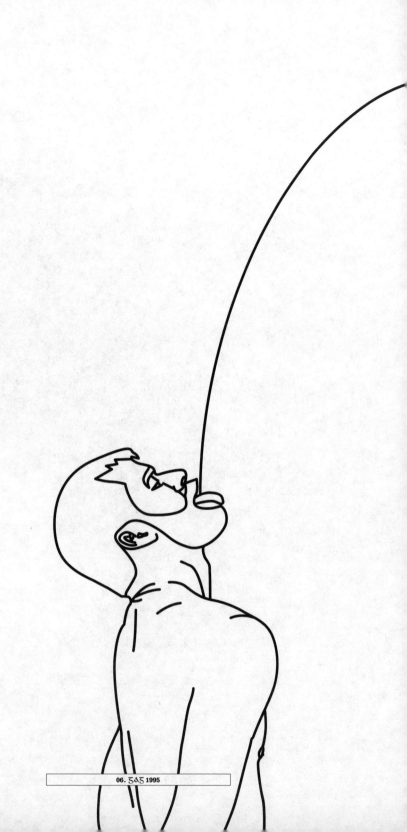

06. БАБ 1995

07. PANTI ALTERNATIVE MISS IRELAND - AMI XIV 2008

08. PETITES-MAINS [TONY FLYNN] REVOLVER 2009

10. MISS SHIRLEY TEMPLE BAR ∆MI 111 1997

11. MISS DEMEANOUR RATHMINES ∆MI 1 1987

13. KAERMY WHITE powderbubble 1997

14. MISS VEDA BEAUX RÊVES ∆MI V 1999

12. MAN IN A P-SUIT ᚷᚨᚷ 1996

15. KITCHEN CROWD (THE LADY CITY) GRISTLE 2001

16. MISS HEIDI HONNT ΛM1 ƆC1 2005

20. powderbubble 1997
21. ROSEBUD ЗДБ 1996

ALL IMAGES: Niall Sweeney

ADDITIONAL PHOTO CREDITS: 03, 04. Marcus Lynam / 07. Eamonn Doyle / 10, 14, 16. Mary Furlong / 08, 19. Fiona Morgan & THISISPOPBABY / 13, 20. Trish Brennan

Victor and Gord,
Ali and Michael

ÚNA McKEVITT
with cast

This version of *Victor and Gord, Ali and Michael* was first presented at the Project Arts Centre, Dublin, as part of the Queer Notions festival, run by THISISPOPBABY and Calipo, on 24 June 2009.

CAST

Ali	Ali Barron
Michael	Michael Barron
Victor	Vickey Curtis
Gord	Áine McKevitt

PRODUCTION TEAM

Conceived and directed by Úna McKevitt
Devised by Úna McKevitt, with cast

The movement of this piece is informed by the personal dynamic of the pairs which emerged during the devising process. VICTOR *and* GORD, *for instance, are not very comfortable looking at each other in performance. When early in the show they tell the audience where they lived in relation to each other growing up (*VICTOR'*s house is behind* GORD'*s),* VICTOR *moves upstage right saying, 'My house was here.'* GORD *stays downstage left, saying, 'My house was here.' During the show they return to these positions frequently to represent the proximity of their past homes, while also allowing them to maintain a comfortable distance from each other in performance. The one time they do look at each other is during the scenario 'If I was Vickey/If I was Áine'.*

ALI *and* MICHAEL *like to look at each other and like to be beside each other as much as possible. They are directed to move towards the audience when they are speaking but otherwise can move anywhere in the space.*

When the pairs talk among themselves, they tend to form a line in the middle of the stage.

During this production there was no set and no props other than the water bottles the participants brought out onstage with them. The stage is very well lit with a general wash. There are only two lighting transitions; during the introductions centre stage is lit; however, once VICTOR *moves to her house all the lights come up. Near the end, when* ALI *and* MICHAEL *begin 'Michael's room/Ali's room', the lights come down again to fill only the centre of the stage.*

There are no acts or scenes, but rather episodes, marked here by styled breaks.

ALI: Hi, I'm Ali and this is my brother Michael. We're a year and four months apart in age. We grew up in Carrickcloney, Glenmore, Co. Kilkenny.

MICHAEL: We're the youngest two in a family of six. Our older brother and sisters left home when we were quite young, so we were kind of like a second family: Ali, me, Mam, Da and our granny.

ALI: And when we were little, we used to like to pretend that we were twins.

VICTOR: Hi, how's it going? I'm Victor, born Victoria Elizabeth Margaret Mary Jessica Curtis, and this here is Gord. (VICTOR *motions in* GORD's *direction.*) Gord is short for Gorgeous. I'll let yiz make your own minds up about that one, though. Her real name is Áine McKevitt.

GORD: The reason we're here tonight is because my sister, Úna, who christened us the names Victor and Gord, had seen a picture of us in my bedroom in our school uniforms when we're about sixteen, like this . . . (VICTOR *and* GORD *put their arms around each other, slouching in a teenage way.* VICTOR *has a manic grin on her face;* GORD *looks sullen.*) . . . and thought it would be interesting to explore further our friendship, which she describes as frustrated, constipated and intense.

MICHAEL: We're here also because of a photograph. Úna saw a picture of Ali and me on Facebook, and in the picture we're doing this . . . (ALI *and* MICHAEL *face each other and, crossing their arms, hold each other's hands*) . . . having a bit of a swing. It was at a family do two years ago in Kennedy Park in Wexford. We still don't know exactly what Úna saw in the picture but she became a little obsessed by it. She used to message me on Facebook quite a lot, come up to me in Pantibar, saying, 'Oh, I really love this picture.' I'd see her coming and try to hide. For some reason or another we've found ourselves here tonight. I'm really interested in other people's lives, in other people's stories but I was quite anxious about doing this because I thought standing up here in front of people might seem a little self-indulgent.

ALI: I had more fears about it. I was kind of worried that something would come out along the way that would cause our relationship to alter forever. So I had some reservations about that.

VICTOR: When we did it first, I didn't know what to expect either, I was really confused about it, and I still am.

GORD: I had no idea what was gonna happen.

VICTOR: I mean, everyone has friends, this is just an insight into another kind of friendship.

GORD: Originally I pictured that me and Vickey would be sitting on two stools and our voices would be played overhead, there'd be a lot of movement and action and not very much talking. We grew up next to each other . . .

VICTOR: . . . It was Ballinclea Heights; it was Killiney.

GORD: My house was here . . . (GORD *stays downstage left.*)

VICTOR: And my house . . . (VICTOR *runs upstage right.*) . . . was here. Between my front garden and Áine's back garden there's a playground.

GORD: It's not really a playground any more, it's just more of a little park now.

༜༜༜༜༜༜

VICTOR: I'm trusting, I'm very trusting. It's a flaw, it can be a flaw. I trust my friends because they're my friends.

ALI: We had these neighbours growing up; they were kind of like our best friends. Their names were Kevin and Ciara, and we played with them nearly every evening.

MICHAEL: Their father was really hot. Really tanned and he always had great hair, an absolutely perfect quiff. In many ways he was my early style icon.

ALI: When we played together, if we were painting they would say . . .

ALL: *. . . Painting, painting, painting . . .*

            (*Everyone moves their right hand up and down in a painting gesture while they chant this.*)

ALI: And if we were running, they would say . . .

ALL: *. . . Running, running, running . . .*

            (*Everyone runs.*)

MICHAEL: Ali and I always hated going to dinner in their house. They only ever seemed to eat shepherd's pie or sausages. And when you'd sit down at the kitchen table, there was this fly paper that hung over the table, so you'd be sitting there eating your dinner with thousands of dead flies staring at you.

ALI: As Kevin got older and became more self-sufficient, he was really good to his mum and dad and one day our mum saw him driving down the road in his new car with a trailer attached to it with a spanking new washing machine for his mum in the back. Our mum immediately phoned me and Michael to say, 'Well, maybe you shouldn't have gone to college after all, maybe you should have got a trade instead.'

MICHAEL: I remember really feeling that dig.

GORD: So, you go out my back door, down my back garden, out my back gate and you're in the playground. My house is there . . . (*Points to where she was standing downstage left*) . . . and Vickey's house is there . . . (*Points to where* VICTOR *is standing upstage right. During the playground scenario,* GORD *moves freely in the space.*) In the playground there were a set of monkey bars that when we were very small we'd crawl over and then when we were bigger we'd walk over them. There was two single metal bars in the playground that we'd do forward rolls and backward rolls on. There was a big, or what seemed big at the time, boat and we used to play, like, boat games on that. One of our friends thought she could go to the front of the boat and jump and somersault in the air and dive into the water, but because there was no water, the poor girl just went head first into the ground and really hurt herself. There was also, where Michael and Ali are standing, a big piece of tarmac and every Halloween we'd have a bonfire and do the hokey-cokey around that. There was a set of wooden kind of blocks that went up in a kind of pyramid and we'd play 'King of the castle, get down you dirty rascal' on that. There was also a singular wooden block where Michael Harbourne made nettle soup one time. Down towards the end of the playground towards Doug's house there was lots of bushes and trees that ran all the way along, and every summer, or what seemed like every summer, we may have only done it once, we'd clear out all the leaves and twigs and set up a den, a camp kind of thing, and behind that there was a garden with an orchard which was very exciting. This part of the playground came in handy when we got a little bit older, and by older I mean sixth class, fifth class, fourth class even, 'cause our parents couldn't see us and we'd started hanging around with four boys; we were four girls, so we'd pick a number between one and four and whoever's number you got you had to kiss, or in Vickey's case, snog.

MICHAEL: Unlike their dad, Kevin and Ciara were kind of postcard Irish; they'd red hair and freckles and every summertime when we'd go out in the sun they'd get so sunburnt they'd get blisters all over their bodies.

ALI: When we would argue, me and Michael would wage a violent war of words, saying such things as 'Get off our property.' They would respond by rolling cow dung into balls and throwing it at us.

MICHAEL: Every summer our cousins from Athlone would come down to visit and because we were country folk, people from Athlone seemed kind of exotic and streetwise. So when they'd come to visit, we used to dress up an old shed like a house of horrors, which included getting our little cousin to dress up as a witch and put him into a barrel and we'd force Kevin and Ciara into the shed and scare the absolute shit out of them. Then to add insult to injury we'd turn a hose pipe on them as they ran screaming down the road.

ALI: Kevin recently got married and when he stood up to make his speech at his wedding, he opened his speech with, 'When we were young, we had no friends and no one to play with, so we always played on our own.'

VICTOR: In front of my house there's a cul de sac where all the cars would come and turn around and then, if you turn right outside my front door, walk to the end of my street, swing a left and walk up the hill, you're on Áine's road. In front of you there used to be this big reservoir, an enclosed one. They've flattened it and turned it into a millennium park with all fancy things in it like basketballs courts and cement tennis tables and things, but when we were kids, it was only slopes and a couple of bunkers. It was great to get up there when we were thirteen or fourteen; our parents couldn't really see us up there at all and if you were in the bunkers, nobody could see you. We used to have cheeky fags, cheeky cans, cheeky snogs, if you were lucky . . .

GORD: Or Vickey . . .

VICTOR: The Res was all sloped and in the winter we'd go tobogganing down the slopes; some people had toboggans, other people had plastic or pieces of carpet; it was great craic. On the grounds of the reservoir there was a pump house and we used to have to jump across onto the roof. We thought the gap was huge, like the Grand Canyon, but it was probably only six inches wide; we thought we were 'mad'. I told Áine one time I'd jumped off the pump house roof; she proceeded to do so, fell on her back, really hurt herself and I had to 'fess up and say I hadn't jumped off it.

MICHAEL: Áine would like you all to know that she didn't jump because Vickey told her to jump; she jumped because she wanted to jump.

VICTOR: And I never did do it either.

ひひひひひひ

ALI: I have a favourite photograph of me and Michael when we're little. It was taken during winter, so we'd big coats on and hats and we're all snuggled up in it. I think it's my favourite photograph because it's really dark and you can't really see what's going on in it, really, and I've always looked at it wanting to know what's going on.

GORD: When we got bored of the Res, we moved on to the backfield. Dave Coffey denies this, but I'm pretty sure he moved us from there because his parents could hear us; so we moved to Mullin's Hill where we had a night of Free Love.

ALI: Free Love. Free Love was when Áine and Vickey and their friends would get together for a night of drinking and snogging; the girls would kiss the girls, the boys would kiss the boys, but not too many boys kissed boys.

GORD: We actually only did Free Love once but talked about it so much it seemed like we did it every weekend.

VICTOR: And I actually wasn't there; I was in Amsterdam making my own kind of Free Love.

ALI: (*Raps, as if to Jennifer Lopez's song 'Jenny from the Block*)
I know you all think that I'm a phoney,
but I'm still Ali from the Cloney.
I used to have little, now I have some moe-nee,
but I'm still Ali from the Cloney.

❧❧❧❧❧

Performers recite jumbled lines about themselves and each other.

ALI: She's funny. She's caring. She's just very warm.

GORD: She gives good hugs apparently.

VICTOR: He makes himself do things. He wants things to be better for people than they are.

MICHAEL: As a teenager, she could recite the movie *Sixteen Candles* line for line.

VICTOR: It took her a long time to get here. She didn't like herself for a while. She kind of likes herself now.

GORD: She's good at cooking, entertaining, cheering people up; she's very good at that.

ALI: She always felt more comfortable with boys and men growing up; she just preferred their company.

MICHAEL: She'd like to think she's good at her job, but she's just not sure.

ALI: She remembers when Elvis died; she was three nearly four. Everyone in the house was crying and it was really interesting as a kid looking at all these adults crying and not knowing why; and it was because Elvis had died.

GORD: She can laugh at herself in a good way, not in a negative way. She can laugh. She can have fun.

VICTOR: She can make a show of herself, but she's come to terms with it.

MICHAEL: His idea of an absolute nightmare is just sitting around drinking and smoking spliffs – somebody says something witty or funny and then it's your turn. The whole thing just seems so contrived and so forced.

≈≈≈≈≈

Everyone sings quietly a line from 'Heartbreak Hotel'.

All: 'I been so lonely, baby, well I'm so lonely. I been so lonely I could die.'

≈≈≈≈≈

MICHAEL: There's a picture of our mam and dad in the 1960s that I really love. They're all dressed up; they're going to a dance and my dad's helping my mam into the car and she looks really beautiful, she looks like Elizabeth Taylor.

ALI: Our mum is really beautiful, but it reminds me; there's a picture hanging in our house at home that I really hated, it's a really, really horrible picture of me. I was trying to get my mum and dad to take the picture down and my dad just couldn't understand at all and he said to me, 'Sure, who do you think you are? Jaysus, you're no Elizabeth Taylor.'

MICHAEL: We had a surprise fortieth wedding anniversary for them a few years ago. It was quite rare to have a party in our house at that stage. When we were growing up, it was quite common the house would always be full of people, but at that stage we'd all left home and it was just the two of them living in the house together. So, anyway, we pulled together this surprise anniversary party for them with all their old friends together, their brothers and sisters and neighbours and all of that. We were all out on the lawn and at one point I saw Mam and Dad together and they looked really happy with each other and it just really struck me, so I climbed up onto the table and looked down at them and took a picture. I really love it; they're in their seventies now, they were in their late sixties at the time, and they look really happy and in love with each other.

ALI: For their fortieth wedding anniversary our sister had a cake made and she brought it home from England. The cake was made from a wedding photograph, so it was in the shape of a Morris Minor car and it had little pastry figures, so there was a pastry figure of our dad lounging casually on the bonnet of the car and our mum sat gracefully on the ground with her dress draped all around her. At the party no one dared touch the cake. But, by the next day, we all really wanted a slice, so we decided to dig in and I have this lasting memory of our little niece with the pastry figure of my mother head first in her mouth.

MICHAEL: In our family we've all these snapshots and great memories we like to talk about but there's always been all the messy bits as well and sometimes I wish I could look back and just remember the snapshots and forget all the messy bits.

రుసరుసరుసరుస

VICTOR *and* GORD *run to their 'homes' or stay in their 'homes' if already there.*

GORD: Vickey's house had a porch.

VICTOR: Áine's house had a toasted cheese sandwich-maker.

GORD: Vickey's house had a closet under the stairs.

VICTOR: Áine's house had a high stool.

GORD: Vickey's house had a string on the downstairs bathroom to turn on the light.

VICTOR: Áine's house had a downstairs bedroom.

GORD: Vickey's house had lots of nice food.

VICTOR: Áine's house had a glass door and panels going into her sitting room.

GORD: Vickey's house had a silence button on her phone.

VICTOR: Áine's house had wooden stairs.

GORD: Vickey's house had lots of footage of her eating beans on toast as a child.

VICTOR: Áine's house had bunk beds.

GORD: Vickey's house had a disgusting yellow quilt.

VICTOR: Áine's house had a dog.

GORD: Vickey's house had sliding doors in the kitchen.

VICTOR: Áine's house had a pay phone.

GORD: Vickey's house had Michael Jackson's *HIStory* album.

రుసరుసరుసరుస

GORD: Michael met Jaime on Gaydar.

MICHAEL: Jaime sings to Michael.

GORD: Michael can say things in this relationship that he could never say before. Michael trusts Jaime with insanity. Michael and Jaime have a dog called Sailor.

VICTOR: Ali met her partner, Vin, when she was a teenager. They're together nearly eighteen years. Michael introduced them in the family pub. Vin was Ali's first boyfriend who wasn't gay.

ALI: Vin makes Ali laugh.

VICTOR: Vin and Michael are Ali's best friends. She calls them her boys.

ᘔᘓᘔᘓᘔᘓ

GORD: When me and my sisters were growing up and grown-up, in fact, we were obsessed with who had the biggest head in the family. We all have quite large heads. Between ourselves we had a measuring technique that we'd do with one another on quite a daily occurrence to see who had the biggest head. I'll show you with Michael . . . (GORD *and* MICHAEL *follow* GORD'*s instructions.*) We'd put our chin to chin, nose to nose, go up and check whose goes the highest. In our families it was quite hard to decide, as some foreheads are straight and some go back. No one would ever admit to having the biggest head.

VICTOR: One of the McKevitt sisters actually had to get her graduation hat from college expanded because her head was so big.

ᘔᘓᘔᘓᘔᘓ

GORD: If I was Vickey, I wouldn't be so paranoid or sensitive about throwaway comments I make about her.

VICTOR: If I was Áine, I wouldn't be so worried about our friendship.

GORD: If I was Vickey, I wouldn't make me feel like a bimbo sometimes.

VICTOR: If I was Áine, I'd be less OCD.

GORD: If I was Vickey, I wouldn't drink so much.

VICTOR: If I was Áine, I'd get off my high horse.

GORD: If I was Vickey, I wouldn't feel the need every time I made a cup of tea to mention I was a lesbian.

VICTOR: And if I was Áine, I'd get my leg over more often.

MICHAEL: Both Áine and Vickey are single, by the way.

ᘔᘓᘔᘓᘔᘓ

MICHAEL: When we were growing up, my room was here . . . (*Indicates where he is standing; it doesn't matter which side each of them are on. Their rooms were parallel.*)

ALI: And my room was about here . . . (*If* ALI *is not beside* MICHAEL, *she moves towards him.*) When we were little, we used to go on our holidays to our granny's room, which was just down the corridor from our rooms.

(ALI *and* MICHAEL *each begin to tell their stories at the same time.* ALI *begins the piece with, 'You'd come out of my room . . .' and finishes before* MICHAEL.)

ALI:

You'd come out of my room, walk down the corridor. On the left was a big blue altar with statues of the Virgin Mary that we would decorate with our granny in May. Continue down the corridor and at the very end there was a big window in the middle. Our parents' room was on the right and our granny's room was on the left. When you'd walk into our granny's room, the first thing you'd see was an old antique sewing machine that our granny used all the time. In the corner facing you was a big old wardrobe that we used to think we could go to Narnia through. Beside that, on the wall, was a Sacred Heart light. That was really nice as a child, as it made you feel safe at night when you were on your holidays. It was like a night-light. Beside that, in the corner, there were two trunks that had hat boxes on top. Our granny wore lots of great hats. In the middle of the room was a big brass bed that had knobs on either end and I used to think that if I twisted them at night I could call my Fairy Godmother. In the other corner there was a single bed that our parents bought for our aunt who was a nun on the missions in Africa, so that she would have somewhere to sleep when she came home every few years. That was where me and Michael would sleep. So we'd pack our little bags, walk down the corridor and hop into the single bed in our granny's room for our summer holidays.

MICHAEL:

So if you walk out of my room and turn right, in front of you was a blue altar. It had a statue of the Virgin Mary and another saint, I think St. Joseph. Walk past the altar and the door on the left is into our granny's room. If you open the door, in front of you is a huge wooden wardrobe with a round mirror. It was a kind of Walt Disney mirror and we used to think we could see a wicked witch in it. In the middle of the room was granny's bed. It was a brass bed. There was a big dip in the middle of it and we used to play fairies and pretend it was a phone. I can't remember why. Beside the bed there were two big wooden trunks. They were full of religious materials from my Auntie Mary, who's a nun, some-times we used just call her 'The Nun'. Anyway they were full of religious stuff and we were never allowed to go near them. I always thought it was because I wasn't holy enough. If you hop back over granny's bed, there was another small single bed there. This is where Auntie Mary the Nun used to sleep when she stayed. Now, if you go back to the wardrobe and open it up, inside there were fur coats. We used to climb in and play Narnia, thinking we could see lions and all that. I kind of loved the coats because they felt really cosy but at the same time they were really dusty and I had asthma, so it was sometimes hard to breath. If you get back out of the wardrobe and open up its side door, there were shelves there with jars full of old money and zips and buttons; I never knew why they were there, no one ever seemed to do anything with them, but they were always just there.

ʕ҃ʕ҃ʕ҃ʕ҃ʕ

GORD: Sometimes you have to be stronger than someone. It's like the
            aeroplane theory: if someone's frightened on the plane, you're
            not going to be frightened; and if they're not frightened, you
            take on that role of being frightened; taking on different roles
            to aid people, I suppose. Like, if a crisis hits and someone's
            really upset, you then take on the role of making them feel
            better. Kind of like when me and Vickey first rehearsed for
            this show. Vickey took on the role, or just was more laid back
            and easy-going and easy-breezy. More chilled out, 'I don't
            mind, whatever' about the whole thing. Whereas I was a bit
            more uptight, highly strung, paranoid and upset and worried
            and pedantic about how it was going to work out and wanted
            to talk about it the whole time and explore it more with each
            other. But maybe if Vickey had worked with someone more
            like herself, she might have been a little bit more like me; and
            if I'd worked with someone more like me, I might have been a
            little bit more relaxed.

ALI: Rehearsals were kind of like a whole new experience for
            Michael and me. It was all really good at first. It was fun. It
            was interesting. It was exciting. Then Áine and Vickey joined
            us. It was just that when Áine and Vickey came, they knew
            what they were doing and were very comfortable with what
            they were doing, so that's when my anxieties took off.

MICHAEL: My anxieties were about performing all the way along, so I
            don't think I got that freaked out or that nervous until about
            two days ago. Up until then I kind of enjoyed the rehearsals
            overall, including working with Áine and Vickey, until my
            meltdown two days ago. But I'm over that now.

VICTOR: I had *the maddest* dream about Áine. We were on *Mastermind*
            and she was the host, of course, and she kept hounding me
            and I only remember two questions she asked me – why was I
            so independent? And why had I let Killiney down? I woke up
            sweating my head off.

ʕ҃ʕ҃ʕ҃ʕ҃ʕ

VICTOR: Áine. Áine. Áine.
GORD: What?
VICTOR: Awnee!

GORD: What?!

VICTOR: Áine!

GORD: What, Vickey?

VICTOR: Awww Nyah!

GORD: What!

VICTOR: *Áine!*

GORD: *What!*

VICTOR: Do you even like me any more?

❧❧❧❧❧❧

MICHAEL: I remember she brought Ali plastic flowers when she was pretending to be sick. (*Pause*) I remember she carried coal buckets when she was way too old. (*Pause*) I remember she used to find us hiding in the shed and drag us in to say the Rosary. (*Pause*) I remember she was really proud of a coat she bought in Shaws in Waterford, but when she brought it home, she realized the pockets were in the wrong place. (*Michael places one hand on his breast and one hand on his groin.*) I remember she used to exercise in the living room to *Live at 3*. (*Pause*) I remember she never judged people.

ALI: She died on the darkest day of the year.

❧❧❧❧❧❧

MICHAEL: I wrote a letter to my friend Brian fourteen years ago and at a Christmas party recently he gave it back to me again. It's actually really painful to read in lots of ways. We were both English students at the time, so there's lots of inverted commas, like 'po-mo' for postmodernism. (*Michael makes air quotes with his fingers.*) But I kind of love it. The general gist of the letter is: 'Dear Brian, you know the way you're gay, well I'm gay too.' The reason why I love the letter is, I'd just come back from New York, I'd discovered a whole new world and was clearly having the time of my life. Brian wrote back a very nice letter saying, 'Dear Michael, I'm delighted for you, but I'm not gay.'

A & M: (*Singing*)
       Everywhere we go . . .

V & G: (*Also singing*)
       Everywhere we go.

A & M: *People always ask us!*
V & G: *People always ask us!*
A & M: *Who we are.*
V & G: *Who we are.*
A & M: *Where do we come from?*
V & G: *Where do we come from?*
A & M: *And we always tell them!*
V & G: *And we always tell them!*
A & M: *We're from Kilkenny.*
V & G: *We're from Killiney.*
A & M: *Glenmore, Kilkenny.*
V & G: *Ballinclea, Killiney.*

ᘔᘔᘔᘔᘔᘔ

VICTOR: I can get down, but so can anyone, but that pisses me off because it's so bloody annoying.

GORD: I can say what I think, how I feel; I have my own opinions.

VICTOR: I give too much of myself away, especially with new people.

GORD: I don't really hold back about myself and I don't really like that.

VICTOR: I do like it, but when it's just you giving it all away, it's one-sided and then you kind of leave yourself a bit open.

GORD: I like it in other people, I love it; I love people who are completely open and say anything.

VICTOR: I really admire it and I'm a bit like that but I'm not comfortable enough with myself. But I love people like that.

ᘔᘔᘔᘔᘔᘔ

GORD: I lost my mum. That was a big one. I think that defines loss. I resent losing my mum but you can't do anything about that, you know? I always wonder what things would be like if she was around, so I kind of resent her dying. I resent being cheated on. I resent not coming out . . .

VICTOR: . . . or coming to terms with being gay earlier, because I've always known I was gay, so if I'd just dealt with it earlier, I wouldn't have fucked so many things up. You know what I mean?

ALI: I think our mum always wanted us to leave for our own sake. I think losing the youngest in the family was very difficult for her, even though she was always very encouraging around going to college, as an escape route. In the end I just wanted to get the fuck out of there. Our mum tells a story that I don't think is true . . .

MICHAEL: . . . about when she drove me to the train in Waterford when I was leaving home to move to Dublin for the first time, and in the story I hop out of the car and pull my bag out of the boot and skip off into the train station without ever turning around to say goodbye. You see, in the end I really did want to get the fuck out of there, but it really wasn't as simple as that. I think Ali may have been more conflicted than me . . .

ALI: . . . I was more conflicted and it was partly because I missed my gran and my mum so much, but it was also because I wasn't expected to leave.

VICTOR: I spent too long of my teenage life pining after the wrong person. I lost a lot of time. I lost a lot of tears. And I betrayed myself then; I wasn't strong enough and I let it take over me. I lost my enthusiasm; I think I used to be a lot more enthusiastic about things . . .

GORD: . . . I did lose my enthusiasm. I got it back, but it did take too much out of me. But it could have been a hell of a lot worse.

Long pause, after which VICTOR *starts clicking her fingers and begins to sing 'Man in the Mirror' by Michael Jackson. After one or two lines, everyone joins in. This is unaccompanied and not reliant on anyone actually being able to sing.*

☙☙☙☙

ALI: Michael's room had a picture of Marilyn Monroe over his bed.

MICHAEL: Ali's room had a poster of Billy Idol on the ceiling above her bed, so she could see him every morning when she woke up.

ALI: Michael's room had a crucifix with the Jesus pulled off.

MICHAEL: Ali's room had lots of cuddly toys.

ALI: Michael's room had two voodoo dolls.

MICHAEL: Ali's room had encyclopaedias.

ALI: Michael's room had a huge black boom box.

MICHAEL: Ali's room had a white dresser with roundy mirrors on it and make-up all laid out perfectly.

ALI: Michael's room had Madonna's first album on vinyl.

MICHAEL: Ali's room had a hair diffuser.

ALI: Sometimes if I was lonely or scared, I'd go to Michael's room, climb into his bed and go asleep.

ᏒᏕᏒᏕᏒᏕᏒᏕ

ALI: I wish Michael didn't work so hard.

MICHAEL: I wish Ali didn't phone me four times a day to talk about *Home and Away*.

ALI: I wish Michael had more time to talk on the phone.

MICHAEL: I wish Ali didn't make me feel so guilty about that.

ALI: I wish when my friends met Michael, they didn't like him more than me.

MICHAEL: They don't. That's just ridiculous. I wish I didn't have so much responsibility when I was growing up.

ALI: I wish I could turn back time, so I could ask my granny more about herself.

MICHAEL: I wish I needed to wear glasses.

GORD: I wish Vickey was as nice to me as she is to her other friends.

VICTOR: I wish I was taller than Áine.

ᏒᏕᏒᏕᏒᏕᏒᏕ

VICTOR *recites the nicknames she's called* GORD *in the past, all of which originated in* GORD*'s family.*

VICTOR: Fatty. Fats. Slobodan Milosevic. McKevitt.

(GORD *sings to the tune of 'Blackbird' by the Beatles,* VICTOR *joins her on the chorus.*)

V & G: *Fat girl singing in the dead of night*
Take these Fat Girl wings and learn to fly
All your life
You were only waiting for this moment to arise
Fat Girl Fly
Fat Girl Fly.

(*The word 'fat' is not used in reference to* GORD*'s actual weight and is not placed in the piece to make any statement about weight. The word 'fat' has always been a term of endearment in the McKevitt family and the song 'Fat Girl' was sung to* GORD *as a baby.*)

GORD: Vic. Victor. Victor Victoria. Dick. Dick Van Dyke. Vick the Dick. Dickie Rock. Stubs. Stubby.

ตาฝฌ฾ตาฝฌ฾ตาฝฌ

VICTOR *and* GORD *move to their 'homes' or stay in their 'homes' if already there.*

ALI: I remember Vickey's dad getting into a bad temper because she wouldn't go to religion after school and fucking her religion books down the stairs.

VICTOR: I remember we were camping out in Áine's back garden one time and her parents pretended that the kitchen was like an American diner and passed us out toasted cheese sandwiches through the kitchen window in their best New York accents.

ALI: I remember the first time I stayed in Vickey's on a school night under the disgusting yellow quilt and writing a love letter to her boyfriend and posting it to him on the way to school the next day. Vickey had a lot of boyfriends when we were growing up.

VICTOR: I remember every time you went into Áine's house her dad would always greet you with '*Síochán leat*'.

ALI: I remember Vickey's cousin putting a beach ball on my hand and my nail fell off.

VICTOR: I remember one time Áine couldn't get a pair of jeans on her, so we laid her down in the hallway and got a pliers to her zipper and I was reefing the zipper up to try and close it and I let go and I went flying through the glass panels into the sitting room where her parents and her sisters were all watching television.

GORD: I remember practising for our band in Vickey's sitting room. The only part I had to play was to introduce the band: 'There were the Beatles, there were the Monkees, and now there are *the Ants!*'

VICTOR: I remember going Snore Hunting.

MICHAEL: Snore Hunting. Snore Hunting is when Áine and Vickey would spy on adult snorers when they went on sleepovers to each other's houses.

GORD: I remember listening to a lot of Michael Jackson's *HIStory* album on Vickey's bed.

VICTOR: I remember the first time my parents left me to be babysat by the McKevitts and I wet the bed, with Áine and her three sisters in it.

GORD: I remember Vickey's dad always being very grumpy when you went to the house, except when we got older and Vickey had birthday parties and we'd all be drinking, and he'd be drinking too. He'd get drunk and say to me how happy he was that I was friends with Vickey, and how much he loved me, and that always made me feel a little bit guilty.

VICTOR: I remember Áine's mum making me sugary tea and putting me to bed on the day my mum died.

GORD: I remember Vickey had a club in her shed and I wasn't allowed in it.

VICTOR: I remember at a *feis* one year I won the best actress award and Áine turned around and told me it was because of my costume.

GORD: I can't remember the last time I was in Vickey's house.

⨞⨞⨞⨞⨞

GORD: My ideal friendship with Vickey would . . . well, you see, Vickey and me are always going to know each other. We've always known each other and we're always going to be in each other's lives whether we want to or not, so it would be nice if we were less . . . if we argued less and were just nicer to each other and saw each other more and wanted to see each other more.

MICHAEL: It's been funny during this process listening to Áine and Vickey talk so openly about not liking each other at all, but all the way through it's really obvious that they actually do really like each other.

ALI: I find their relationship really intriguing because they're so frank and so blunt with each other and the only person I know as long as they've known each other is Michael but our relationship is, well, pretty much completely different. I think it's because when we were growing up, we kind of always felt we had to look after each other and look out for each other, so our relationship is kind of very protecting and mindful.

MICHAEL: We do fight but our fighting is generally silence. So if we don't talk to each other on the phone twice a day, that means we're fighting.

ALI: That means every day, if Michael doesn't answer.

MICHAEL: I don't always know whether she wants to talk about *Home and Away* or if she's in a crisis . . .

ALI: There could be a crisis in *Home and Away*!

GORD: The way it seems to me is that Ali and Michael treat each other like friends and me and Vickey definitely treat each other like sisters. I always have the same dream, I've had it for the past nine years, and it's that Vickey's mum is alive again and she's back in the house and the green car is there and the hair equipment is there and all her aunts – Geraldine and June – thousands of them, they're all there. In the dream Mary has been dead but she's alive again, she's back and everyone's very happy, and we're all in the kitchen but no one knows how long Mary is back for, but everyone's very happy. I have this dream all the time.

VICTOR: My ideal friendship with Áine would be a lot less like therapy.

A & M: We've been Ali and Michael.

V & G: And we've been Victor and Gord.

   Performers bow.

A Woman in Progress

PANTI

A *Woman in Progress* was first presented at Project Arts Centre, Dublin, on 24 September 2009, as part of the Ulster Bank Dublin Theatre Festival, by THISISPOPBABY and Project Arts Centre. It had an earlier outing as a work in development as part of THISISPOPBABY's and Calipo's Queer Notions festival in June of the same year.

PERFORMER

Panti	Rory O'Neill

PRODUCTION TEAM

Director	Phillip McMahon
Designer	Ciarán O Melia
Dramaturg	Jocelyn Clarke

On stage right is a podium; on stage left a large projector screen. The performance opens with a video montage comprised of images of PANTI *set to a spoken word track that details the products and processes involved in the transformation of the performer into* PANTI: '*Lipstick, powder press, lash curl, eyeliner, and I am, Pandora "Panti" Bliss . . .' When the track is finished,* PANTI *walks on stage.*

PANTI:
Good evening, and thank you all so much for coming. I really mean that because otherwise I'd feel pretty stupid standing here alone . . . looking amazing but alone. Over the next hour or so, if you'll be so indulgent as to allow me, I'm going to tell you some things about me. Not because there's anything particularly special about me – well, apart from my

ability to stand here and talk to you despite the fact that I'm fairly spectacularly drunk – but because I'm not really qualified to tell you about anything else. I am my own, and only, specialist subject. Some of you may now be rolling your eyes and silently screaming inside, especially those of you who have suddenly realized there's been a ticket mix-up and this isn't Chekhov's *Three Sisters*! Because listening to people talk about themselves is rarely interesting and almost never illuminating. Just ask my therapist.

But then again . . . *look* at me. Chances are my story isn't going to be the usual boy-meets-girl-becomes-computer-programmer-moves-to-Balbriggan, so really, what do you have to lose, apart from the will to live?

And anyway, although I am going to be telling you a few things about me, and how I got here, the show isn't really about me. I am merely using me as a theatrical device, through which I hope to illuminate a larger truth. In fact, it could be argued that that's *all* I am: a big, drunk, devastatingly attractive, theatrical device. But I'm OK with that. I am my own life's work. The fruit of my own creative endeavours. And anyway, there are worse things I could be.

Passes a letter to an audience member, the contents of which will be read aloud at the end of the show.

I think sometimes when people look at me, this giant-pig-dog-man woman, they find it hard to imagine that I came from anywhere. They imagine that I just appeared, fully formed, like the Good Witch Glinda from her bubble. But of course I am from somewhere. I'm from a small town in Mayo called Ballinrobe. Do any of you know Ballinrobe? Actually, I suspect you *all* know Ballinrobe. Many of you are probably *from* Ballinrobe. Ballinrobe is your typical, Irish, country, market town. It has a couple of streets, a church, a town hall, a cattle mart, and there was great excitement when Tesco came to town. I grew up in a typical large Mayo family – five brothers and sisters; my mother: flat shoes, tweed skirt, pillar of the local community; and my father: the local vet, didn't go to the pub, so people considered us privileged. And even though Ballinrobe now has a Tesco, and a black family, it hasn't really changed much since I was growing up there, a young boy called Rory, in the 1970s.

Shows video of bull in Ballinrobe shop.

John Cummins's brother was in my class in school, Vincent Cummins.

The Cumminses practically owned the town. They have the Supervalu, a pub, and a funeral parlour, Cummins & Goins.

ᘔᘖᘔᘖᘔᘖ

PANTI *steps from centre stage to the podium on stage right and reads aloud a letter.*

Dear Rory,

I turned forty last year. I suppose I should say 'we' turned forty last year, but it doesn't feel that way. Somewhere along the years between us, we slipped apart. Turning forty didn't feel like a big deal, and I didn't make it into a big deal. We had a small party in my flat. Though all our siblings turned up from Mayo – you know what Edel is like, she's such an organizer.

I was determined to avoid the clichés – the midlife crisis – but I have found myself ruminating. Thinking about you, actually.

I suppose I have an unfair advantage here, because I know you, but you don't know me. Or at least, not yet. But of course, you don't know anyone like me yet. I'm writing to you because you did an amazing thing for me. I think you probably had to do it, but whether you had any choice or not is irrelevant – either way, I'm grateful. So I hope that in some small way I can make it easier for you. After all, you did all the hard stuff and I got all the rewards.

You know, if we could swap places right now, swap times, things would be a lot easier for you. You wouldn't have to search so long, struggle and kick so hard, to be who we are. But if things had been easier for you, what would I be? I think I'd be less. I know that right now – right then – in Ballinrobe you're not exactly sure what it is you're looking for. But you're right about needing to find it. There is more to life than this. You are your own pope.

Yours gratefully,
Panti

ᘔᘖᘔᘖᘔᘖ

In 1979 I started to think for myself.

That was the year the pope came to Ireland, and when he did, there were no dissenting voices. Or if there were, I was too young to hear them.

Everyone was on board – even I was on board. After all, I was already putting my latent drag tendencies to work as Ballinrobe's pre-eminent altar lady/boy. But even my enthusiasm, driven as it was by the perceived glamour of the occasion, paled into insignificance beside my devout mother's papal devotion.

For days beforehand, our house, like every other house in Ballinrobe, was a hive of activity and nervous excitement, my mother a sandwich-making tweedy blur, and at the crack of dawn on the big day she piled the Volkswagen high with egg sandwiches, brown bread, flasks of tea, pope stools, Holy See flags, and giddy children, and drove to Claremorris, where we parked in a field. Claremorris is fifteen miles from Ballinrobe, and is Ballinrobe's arch-enemy. At Claremorris we boarded shuttle buses to the site at Knock, where we were herded off the buses and into our assigned corrals, and in the grey early morning light it was a sight to behold – hundreds of thousands of damp pilgrims, muttering their bovine devotions, stretched out across fields, ironically vacated by their actual bovine residents for the glorious occasion.

We set up camp, miles from the stage, among nodding nuns, stressed mothers, praying shopkeepers, and farmers drinking cold tea from TK lemonade bottles, as an interminable rosary was broadcast over the tannoy system. It reminded me of a badly organized Nuremberg rally.

By the time the pope arrived – or at least someone who sounded like him – it already felt like we'd been at a mass for days on end, but now an actual mass did start, and it was longer and more boring than any mass I'd ever been to.

But during the mass I looked around me – and I had an epiphany of sorts. I didn't belong here. I looked at the hundreds of thousands of people speaking as one, and I didn't feel any wonder. I felt no joy. I felt afraid. There was nothing spiritual or divine about this event; this was a cult, a cult of personality and hype. And had I had the courage, I would have stood up and screamed, 'The pope has no clothes!'

I didn't become an atheist that day – that would be a longer process – but I took the first step . . . and became a Protestant.

When the mass ended, the excitement was palpable, because this was what everyone was really waiting for – *the Popemobile!* It's hard to grasp now, but at the time, the Popemobile was this huge deal. It was basically a jeep with bullet-proof glass at the back, but the way people went on, you'd swear it was *Wanderly Wagon!*

At the end of the mass the pope would drive through the corrals of people and it was our chance to get up quite close to him and take that shaky photograph to be treasured for years to come. But then it was announced over the tannoy that because things were running behind schedule and it was already beginning to get dark, the pope was going to leave immediately. He may have been God's chosen representative on earth, successor to St. Peter, with a direct line to the Virgin – but he still had to be home in time for *Coronation Street*! And everyone was crushed! Nuns looked at each other with stricken faces on the verge of tears, and my mother shrivelled before my very eyes. And hundreds upon hundreds of thousands of cold, wet people looked at each other and said, 'Feck this crap', and left. All at the same time. In the dark. It was total chaos. There was no way they could get the buses through the frustrated throngs, so everyone had to walk the eight miles back to Claremorris, down tiny Mayo country roads, in the pitch dark, jostled by hundreds of thousands of other people. My mother – cold, wet, miserable, disappointed – made us kids – cold, wet, miserable, tired and cranky – hold hands as we stumbled and bumped and cried our way the eight miles back to the car. It was a frightening experience. Old people were stumbling, children were crying, treasured pope stools were tossed into ditches, and my mother, even in the dark, looked tired and disappointed. On the drive home in the dark I was exhausted but I couldn't sleep. I remember seeing my mother's hands illuminated by the light from the dashboard – I could see the blood in her veins. I'd never even noticed she had veins before, and for the first time in my life, she looked to me like a real person.

The pope's visit made me think – really *think* – for the very first time. It made me question what was presented to me. Made me wary of accepted truths. That day, a crack opened up between me and the world around me. A crack that over the years became a crevasse, then a gorge, and then a chasm. A chasm I've come to treasure. The pope's visit unhooked me from the deadweight of religion and pushed me into the stream of my own consciousness. It gave me a mind of my own.

Knock is the world's worst Marian shrine, and coming from Mayo, I don't say that lightly. I don't know if you've ever been to Lourdes, but it's so much better; even the apparition is so much better than Knock's. In Lourdes, the Virgin pulled out all the stops, all the big special effects – the sun was spinning, water was gushing and she kept reappearing to a very strict schedule, whispering very important secrets. In Knock she appeared once, in the middle of the night in the lashing rain, and ruined the drama of it by bringing a bunch of vaguely recognizable back-up saints. And possibly because of the weather, she didn't bring the actual baby Jesus, she brought a lamb. Oh c'mon, Mary – if you're going to appear in a bog in the middle of the night, you could at least bring the baby Jesus and not a bloody metaphor.

∂♃∂♃∂♃∂♃

PANTI *steps from centre stage to the podium on stage right and reads aloud a letter.*

Dear Rory,

It's funny how life turns out – the things you leave behind; the things you take with you.

You're taking Aunty Qy with you.

You're not going to be a cartoonist when you grow up. But don't worry. I don't think you really want to be a cartoonist. It's just that it's the only obvious use of the things you're good at that you can think of right now.

You're going to be an entertainer of sorts. An entertainer that uses all the things you are good at: talking, painting, dressing up, not doing what's expected of you, disappointing your poor mother . . . and imitating Aunty Qy.

Next time she comes to visit, study her closely. The way she talks, the way she moves. It'll all be useful to you in the end. And it'll be fun. Trust me.

Yours,

Panti

∂♃∂♃∂♃∂♃

There's a lot to be said for growing up in 1970s Mayo. It was fun and carefree. The weather seemed better. The summers longer. You'd go out in the morning and spend the day exploring the woods, swimming in the lake, kissing boys at the bottom of the garden, as if it was the most natural thing in the world, and your mother wouldn't worry or care where you were as long as you were back by teatime. Even now, they have a very relaxed attitude to child safety in Co. Mayo. Like the rest of the country, every Mayo garden seems to have a trampoline these days, except, in Mayo, nobody has a safety net.

The one thing Mayo didn't have was glamour. It had grass and cows and fish and football, but no glamour. Glamour was in short supply in 1970s Ireland, anyway, but what little there was rarely made it past the Shannon and usually came from abroad. When Mrs. Nixon, the wife of the disgraced president, came to Ballinrobe in a helicopter and shook hands with people at the local agricultural show, the whole town nearly had a stroke. She was like something out of a 'filim'.

But glamour came to our house once every few years in the shape of Aunty Qy, my mother's glamorous younger sister. She even had the glamorous name – Columba – which everyone shortened to Q or Qy for some reason. Aunty Qy. She was gorgeous, and had this rich husky voice, redolent of Katharine Hepburn. She wanted to be an actress, and did a little bit on radio, but mostly, she was just beautiful. Seven different men proposed to her but she said no to all her suitors until a wealthy American, an ex-naval officer, proposed. He was twenty-five years her senior, but he was dashing and exciting, and in grey 1950s Ireland, he was in Technicolor, and he took her to America.

Aunty Qy would arrive home with her husky drawl, in a swirl of beige pant-suits and menthol cigarettes, cigarettes with mint in them! And the glamour would almost knock me over. She'd smoke and drawl and sing 'W-O-M-A-N'. She'd clank bracelets as she took out gifts wrapped like gifts in movies, and inside we'd discover new and amazing things; a battery-operated game called Simon . . . a computer, really. A jumper with a hood on it! America had everything. We'd never seen the like! The whole town was talking about us and our jumpers with hoods on them.

All the other kids wanted an Aunty Qy. I wanted to *be* Aunty Qy.

She was like no one else I'd ever met. She was exotic and glamorous and *different*. She was like a character from a movie, a 3D emissary from a 2D world I'd only ever seen on screen or in books. But she was flesh and blood, undeniable, tangible evidence of a big world out there, some-where past Roscommon. I feverishly imagined this world and fevered to be part of it. This bigger, brighter world full of new and different things, exciting and full of possibilities – where people wore jumpers with hoods on them.

ↄᴙↄᴙↄᴙↄᴙↄᴙ

PANTI *steps from centre stage to the podium on stage right and reads aloud a letter.*

Dear Rory,

There is no such thing as fate. Life is plastic, malleable, and you have to shape your own.

Americans like to say that you can be whatever you want to be, but they're wrong of course. There are too many variables outside your control:

luck, talent, opportunity, privilege. But you can be whoever you want to be.

The question is, who do you want to be? The possibilities are infinite, but to see them you need to look beyond Ballinrobe. Everyone is different, Rory, and some people will find their answer in Ballinrobe; Damien will, Fergal will, Deirdre will, but you won't. I know that seems a bit daunting now – you think you're unlucky – but I think you're lucky. Your gay necessity will push you further, but the journey is where all the fun is.

Yours,

Panti

⅀⅂⅀⅂⅀⅂⅀⅂

When I was twelve, my parents encouraged me to go to boarding school near my grandmother. They didn't need to. I took one look at the collection of rundown prefabs and Christian Brothers with drink problems that made up the Ballinrobe Secondary School for Boys and I ran for the train.

The school was rigid, run by Franciscans who were only interested in answers, not questions. Independent thought was discouraged, foreign sports frowned upon, and art was considered a suspicious activity. But at least I met people who were from places other than Ballinrobe – a few were even from 'abroad', and I eked out my own small freedoms. Not considered a real subject, I studied art on my own at night and sat the Leaving Cert art exam alone in an empty exam hall.

After school, I went to art college. I still had no idea what it was I was looking for but I figured art college would be a good place to start looking. Here, surely, I thought, questions would be valued over answers.

On my first day I sat in the queue for registration beside a handsome mohawked punk wearing a pair of pyjamas with a *Playboy* centrefold safety-pinned to the back. Finally! I thought, and had to literally stop myself leaning over and kissing him full on the mouth.

But even art college had its own rules, its own accepted truths, its own collection of moulds, and none of them seemed to fit me. But at least it gave me time and space to ask my own questions, and among the students I found a couple of other gays in whom I saw parts of myself reflected for the very first time, and that was a start.

In the summer of my final year, I went to London to stay with my brother, and on my first night he threw a party. In his kitchen I met a large, imposing Australian, wearing a ridiculous wig and a tweed jacket with tiny swastikas embroidered on it.

This was Leigh Bowery.

As an art student in the 1980s, I was already aware of Leigh Bowery. He was already a club legend, a living work of art, a flesh-and-blood sculpture, a towering installation of skin and costume that moved with surprising grace through crowded rooms of startled clubbers. And at that time, he was making inroads into the 'serious' art world as a performance artist and muse.

For Leigh, his body wasn't an end, it was a beginning. His very flesh a medium of alchemy, an opportunity. With paint and fabric and movement and performance, he pushed against the boundaries of his own form, his own biology – and *transformed* himself.

For the rest of the summer I would turn up at gay clubs, wide-eyed with the possibilities, and this huge magnificent creature would greet me with a squeal and encourage me to get into as much trouble as possible. I've often wondered if he was that sweet to me, this young gay boy from Ireland, because Leigh understood where I was from. He was a fat gay boy from the asshole of Australia, but he had, through his own creativity, transformed himself into the most fabulous creature in a world full of fabulous creatures.

Leigh died of an AIDS-related illness in 1994 at the age of thirty-three.

In Leigh I saw all sorts of new possibilities: that life was for creating, not consuming, that convention was for wimps, and that being gay, far from being a burden or a limitation, was a gift! For the first time in my life I realized that I didn't have to be defined by Ballinrobe, Co. Mayo. I could define *myself*.

And for the second time in my life, a man in an elaborate costume had made me *think*.

That summer of fun changed everything for me, and when I came back to Dublin to finish college, I was no longer interested in cutting paper and drawing pretty pictures. I was going to be, in the words of the song, 'My own special creation', and I threw myself into it with gusto. Much to the consternation of my college tutors, I spent the rest of the year working on a drag show – but I didn't care if I failed my degree any more. I was on a mission to find a new, more fabulous me, and people could get on board or not.

I didn't care, and not caring was amazing.

≈≈≈≈≈

PANTI *steps from centre stage to the podium on stage right and reads aloud a letter.*

Dear Rory,

Sex. Grab it – with both hands.

Right now, I know, sex to you is a fumbled, tortured activity, laden with guilt. But very soon, sex – real, messy, exciting, dangerous, funny, life-affirming, liberating sex – is about to hit you like a tonne of gay bricks.

Lucky you. I'd love to have all that ahead of me, rather than behind me. (Which makes a change!) Not that I never have sex any more – I'm not a completely dried-up old husk yet. But it's less.

It's partly through my own choosing, of course. I've lost some of your youthful drive. You'll forgive a multitude of sins for the lay. I'm less forgiving. Which is a pity perhaps. Even dreadful sex can be the prelude to an adventure, as you'll soon discover.

Spending the evening scratching the dog's belly has an appeal now that it used not to have. But it's not all my own choosing. There's no denying that a forty-year-old drag queen isn't top of most people's wish-list. I like to tell myself it's a filter. That it strains out the chaff. But you have all the good stuff still ahead of you! Sex, for a while, will define you – define you as an outsider to everything you've been presented with till now. It will liberate you and reinforce for you the need to question everything you think you know, and find your own self-defined life. This is not something to be afraid of. It's something to be embraced and treasured.

Panti

❧❧❧❧

Grey, depressed, 1980s Dublin was a difficult place to be fabulous, so with the energy and enthusiasm and blind confidence that comes with being young and drunk, I set off to travel the world that Aunty Qy had once represented. At the time I had developed a bit of an obsession with train journeys, so I just kept taking trains until I found myself, by accident more than design, in Tokyo.

❧❧❧❧

Video of PANTI *performing in Tokyo, while* PANTI *reads aloud a letter she sent to her friend Niall at the time.*

Tokyo – Japan – 1993.

The club: big, dark, lights, sweat, beats, smells . . . sensory overload.

This is Tokyo.

My heart is pounding with the music and I'm covered in dance sweat. A friend is beside me but we don't talk.

I move to the bar.

I pass a cute guy I know. He smiles, a big cute smile, but doesn't wave. His left hand has no fingers and he keeps it in his pocket self-consciously. I consider kissing him . . . maybe later.

I need a drink.

I buy a beer, drink it down in two, and move onto the dance-floor and begin to dance. At first with little effort or energy, but before long my body is jerking and pumping. The beat is loud and I can feel it inside me. I push my hand through my sweat-drenched hair, and though I can't see it, I know it sprays droplets over the people around me. How long have I been dancing? I don't know. I move across the floor towards where a wide, curving, metal stair winds up off the dance-floor.

Upstairs there is a cooler, quieter bar. I meet a girlfriend and we sit and drink and talk. A transsexual woman leans over as she squeezes by and the nipples of her exposed breasts brush against my elbow. I talk to my friend about Ireland and Catholicism and abortion. The case of a fourteen-year-old Irish girl, molested and pregnant, is getting a lot of coverage in the international press here. The articles say things like 'in this ultra-conservative society . . .' or 'it may be difficult for outsiders to grasp how much power the Catholic Church wields in this secular state'. The transsexual squeezes by again, though this time she is careful not to brush me with her nipples. She grins.

I'm standing between the bar and the dance-floor, a drink in my hand, when someone greets me. 'Konbanwa.' I recognize him from the gay area of Tokyo. He doesn't waste time. He wants to take me home and fist me. I'm too drunk to be surprised. I decline the offer. He doesn't give up. He tells me it's easy. To prove it he produces a Polaroid. The picture is of two fore-arms buried in an asshole. Now I am surprised. Mildly shocked even. He says something about the technique. 'Curling' the arms. That's lovely, I tell him, but I still decline, now even more sure than before. I walk away.

There is a guy blocking my way. I go to squeeze by him. He turns around: mid-twenties, the same height as me. Unusual for a Japanese. He's handsome. He smiles. I lean forward. His tongue is in my mouth. At first it's cool against my own warm tongue. He's been drinking something with ice in it. I can taste citrus and alcohol. Then it's warm. I feel his teeth with my tongue. I can feel the heat of his chest against mine. I can smell the sweat on his neck. I can feel the hardness of his erection against my hip, his hand in the small of my back, the edge of his eyebrow on mine. I give him my it's-early-yet-but-I'll-see-you-later smile. He smiles and his teeth are caught in a flash of UV. It's a wolfish effect. I linger. His fingers touch mine. I move on.

A girl is looking at me as I begin to dance. She is moving to the music, but not a single bead of sweat mars her pretty face. Her hair (thick, long, glossy, black, like everyone else's) is pulled tightly off her face. Her eyeliner is thick, in perfect sweeps along her upper lids. She is looking appreciatively at me. I give her the smile that says, 'You're very pretty, I'm very gay.' She smiles, laughs, and jokingly imitates my dancing. I speak a few words to her. She's funny. What are we talking about?

I'm tired now. My head against the wall, my eyes closed. I can feel the beat resonate in my chest. I feel very much alive, but I'm tired. My senses confused. Am I smelling the sweat, or tasting it? Feeling it? Hearing it? I light a cigarette and take a deep drag. I feel it in my mouth, hear it in my throat, taste it in my lungs, I see it.

It's 5 a.m. It's Tokyo. I'm tired. Time to go home. Where's that boy? The one with the citrus-coated tongue.

᷉ᘒᕱᘒᕱᘒᕱᘒ

There are no expectations of a gay, foreign, drag queen in Tokyo. I was free to be whoever and whatever I wanted to be. I'd arrived there full of youthful energy, full of questions – in a way, I was a question – and in Tokyo I looked for my answer. No experience would be left unturned, no offer rejected, nothing ventured, nothing gained. I threw myself at life, hard, over and over till I ached.

Painted and teased and tottering in heels, I tripped and ran and stumbled and flew and crawled my way through the emporium of night-time iniquity. And somehow got paid for it. I devoured everything I came into contact with like a huge, glamorous Ebola virus: art, drugs, boys, men, music, gangsters, dykes, trannies, love, sex, beauty. And my appetite was insatiable. I just kept eating and eating and I never threw up.

But after five years, I ran out of steam. It's not necessarily a course I'd recommend to everyone. But it worked for me. Because when I finally did stop and look in the mirror, I was a bit battered and bruised (though some of that was probably just lipstick), but the person looking back at me – was me – and for maybe the first time – was someone I recognized as me. Even under all the make-up.

I was, at last, my own special creation.

≈≈≈≈≈≈

PANTI *steps from centre stage to the podium on stage right and reads aloud a letter.*

Dear Rory,

Take risks.

Life isn't meant to be safe – that's how people end up in seminaries, scientology, or, God forbid, Lucan.

We have a contrary streak in us, which you should know by now, because God knows Mammy has pointed it out often enough. It can be exasperating for other people sometimes, but that contrary streak is going to save you, time and time again, Rory, so treasure it.

It's that contrary streak that makes you think for yourself. It's that contrary streak that will push you to leap into the dark despite your fear. It's that contrary streak that will push you down the path least followed. And it's that contrary streak that other people will sometimes mistake for courage when it's no such thing . . . but it doesn't matter; the end result is the same. Your own self-realized life.

P

≈≈≈≈≈≈

When I came back to Dublin in the mid-90s, I found a city bursting with energy and possibilities. Creative and fun. And fun is my signature dish. Homosexuality had only just been decriminalized, and the gays, full of a new confidence, were at the forefront of all this explosive energy. No idea was too stupid or too outrageous or too beautiful, here, where fun and art collided.

We started clubs without a thought as to whether they were commercially viable or not. We weren't interested in consumers, we were interested in participants. This was night-clubbing as performance art.

At GAG, a fetish club in the docks, I gave myself paint enemas and squirted onto canvasses, or pulled the lyrics of songs from my ass. A painted and fleshy karaoke machine. For a glorious and messy year, we pushed the envelope of decency, until we attracted the attentions of the press and Store Street Garda Station.

At Powderbubble on Harcourt Street, we put trees on the dance-floor and people in plastic bubbles. Like Lady Godiva, I rode a horse on to the dance-floor and, at Christmas, tried unsuccessfully to get a donkey to do the same, so my Virgin birth took place in the car park.

At HAM in the POD, we covered ourselves in fake blood and covered our bloody nudity with rubber aprons, and plastered the city with ambiguous posters proclaiming 'Butcher Queers' and were accosted by outraged middle-aged American tourists.

And there was no shortage of people, unemployed and underemployed and bored, to help us do it: Create. Think. Do.

My gayness was making me question everything around me – everything I'd been told, everything that was expected of me. And underground gay club-land was populated by people just like me. People who'd thrown off everything to be there; who'd found a place full of people just like them, where the rules were vague and there to be made up as we went along, where creativity and outrageous investigation was prized above all else, where even gender was up for grabs. A place with its own secret codes; disco, poppers and sidelong glances. When I found this world, I exploded! I threw myself into its every dark and exciting corner. I revelled in the lights, the music, the smoke, the fun and the sex. And there was plenty of that! And every sex act was a liberation, another push to question everything, to accept nothing as given, to assume everything is bullshit till I'd worked it out for myself. I was young and gay and free and proving to myself, and the world, that everything you'd ever told me about sex and my sexuality was bullshit! 'Fuck you and your Popemobile!' I was saying to the world every time I got fucked.

And in this heady atmosphere of sex and colour and creativity and drugs and fun I continued to question everything I'd ever been told.

Being gay pushed me, pushed us, to think. And from it came an explosion of art, politics, passion. A lust for life and all it could be.

And I wouldn't change a single thing about it, because I was forged in that chaotic world and it made me the fabulous creature I am today; which I admit is a matter of opinion, but it's my show, so we're going with my opinion.

I'm forty years old. I should be putting my large feet up in a world I did my tiny part to create. And instead my world is disappearing and leaving me stranded. Castaway. A relic of a disappearing world. A bloody dinosaur! Granted, I'm a gorgeous dinosaur, but I'm not meant to be a dinosaur! Dinosaurs are fat.

Being gay saved me, but now the New Gay is killing me.

Because the New Gay is the opposite of creativity, the opposite of passion. An inoffensive, sickly sweet candyfloss of blandness created by corporations.

The gay culture that rescued me is being replaced by a culture that questions nothing. The New Gay doesn't question. It doesn't search – Google does that. It has the whole world at its mouse tip but it only clicks on Hannah bloody Montana. Fifteen-year-old Rory, starved of anything that reflected him, read and reread the section on homosexuality in Desmond Morris's *Manwatching*, thrilling at the clinical descriptions of sex acts, excited by the non-judgemental tone, clutching at the hard evidence of a gay world somewhere 'out there'. Today, any fourteen-year-old can watch Brazilian boys fingering each other, before reading all about Stephen Gately's painful break-up in *Heat* magazine. The New Gay hasn't struggled and fought and searched to find 'the gay'. Bits of 'the gay' have seeped into its world. Corporate-friendly bits. Graham Norton is on the telly; *Will and Grace* is at teatime. Every evening, desexualized gay men are beamed into your living room as they decorate your dreary houses or refurbish your middle-aged women. Your best friend and eunuch. Your granny knows where the George is, and young gay boys in Mayo can friend-request any tranny on Facebook.

The underground has come overground and shrivelled and died in the light.

Being gay has been emasculated. It's no longer a rejection of the status quo – it's embracing the status quo and adding a few throw pillows. Being gay is no longer dangerous and exciting and anti-establishment and mother-horrifying. It's easy and inoffensive and brings its mother to gay bars because she'll love it.

But your mother shouldn't love it. When you're gay and twenty (hell! when you're straight and twenty!), your mother should be horrified at everything you do. If she even suspects a small portion of what you're up to, she should be pulling her hair out in despair, frantic with worry, gnashing of teeth and beating of breast, howling with rage and praying for the courage to disown you.

The New Gay is sitting on the sofa with its granny, tut-tutting at cruising and bath houses and casual sex. What was liberating and full of honesty to me, is sad and shameful to the New Gay. The New Gay wants to bring a boyfriend home at Christmas. I wanted to fuck Christmas.

The New Gay wants to go to sexless, shiny, over-decorated bars, and drink Bacardi Breezers on glass table tops; I wanted to smash the glass table tops and fuck on the shards.

Gay culture is being stripped of everything that made it interesting and dangerous, and offensive. Plucked, shaved and polished till it's a sexless child of indeterminate gender. Instead of liberating you from a rigid world, being gay now gives you a new set of rules designed for children – packaged, anodyne, domestic. Even the New Gay's icons are children's entertainers: Steps, Miley Cyrus, Britney. Entertainments designed for children, filling dance-floors in gay clubs. Britney is carrying around children and twittering about watching *Nemo*. Debbie Harry didn't have kids. She had sex. Domesticity is the New Gay. That's not the gay I signed up for.

The New Gay even rejects being gay! It wants to be 'straight acting'. '*I'm not a gay man,*' it screams, '*I'm a man who happens to be gay!*', as if their sexuality is nothing more than a haircut. Something to be glossed over, rather than an intrinsic, integral, and powerful part of themselves that shapes and colours everything they do and are. Assimilation, not revolution, is the New Gays' dreary goal.

My generation was the generation who came of age under the shadow of AIDS. We grew up with sex and death inexorably linked. AIDS was here to kill us for going against nature, to punish us for our promiscuity. And we adapted. We had ourselves tested, and watched friends die, but we never turned against sex and the liberation it had brought us. Sex defined us – and why not? Sex defines us all. Straight people, you just don't notice it so much, because your sexuality is simply part of the background, incorporated into every nook and cranny of everyday life. It's less obvious because it's ubiquitous. It's only gay sexuality that's thrown into relief against the heterosexual background.

Our sexuality awakened us, and sex itself was the physical, emotional, and even political expression of our sexuality and ourselves.

Being gay used to mean being part of a fire of creativity and exploration, but rather than burning bigger and brighter, it seems like now the fire has dwindled and burned to a barely smouldering ember.

⤳⥂⤳⥂⤳⥂⤳⥂

PANTI *steps from centre stage to the podium on stage right and reads aloud a letter.*

Dear Rory,

I'm tempted to save you a lot of heartache here by giving you a list of all the fellas who aren't 'the one' – but you'll figure that out in your own time, and once the hard part is over, you'll have learned a lot from each. Though I will tell you that Paul the music guy is not the one, so don't even bother. That's eleven weeks of our life you could use more productively.

A gardener with a Labrador and a picket fence – but that's just not you. Me. Us. We're not very 'coupley'. You're a very independent young man, and for the most part, it suits you. You'll be happy in your own company – and rather be on your own than with someone who doesn't meet your exacting standards. Not that we look exacting from the outside! – it's just that the things that are important to you are not necessarily what's important to most people.

However, there is one thing. This thing for small fellas! I'm not even sure you're particularly aware of it yet, but we're mad for small fellas. And we're not small, so it's a little limiting. Awkward even. I'm not even sure how it all started, but if you could be aware of it and try and nip it in the bud, that'd be great, thanks.

Oh, and one last thing. I've put a small envelope inside this letter. In it there's a name and address. He's the one. Or at least I'm as sure of that as I can be. Don't open it yet, 'cause he's only just started primary school and you could get in trouble. But when you're in your late twenties, go look him up. I wasted too much time before I found him, and then, when I did, I fucked it up. And he fucked it up – little shit.

Anyway,

Love,

Panti

෴෴෴෴

Video of PANTI*'s Pride speech, delivered at the Civic Offices in Dublin in June 2009. This speech was picked up by Brenda Power, an opinion columnist for* The Sunday Times, *who used the occasion to argue against the provision of marriage to same-sex couples.*

It's funny, but sometimes you don't recognize the cavalry at first, because the cavalry is dressed up as an ill-informed, middle-aged reactionary.

There I was, despairing that the New Gay, like the grey squirrel, had routed the revolutionary, creative passion of the red squirrel, when out of nowhere, the gay marriage debate comes along, and I find myself in the middle of a gay shit-storm. Somehow I've accidentally become some sort of touchstone in a debate I didn't even see coming, and like Linda Martin at the *Eurovision*, I'm left wondering, 'Why me?'

Online gay-bashers are telling me to kill myself; my potential parenting skills are being debated by late-night taxi drivers; New Gays from Maynooth are calling Joe Duffy to say I'm a terrible role model; and worse, other gays are looking to me to be an erudite and eloquent spokesperson for every-gay. Suddenly, my personal has become political.

But when the shit-twister moves on and I poke my head out of my tranny storm shelter and look around, I realize something wonderful has happened. The New Gay has been shaken from its stupor. Its comfortable gay bubble has burst, and it's found itself in a struggle. And what that struggle is, what the issue is, could be anything really. What matters is that, suddenly, the New Gay is taking to the streets, in its thousands, it's organizing and agitating and expressing itself. It's climbing the barricades, and arguing, not just with the forces arrayed against it, but with other gays! The New Gay has been forced to *think*, to be creative, to consider its place in the world and what that world should look like. For the first time, the New Gay is political. It's making, not consuming, doing, not buying, and finally asking questions . . .

A fire has been re-lit and I promise to do my part to keep that fire burning, fan the flames till they spread beyond the gay marriage debate and incinerate the unquestioning, unthinking, uncreative citadel of the New Gay. Because we are at our best when we're flaming!

ನ್ಯನ್ಯನ್ಯನ್ಯ

Audience member is asked to read out the letter she or he was handed at the beginning of the show. As it's read, lights fade on PANTI.

Dear Panti,

Thank you so much for writing, even though I did have some trouble reading your old lady handwriting! It was interesting to hear all that stuff, but I'd prefer if you didn't write to me any more. Partly because Mammy is all suspicious about these perfumed letters I'm getting – I think you're getting her hopes up – but mostly I don't want you to write for my sake; or our sake, I suppose. Because I think it's better if I find this stuff out for myself. It sounds to me like the finding out was the best part, and you seem to have turned out OK (if a bit weird), so thanks, but I think I have to do this by myself.

But I am sorry to hear about your love life and that fella. I promise I'll do my best.

Rory

P.S. I don't know what an Internet is. Or AIDS. But they sound fun.

Notes on Contributors

LOUGHLIN DEEGAN's first play, *The Stomping Ground* (1997), was a finalist in the National Association of Youth Drama's Stage-it competition, and it was subsequently produced by Red Kettle Theatre Company, which also commissioned and produced his second play, *The Queen & Peacock* in 2000. He has worked for various theatre companies, including Druid and the Belltable Arts Centre, as well as for Rough Magic, where he worked as literary manager and later as executive producer (2003–16). For the Irish Theatre Institute he was editor of the *Irish Theatre Handbook* and director of the Irish Playography project, a comprehensive database for new Irish plays, from 2000 to 2003. He was appointed artistic director and chief executive of the Dublin Theatre Festival in 2006 and still holds this position.

DEIRDRE KINAHAN is artistic director of Tall Tales Theatre Company. She began writing for theatre in 1999 and has written many plays, including *Bé Carna* (1999), *Summer Fruits* (2001), *Knocknashee* (2001), *Passage* (2001), *Attaboy Mr. Synge* (2002), *Rum & Raisin* (2003), *Melody* (2005), *Hue & Cry* (2007) and *Moment* (2009). Plays for children include *The Tale of the Blue Eyed Cat* (2004), *Snow Child* (2005), *Rebecca's Robin* (2006), *Maisy Daly's Rainbow* (2008), and *Bogboy* (2008) for RTÉ Radio 1. In 2009 Kinahan was the winner of the Tony Doyle Bursary with BBC Northern Ireland and won a bursary from the Arts Council of Ireland for playwriting in 2008. She is under commission to the Abbey Theatre, Semper Fi (Ireland) and RTÉ Radio in 2010. She holds a BA in English Literature and an MA in Modern European Drama. Her plays receive regular production both in Ireland and internationally, and some have been published by Samuel French and Tall Tales/Liberty Press.

ÚNA MCKEVITT is a Dublin-based theatre-maker interested in making theatre from everyday life. McKevitt is an associate artist of the Project

Arts Centre and a graduate of Drama and Theatre Studies at Trinity College Dublin. In January 2009 she directed *Victor and Gord*, a durational work in progress devised with Vickey Curtis and Áine McKevitt for Project Brand New 3 at the Project Arts Centre. In June of the same year, she presented an extended version of the performance entitled *Victor and Gord, Ali and Michael* as part of the Queer Notions Festival, also at the Project Arts Centre. In September 2009, as part of the Dublin Fringe Festival, she presented a further extended version of this show, *Victor and Gord CUBED*, which was nominated for the Spirit of the Fringe Award. A new version of the show took place in February 2010 at the Project Arts Centre.

PHILLIP MCMAHON began acting with Dublin Youth Theatre, National Youth Theatre, and Australian Theatre for Young People. Since then he has acted with many companies, including THISISPOPBABY, Calipo, RAW, Randolf SD, PanPan, the Abbey/Peacock, Barnstorm, and TEAM. McMahon has directed the performer Panti in three productions: *In These Shoes?* (2007), *All Dolled Up* (2007) and *A Woman in Progress* (2009). *Danny and Chantelle (Still Here)* is McMahon's first play, and it won a Spirit of the Fringe Award when first staged at the Dublin Fringe Festival in 2006. Other playwriting credits include: *All Over Town* (2007), *Investment Potential* (2008) and *Pineapple* (2010). He has written one short film, *Round Here* (2007). He is cofounder of the theatre and performance company THISISPOPBABY. McMahon held the position of writer in association at the Abbey Theatre for 2009–10.

VERITY-ALICIA MAVENAWITZ was born in Ireland in 1957. She spent part of her childhood in the Middle East. She has also lived in the Netherlands and Greece. Mavenawitz has written scripts for television and radio and has written several stage plays. She was twice nominated for the Oscar Wilde Award for Outstanding Achievement in New Writing for the Theatre, in the International Dublin Gay Theatre Festival, and also worked for a short time as a journalist and critic. Her plays include . . . *And Then There Was Me!*, nominated for the Wilde award in 2005, and *The Drowning Room*, nominated for the same award in 2006. Other plays include *Counting Saturday* (2006), *Damelza Eating Apples* (2007), *The Smokestown Rendezvous* (2008) and *Abel and His Brother* (2009). She is currently working on her first book, entitled *The Very Beautiful*, and a play, *The Panic of Water Rising*.

PANTI began life as the art college project of Rory O'Neill in Dublin in the late 1980s, before moving to Tokyo, where she spent four years performing on the club scene as one half of double act CandiPanti. Returning to Dublin in 1995, she became part of the emerging club scene, both as a performer and a promoter of seminal clubs such as GAG, Powderbubble and HAM, among many others, eventually opening her own venue, Pantibar, in 2007. She has been the host of the annual Alternative Miss Ireland (AMI) since 1996, and has played roles on stage and screen, including RTÉ's *The Clinic*. She has written and performed three one-woman shows: *In These Shoes?* (2007), *All Dolled Up* (2007) and *A Woman in Progress* (2009).

NIALL SWEENEY founded the first Alternative Miss Ireland in 1987. AMI was recently presented at the Brno International Design Biennale as an example of alternative working practice. Sweeney is a long-time collaborator with Panti, and together they are the creative force behind many of Ireland's radical clubs and events – such as GAG, HAM, Gristle, and Powderbubble – through to Panti's emergence as Dublin's favourite landlady in the pub Pantibar. He continues to be involved in art/technology/music events and has been working with the dynamic THISISPOPBABY and its bright new wave of theatre. Sweeney is also one half of Pony Ltd., an award-winning graphic design studio based in London which is under the partnership of Sweeney and Nigel Truswell. Their clients run the gamut from major cultural institutions and academic research units to local social enterprises and many international contemporary artists and friends. With a keen interest in words, pictures and the chance of a dance, they present beautiful work – as talk, exhibition and performance – internationally.

NEIL WATKINS commenced his theatre education in Dublin Youth Theatre. He went on to train at the Drama Centre London, where he obtained a BA Hons degree in acting. He has also studied singing at the Bel Canto School of Singing in Belfast. As an actor, Watkins has performed in *The Seven Deadly Sins* (2003) with Performance Corporation and *And They Used to Star in Movies* (2006) with Bewley's Café Theatre. For Dublin Youth Theatre, he has written and directed three one-act plays. Supported by the British Council, Watkins was mentored by renowned performance artist David Hoyle in 2007. His controversial alter ego, Heidi Konnt, won Alternative Miss Ireland in 2005. Heidi has collaborated with many theatre and performances groups, including

Coiscéim, Opera Ireland, Corn Exchange, Gloria and Anúna. In 2009, he sang and played John Mac Neill in Brokentalker's production of Seán Millar's *Silver Stars*, which subsequently toured internationally. Acting for television, Watkins has appeared in *The Savage Eye*, *Val Falvey T.D.*, *Fair City*, *The Unbelievable Truth*, *Love is the Drug* and the highly acclaimed drama-documentary *Stardust* for RTÉ. His playwriting credits include *The Ugly Penguin Scenario* (2002), *Love in a Time of Affluence* (Stewart Parker Award nominee, 2003), *A Cure for Homosexuality* (2005), *Dublin City Counselling* (2007) and *The Dark Room* (2008).